The Rastafarians

the rastafarians

sounds of cultural dissonance

Leonard E. Barrett, Ph.D.

Beacon Press : Boston

Beacon Press books are published under the auspices
of the Unitarian Universalist Association
Simultaneous publication in casebound and paperback editions
Published simultaneously in Canada by
Fitzhenry & Whiteside Limited, Toronto

(hardcover) 9 8 7 6 5 4 3 2 1
(paperback) 9 8 7 6 5 4 3 2 1

All photographs appear by courtesy of the author.
The print "Not Far Away" and the jacket and cover
art are courtesy of Ras Daniel Heartman.

Library of Congress Cataloging in Publication Data

Barrett, Leonard E
  The Rastafarians
  Bibliography: p.
  Includes index.
  1. Ras Tafari movement. 2. Jamaica—Religion.
3. Jamaica—History. I. Title.
BL2530.J3B37   299'.6   76-48491
ISBN 0-8070-1114-2
ISBN 0-8070-1115-0 (pbk.)

Dedicated to the Honorable Rex M. Nettleford O.M.

*Whose exemplary contribution to the cultural
life of Jamaica in Arts, Letters, and Folklife won
for him the Jamaica Order of Merit, 1975.
He remains an inspiration to all Jamaicans.*

Contents

An Introduction to the Rastafarian Movement

BY C. ERIC LINCOLN

On August 6, 1962, the island of Jamaica became a sovereign state. While there was general rejoicing that the cold waters of European colonialism had receded from the shores of one more Black community, the event took on added significance in America where the Black freedom struggle had already captured the attention of the world. Hopes for the new Black nation were high, and have remained so. But expectations were high too, and nowhere were they higher than in Jamaica itself. "Emergent" nations have typically found an abundance of challenges facing them in their efforts to make their new status secure at home and abroad.

Jamaica, with a population of about two million and an area somewhat smaller than the state of Maryland, is not an exception. Despite the patina of affluence which radiates from selected areas of Kingston, the capital city, Jamaica is not a wealthy country. Much of its economy depends on tourism and the export of bauxite, sugar, bananas, and rum. The rest depends on the production of large numbers of small farmers with meagre holdings. The population of Jamaica is essentially rural; illiteracy is high. Unemployment, substandard housing, and low wages are perennial features. There are other problems. The legacy left by colonialism was not designed to engender broad agreement on national or personal identity, or on the identity of the issues most critical to the total welfare of Jamaica and Jamaicans. Jamaica has produced some very able political leadership since its independence. However, Jamaica, (as most other emergent states) suffers from the inability to translate absolute sovereignty into instant, absolute prosperity. Hence, it is fertile soil for a variety of indigenous efforts to monitor the process of making dreams real, to hurry it along, or to create alternatives for those who cannot wait any longer.

The Rastafarians are prominent among those who dissent from the "system" in Jamaica, and who offer spiritual and ideological alternatives to those which prevail in the larger society. The Rastafarians have deep roots in the protests of the maroon societies which excepted themselves from Jamaica's turbulent master-slave arrangement in the middle of the seventeenth century, and they remember Africa as the homeland from which they came and to which they must eventually return. In the interim, their temporary sojourn in Jamaica has gained increasing attention. This book by Professor Leonard Barrett is the fruit of an extended study of the Rastafarians, their history, their ideology, and their impact on Jamaica. It is an important contribution to the sociology of religion, and to the continuing effort of a distinguished cadre of Black scholars to document the variety of religious expressions which mark the dispersion of the West African Diaspora in the Western Hemisphere.

The first response to Professor Barrett's study of the Rastafarian movement is likely to be a sudden realization of the essential kinship of Blackamericans and Black Jamaicans, followed by a question of why so little thought has been given the matter before. While there has always been a general recognition of the fact that the West African Diaspora is dispersed throughout the Caribbean and in Central and South America as well, this sort of "general understanding" has seldom been of sufficient depth or intensity to make that recognition functional to the Blackamerican's consciousness of kind, or the recognition of common obstacles to a common destiny. Perhaps the reason lies first in the tribal differences of the slaves who were predominant in Jamaica and those who were brought to the American mainland. But this supposition is unconvincing because many slaves imported to America were purchased in Jamaica rather than in Africa, and even if that were not so, the ultimate African sources were not mutually exclusive.

Again, one might look at the essential insularity of the separate slave systems of America and Jamaica—an insularity to which distance, water, and the political style and religious and economic commitments of the slaveholding establishments made the significant contributions. So discrete and so insular were the slave systems of these two Atlantic communities that slaves of the same tribe, or even of the same family who were split between the two, could expect to live out their destinies as differently as if they were on separate planets. One factor of notable consequence bequeathed by this quirk of history has been the Jamaican's traditional recognition of color as a social and political value while the Blackamerican has struggled to suppress or deny it. Another has been the Jamaican's preoccupation with British culture while the Blackamerican has been trying to identify and establish his own. It would be incautious to assert, of course, that in either instance the orientations I have mentioned have been *exclusive.* They have not. But they are—or they have been—*prevailing* characteristics of the Jamaicans and the Blackamericans respectively. Even in the seaboard cities of America to which large numbers of Jamaicans have immigrated (except for a few intellectuals and professionals), mutual exclusiveness, encouraged by a panoply of myth and counter-myth, has been the usual social arrangement for most first generation Jamaican immigrants and indigenous American Blacks. How anomalous this would seem to be for peoples of a common ancestry, a common adopted language, and a common experience in chattel slavery!

Marcus Mosiah Garvey, who was considerably ahead of his detractors (at home and abroad) in his social insight and political daring, sensed the tragedy of the cultural and psychological isolationism which fragmented the Black Diaspora and sought to unite them under the banner of "One God! One Aim! One Destiny!" for eventual repatriation to Africa. African Zionism was not new, of course. It has probably been a feature in every sizeable community of displaced people of African descent. Garvey's unique contribution in this instance lay in his efforts to create a sense of kinship among Africans *outside* of Africa—kinship with each other—a functional recognition of the common bonds which, in binding them to the motherland, made them brothers wherever they were. W. E. B. DuBois' Pan-African Congresses were the caucuses of intellectuals on *behalf* of Africa. Garvey's Universal Negro Improvement Association was a commitment to *being* African—in America, or Jamaica, or Haiti, or wherever, and rejoicing in the prospects of complete consummation in Africa itself. This was the perfect expression of the uncluttered identity so common to the common people, but so seldom the comfort of the Black elite.

Garvey left an enormous legacy to the Black world. Since religion has always been the chief expression of what concerns Black people most intimately, it is perhaps inevitable that the fundamental teachings of Garvey found their principal survival in religion—in Jamaica where he was born, and in America where he knew his greatest triumphs. In America, the Black Muslims (now known as the Community of Islam in the West) incorporated much of Garvey's philosophy into their own "doctrine of the black man," and Elijah Muhammad spoke of Garvey as "a very fine Muslim." In Jamaica, where Garvey first introduced his strange notions about a worldwide brotherhood of Black people and the development of "Africa for the Africans," he attracted little interest and even less applause, at first. And while neither he nor his doctrines were ever accepted by the Jamaican middle class, the Rastafarians quickly made a prominent place for him in their pantheon.

The Rastafarians and the Black Muslims are both the products of extreme social dislocation, and the similarities

between the movements are very striking indeed. Both revere Marcus Garvey; both are millenarianism-messianic
cults; both received their primary incubation in the depression years of the early 1930s. Both consider the White man
to be the personification of evil, but both are willing to accept and work with White individuals who have overcome
their traditional racist behaviors, or who at least keep them
under restraint. Both have dietary restrictions which set
them apart from the nonbelievers, and both are distinctive
in their physical appearance—the Rastafarian "Dreadlocks,"
tanglehaired and unshaven; the Black Muslims, clean-cut
and neat in white shirts, jackets, and ties. Both the Rastafarians and the Muslims consider their present expatriation to
be temporary. A return to the motherland is the ultimate
goal which figures in every major activity and all planning
for the future. And both believe in a Black god, or more accurately, a Black man who *is* god. For the Rastafarians, god is
Haile Selassie, King of Ethiopia. For the Muslims, he is Wallace D. Fard who is considered to be "Allah in Person." Both
groups believe that God sent prophets, including Abraham,
Moses, and Jesus, and that eventually they were favored
with a visit from the deity himself—Farad having come to
Detroit in 1930, and Haile Selassie having visited Jamaica in
1966.

More important than anything else perhaps, is that both
movements accept the finality of death on this earth. This
lends a certain urgency to the changes they want to see
brought about, and it contributes to the impatience with
existing circumstances. To the Rastafarian, Jamaica is
"Babylon," and to the Black Muslim, America is the
"Wilderness in the West." Of course, Babylon must be destroyed, and the Muslims faithfully look forward to their
own "Battle of Armageddon," not in some mythical Es-
draelon, but "right here in the Wilderness of North
America."

Movements such as the Rastafarians and the Black Muslims are visible and insistent symbols of the failure of society to make its prevailing interests conform to the needs of

substantial numbers of the people who comprise it. It is impossible to tell how many members there are in either cult, for converts drift in and drift out in relation to their own sense of fulfillment, or lack of it as they experience the rituals, the fellowship, the common struggle, and the common hope. In any case, the real strength of such a movement does not lie in whatever number of formally enrolled adherents, but in the amorphous, faceless masses of the people who share their discontent and who share their hope for reversal. Of the Black Muslim membership, Malcolm X was fond of saying, "those who know don't say, and those who say don't know," but the Muslims' greatest security was in the knowledge that out there in the streets of the Black ghetto the line between the Black Muslims and the Black masses became progressively less distinct. So it is with the Rastafarians who have become the visible, cutting edge of the restlessness, the frustration, the discontent, and the creativity of the masses for whom society has no place except the bottom of the socioeconomic heap.

Social rejection may take one of two forms: those to be rejected may be stereotyped and labeled (e.g. "lazy Negro" or "greedy Jew") for ready identification and exclusion; or they may be consigned to a sort of anonymous oblivion which makes it easier for them to be simply ignored or forgotten. These psychological strategies often function to reinforce each other. A typical instance is the common observation of prejudiced Whites that "all Negroes look alike," or "a coon is a coon"—which is a more vicious rendering of the same idea. In either case, whether marked by stereotyping or marked by facelessness, the primary struggle of the disinherited is to select and project an identity. If society has chosen to be oblivious of them, the first task is to get on the record of human existence. If they have been negatively stereotyped and burdened with a pejorative label, they must either find a hidden, superior virtue in the stereotype (e.g. "greedy Jews" are really "astute businessmen") and superior value in the label (e.g. "black is beautiful"), or they must disavow the stereotype *and* the label by creating a counterimage and adopting a name engendering veneration and respect. Thus the Black Muslims refute the "Negro" stereotype by their industriousness, and they call themselves "Bilallians," after an African Muslim, which is to them a more distinguished and acceptable appellation than the despised "Negro"—a code name fastened on them by the White man to identify them as people to be scorned, exploited, and abused.

In Jamaica, as in the United States, an acceptable social identity is not to be taken for granted. The problem is compounded by the fact that the African intaglio has been spangled with multiethnic impingements, both biological and cultural for well over three hundred years—more than enough time for lips to be thinned, colors to be blended, hair to be modified, and memories to be blurred. Since the educated elite are themselves quite often confused regarding identity, and not infrequently attempt to assume identities inconsistent with more palpable realities, the struggle for identity among the masses becomes a critical aspect of the struggle for survival and for reasonable participation in whatever values the society has to offer. In Jamaica, "Ethiopianism" is the search for an identity which is both venerable and stable. Ethiopia represents not only a glorious past and a continuing civilization universally respected in the political and cultural councils of the world, but Ethiopia is also intimately associated with the world's great religious traditions, even with the dawn of civilization itself. Beyond that, the Ethiopians are a *Black* people, an *African* people, and the most singular heritage of the common people of Jamaica is that they are Black and African. Hence, Ethiopianism is a logical element of the Rastafarian movement because it not only accomplishes identity, but it establishes historical continuity as well. It also implies a critical judgment upon the ruling classes "whose self-identity," as Professor Barrett observes, "has been suppressed by alien symbols from the outside."

Rastafarianism is essentially the symbolic projection of the selected identity of Jamaica's peasant class upon the attention and the conscience of Jamaica first, and then the world at large. The rituals, including the use of ganja, the style of dress, and the idiom of speech, the Ethiopianism, the art, and the music are all in the first instance ways of rejecting a consignment to inexistence which the Rastafarians equate with life in Jamaica. Jamaica is "Babylon." Jamaica is a "hopeless hell." The Rastafarians are *in* Babylon, but not *of* it. Ethiopia is heaven; Ethiopia is home. And whatever distinguishes the believer, i.e. the true Rastafarian, ipso facto marks the sojourners and sets them apart from the prodigals of Babylon. Hence, the Rastafarians represent the insistent, vital signs of a class of people in Jamaica who have been written off by the politics and the economics of contemporary times. They have their counterparts in many corners of the world, for there are always dissenters who refuse to capitulate without a struggle to the pressures and powers which determine the fate of the poor and the weak.

Professor Barrett, who is himself a Jamaican, a student of history, and an acute observer, has witnessed for himself the turbulence and the uncertainty of an island cosmos in continuous transition. Yet, he is cautiously optimistic about the role the "functional" Rastafarians will play in the future of Jamaica. There are some encouraging signs, but Professor Barrett is also mindful of the explosive pressures within and without the movement which could give it a dramatic change in direction.

It is a very long way from the simple society of the Arawaks to a vote in the United Nations. The long pilgrimage has been made exceedingly complex by the distinctive interests of Spaniards, Africans, Englishmen, Chinese, East Indians, Jews, slaves, laborers, Planters, patricians, petite bourgeoisie, maroons, mulattoes, Blacks, and the educated and the uneducated in varying combinations. The stresses of transition were too great for the indigenous Arawaks, and they soon became extinct. In contrast, the proliferation of the African Diaspora would seem to suggest a persistence and a staying power which does indeed augur well for Jamaica, and for African societies elsewhere in the world. It was the Africans who came to Jamaica under the most inhospitable conditions, whose lives were the most expendable, whose welfare was always incidental, and whose presence was the basis of the economy, the labor force, and the caste arrangements which provided the psychological security for all the others. To the degree that the Rastafarians are representative of the African penchant for surviving neglect and outlasting oppression, Professor Barrett's optimism would seem to be well grounded.

The place for caution is to avoid a premature conclusion that the Rastafarians, with all their color and their popular impeccancy, do in fact represent the wave of the future in Jamaica. One of the most impressive facts gleaned from the study of such movements is their unpredictability. Doctrines turn on the charisma of leadership; the realization of minor goals often compromises the zeal for more distant and less achievable goals. Ritual and pageantry and the visible symbols of membership have a way of becoming ends in themselves. But the greatest obstacle to movements like the Rastafarians and their desire to find fulfillment in modern times is the lock-step nature of contemporary society. Most societies today are so irretrievably locked into a set of relations and expectations—with forces internal and external to themselves—that they lack the flexibility to respond to such movements unless, and until, they become cataclysmic. Even then the desired response may either be obsolete or past delivery. Ironic as it may seem, a major reason why these movements come into being in the first place is that the faceless masses have not been heard, or are convinced that they have not been heard by the powers which condition their lives and the circumstances of their being. When those powers fail to respond because they *cannot*—having been in effect automated by reciprocating systems of relationships which exclude the interests of the poor and the weak—the social mechanism has become an automaton programmed for its own destruction. Barring a transformation which changes the nature and the style of its coercive potential, messianic-millenarianism is unlikely to be able to either rescue an errant modern society, or deflect it from its course. Hence, a movement like the Rastafarians is more realistically limited to avoidance and rebuke of the offending society while waiting for its predicted demise. And when the end comes, the disinherited will survey the ruins and gather themselves to await their leader's call to come home—in the case of the Rastafarians, to Africa. To Ethiopia. To be with Ras Tafari, Negus Negast, the Conquering Lion of Judah.

Preface

From North America to mother Africa, a new sound can be heard from the Caribbean haunting the places where Black people get together for music and dancing. From the prestigious Hotel Ivoire in Abidjan on the Ivory Coast to the secluded Meridian Hotel built by Kwame Nkrumah in the seaside city of Tema in Ghana, wherever the reggae is heard, its lighthearted mysterious sound always evokes an emotional reaction. Beginning with a slow, undulating, hesitant beat, the music of reggae assaults the primitive brain stem where emotions originate. Before the brain can decipher the new beat, the driving Trench Town music captures and transports the listener. The effect of reggae is magic; it is Africa, Jamaica, soul, nature, sorrow, hate, and love all mingled together. It sprang from the hearts of Africa's children in "Babylon"—Jamaica. It is liminal music that sings of oppression in exile, a longing for home, or for a place to feel at home.

Reggae, like its earlier counterpart calypso, quickly became a medium of social commentary as part of the African cultural tradition transported to the Caribbean by the slaves. It still serves as a social safety valve through which oppressed peoples express their discontent. Like the music of Africa, the reggae is for dancing, but the lyrics elicit a variety of responsive emotions—crying, rage, and rejoicing. As Bob Marley sings in "Them Belly Full (But We Hungry)":

> Forget your troubles and dance
> Forget your sorrows and dance
> Forget your sickness and dance
> Forget your weakness and dance.[1]

Reggae is a cultic expression that is both entertaining, revolutionary, and filled with Rastafarian symbolism. The symbols are readily understood in the Jamaican society, but the real cultic dimension of reggae was unknown until the Rastafarian song-prophet, Bob Marley, made his debut in New York. Marley stamped his personality on reggae until the sound became identified with the Rastafarian movement. Reggae music is now a multimillion-dollar industry, but its cultural significance derives from that unique sect whose music is an inseparable and expressive ingredient. This book is about this sect—the Rastafarians.

The Jamaican Rastafarian cult is the largest, most identifiable, indigenous movement in Jamaica. As such, it has a philosophy and structure capable of providing a rallying point for the masses in search of social change. In the last ten years, the movement has attracted much attention, not only in this West Indian island where it originated, but also in the United States, Great Britain, Canada, and Africa. Although the movement has been in existence since 1930, very little—and that mostly sensational—has been written about it. Consequently, the movement is generally misunderstood, not only in Jamaica, but also in America and Canada, where many members and affiliates have migrated. Some of the reasons for the Rastafarian's bad publicity in the early days of the movement may be due to some provocative incidents associated with fringe groups of the movement. Two incidents worth mentioning are the "Henry Fiasco" of 1960 (which created an islandwide emergency after the shooting of two soldiers of the Royal Hampshire Regiment and three Rastafarians under the leadership of Ronald Henry), and the so-called "Holy Thursday Massacre" of

April 1963 (in which several police and civilians were killed on the North Coast near Montego Bay).

Another reason contributing to the negative image of the Rastafarians is their strange hairstyle known as "dreadlocks," which some people feel is wild and unattractive. The Rastas adopted the dreadlocks during their "jungle existence" in the hill country where the movement developed its early characteristics. This dreadlock appearance is the distinguishing mark of the movement. Another trait contributing to the Rastafarian's negative image is their members' use of "ganja" (marijuana) in their sacred rituals.

Despite the early adverse publicity of the movement, the negative reaction to the members' hairstyle, and their constant use of the "weed," this Jamaican movement has evolved into a dynamic, creative instrument for social change. The Rastas are admired by the masses and have received praises from the current prime minister of Jamaica, who sees them as a "beautiful and remarkable people."

But while the Rastafarians have quieted down in Jamaica, a new wave of adverse publicity has surrounded some of their followers in New York City where the movement appeared after Jamaica's independence in 1962. Some Jamaicans who immigrated to the United States during this post-independence period were either Rastafarians or marginal followers of the movement. After reaching New York, they found themselves psychologically uprooted in a strange land and, for the most part, out of work and homesick. The dreadlocks' appearance in New York and in other North American cities where the cultists were relatively unknown compounded the isolation of the newcomers. As nostalgia set in, these new immigrants became convinced that only a Jamaican movement could offer them identity. Today, there is nothing more Jamaican than the Rastafarians. The assumption of Rasta garb and habits was natural.

This New York version of the Rastas—mostly youth-oriented and ganglike in characteristic—soon adopted the prevailing patterns of the big city youth culture. Several groups began opposing each other for separate ganja-turfs which resulted in a wave of shooting and killing. The behavior of these immigrant Rastafarians brought unwelcome publicity to their middle-class Jamaican counterparts living in New York who felt their prestige was threatened by the cultists' Jamaican identification. However, much of this negative behavior is changing and, in time, the creative dynamics of these Rastas will probably be turned toward creative channels like the "Old Settler" Jamaicans who are known for their industry and achievement.

Aims of the Book

This study will show the emergence and development of the Rastafarians cult from its inception in 1930 to the present. Particular attention will be paid to the socioeconomic conditions from which this cult emerged; its ideology; its function as a socioreligious movement within the Jamaican community; and its impact on the Western world. This book will also explore some of the myths surrounding the movement, as well as discussing some of the more serious contributions the Rastafarians have made to Jamaican society.

The book has four aims: *First*, to make an original contribution to Caribbean studies—an increasingly important topic—in which there is a scarcity of indigenous research. Many of the previous studies of the Rastafarians' beliefs and practices are limited and outdated. Among these earlier investigations are: a short paper by George Eaton Simpson, 1953; the small monograph by Smith, Augier, and Nettleford, 1960; and the author's monograph, 1968. "The Report on the Rastafari Movement" by Smith, Augier, and Nettleford, 1960, has become a classic, although only fifty pages long. Professor Rex Nettleford's recent book *Race, Identity and Protest* (1973), contains an excellent chapter on the movement. Also *Soul-Force: African Heritage in Afro-American Religion*, 1974, includes a chapter on the movement.[2]

Second, to show that the Rastafarian movement—

although assimilating much of the native religious culture
of Jamaica—has rejected most of what is considered typically Jamaican, even to the point of spurning Jamaican nationality. It is unlike the Revival and Pukumina cults which
can be considered Christian-oriented cults. The Rastafarians
reject Christianity and firmly believe in Haile Selassie as the
returned Messiah and Ethiopia as the promised land of all
Black people.

Third, to show the effects of cultural deprivation and what
can result in a society when individual members are denied
the opportunities to perform the cultural roles which are
normally expected of them—hindered by adverse socioeconomic and political conditions—and the environment
necessary for their fulfillment.

Fourth, to study the nature and dynamics of a
millenarian-messianic movement and its function and impact on a typical Caribbean community. An investigation of
this nature will reveal that the Rastafarian movement in
Jamaica is only one of thousands of such movements which
have emerged throughout the world.

A study of these movements has considerable significance
in understanding the dynamics of the so-called Third World.
Between local ethnic (or native traditional) religions and the
missionary religious faiths, religious movements such as the
Rastafarian cult are of great interest to scholars of
phenomenology and the history of religion. They also con-
tribute important biographies of prophets and martyrs. To
the sociologists and anthropologists, they provide studies in
the dynamics of culture contacts and social change; and to
political scientists, they provide the studies of ideologies.
Some of these movements may be seen as reactions against
colonialism, interest groups, and the emergence of
nationalism. To the psychologists, they may exemplify
stress and adjustive phenomena. Linguists may find the
emergence of new symbolic language formations—an
evolving field—not to mention the potential for students of
theology.

The present work is the product of over ten years of research. The original research covers the years 1963–1966, from which a monograph was published in 1968—only a limited number of copies were distributed. Encouraged by the persistent demand for this initial study, the author returned to the project in 1966 to update the original monograph. This book is the culmination of that undertaking.

My thanks to my many Rastafarians friends in Jamaica who helped me in my research over the years. To cite each name individually would be impossible, although many of their names appear in this book. As usual, my wife, Theodora, has been of great help typing and retyping the early drafts of this book and offering constructive criticisms which are incorporated into the work.

My thanks to Miss Nancy Krody of the *Journal of Ecumenical Studies*, Temple University, for reading and correcting the manuscript; and to Mrs. Grace Stuart for the final typing.

1

Paradise Island

Who Are the Rastafarians?

The Rastafarian cult is a messianic movement unique to Jamaica. Its members believe that Haile Selassie, Emperor of Ethiopia, is the Black Messiah who appeared in the flesh for the redemption of all Blacks exiled in the world of White oppressors. The movement views Ethiopia as the promised land, the place where Black people will be repatriated through a wholesale exodus from all Western countries where they have been in exile (slavery). Repatriation is inevitable, and the time awaits only the decision of Haile Selassie. Known only to the true believers, the details of the actual departure are secret. In the past some fantasies called for planes to the United States, and then ships from there to Africa. Some envision the operation being launched from the shores of Jamaica by at least ten British ships at a time, while others see the operation being undertaken in Ethiopian vessels at Jamaican expense.

The destination of this great migration is also vague in the minds of some speculators. The majority see Ethiopia as their homeland; others view Africa as the true homeland. There is no unanimity about the destination. To many, Ethiopia means Africa, while to others, Ethiopia is the promised land, though they will settle for any part of the continent.[1]

The author, who has observed the Rastafarians since 1946 and has carried out systematic research among them from 1963 to 1966 (on which his first monograph was based), returned recently to Jamaica to study their development from 1966 to the present. The findings of the new search demand that much of what was written in the 1968 monogaph be revised and updated. An up-to-date assessment of the movement may be stated as follows:

The present membership of the Rastafarian movement, including sympathizers, may number one hundred thousand.[2] No census has yet given an accurate account of the membership, but a knowledgeable Rasta leader states that six out of every ten Jamaicans are either Rastas or sympathizers.[3]

The membership is young and has no individual leadership. Up to 80 percent of those seen in the camps and on the streets are between the ages of seventeen and thirty-five. The leading brethren are mostly men from thirty-five to fifty-five years of age. The older members were either ex-Garveyites or sympathizers of his movement.

Most members are male. Women play a very minor role in Rastafarianism and are generally seen only in the background of the camps. In special meetings women act as mistresses of songs or, in the case of the Rastafarian African National Congress, they may be used as recording secretaries. In all other respects the male assumes the responsibilities of the movement, though at present, a large segment of Rastafarian women now sell Rastafarian products such as knitted clothing, baskets, mats, brooms, art works, and other sundries.

Until 1965, the membership was essentially lower class, but this is no longer the case. Once considered "products of the slum," the Rastas have now penetrated the middle class. They are found among civil servants and the elite; some are students at the prestigious University of the West Indies;

some are in the medical profession and other upper-class occupations.

Based on the earlier research, the members were almost all of African stock. At present, the overwhelming majority of members still are, but there are also Chinese, East Indians, Afro-Chinese, Afro-East Indians or Afro-Jews, mulattoes, and a few Whites. Every ethnic minority is now represented in the Rastafarian camps.

The members are predominantly ex-Christians. About 90 percent of the members interviewed were from Protestant or Catholic churches or Pentecostal sects. The minority who said they had no church connection did acknowledge that they came from Christian homes.

As a group the Rastafarians see Jamaica as a land of oppression—Babylon. Their only avenue of escape is by supernatural means or by seizing the power and creating a utopia for the oppressed.

The Place, People, and Language

The island of Jamaica is the third largest in size of the West Indian islands after Cuba and Haiti. Jamaica is 150 miles long and 52 miles wide, subtropical, a land of warm weather without the extremes of climate common to the mainland of the United States. Jamaican harbors are among the world's finest, and Jamaican rivers add beauty and economic value to the island. Hills and mountains form the center of the island, ranging from the gentle Cockpit Mountains of the west to the high John Crow and Blue Mountains of the east, with altitudes exceeding seven thousand feet. These high mountains and the broad, easily drained plains below provide diversity of climate and agriculture.

The population of Jamaica is presently estimated at a little less than two million people, of which nearly a half-million now reside in Kingston, the capital and largest city.[4]

The distribution of people by racial origin can be summarized as follows: those of African origin, 90 percent;

Caucasians, about 1 percent; descendants of East Indians, 3 percent; those of Chinese descent, about 2 percent.[5] Of the remaining 4 percent, the Jews and Lebanese are the largest identifiable groups. Thus the vast majority of Jamaicans are currently of African or Afro-European descent. By contrast, the original inhabitants of the island (when Columbus discovered it in 1494) were the Arawak Indians, a homogeneous people completely different from any group living there now. Columbus' arrival introduced the natives to the Europeans, a meeting which proved catastrophic for the Arawak Indians: by the time the British conquered Jamaica in 1655 the Arawaks were extinct.

English is the formal language of the island. The greater part of the masses, however, speak a Jamaican dialect. Cassidy's *Jamaica Talk*[6] (the first scientific work to deal with the dialect) portrays Jamaica as a place where "a pepperpot of language is concocted." He observes that "Jamaica-talk" is not the same for every Jamaican because of the vast spectrum of dialects. "Jamaica-talk" exists in two main forms which Cassidy illustrates as lying at opposite ends of a scale. At one extreme is the type of "Jamaica-talk" that emulates the "London standard" or educated model spoken among many of the elite. At the other extreme is the inherited talk of peasant and laborer who remain largely unaffected by education and its standards. Their speech is what linguists call "creolized" English; that is, fragmented English speech and syntax assimilated during the days of slavery and mixed with African influences. This Anglo-African admixture continues to be spoken in much the same form today.

There is, though, a third dialectical element in Jamaica located in the middle of the language scale where one discovers an increasing inclusion of local elements of Jamaican rhythm and intonation of words that the Londoner would have no need to know. These characteristics of the language evolved within an island population, which Cassidy calls "Jamaicanism." He defines this term by citing five main divisions:

1. Retention, which includes English words now rare or poetic that are still in common use in Jamaica.
2. New formations, which are in turn subdivided into alterations, compositions, and creations.
3. Borrowings which are French and Portuguese words which came into English as early as the eighteenth century.
4. Onomatopoeic echoisms.
5. Usage of words which, though not exclusively Jamaican, is the preferred term on the island.[7]

Speaking of the greatest influence on "Jamaica-talk," Cassidy concludes:

Of non-British influences it is obvious that the African is the largest and most profound; it appears not only in the vocabulary, but has powerfully affected both pronunciation and grammar. We may feel fairly certain about two hundred and thirty loan-words from various African languages; and if the numerous compounds and derivatives were added, and the large number of untraced terms which are at least quasi-African in form, the total would easily be more than four hundred. Even at its most, the African element in the vocabulary is larger than all the other non-English ones together.[8]

Cassidy's studies, which were carried out in the 1950s, made no mention of the influence of the Rastafarian movement on "Jamaica-talk." Since the 1950s, a new linguistic change has taken place in Jamaica. This is what we may call a "soul language"—highly symbolic and radically revolutionary. The development of this new linguistic component will be discussed in Chapter 5.

Education in Jamaica has generally followed the British pattern. Though understandable from a historical perspective, the system has created much confusion in the social patterns of the Jamaican people. During the colonial period (and to a great extent to the present day), children were taught about the English culture without attempting to relate it to the environment in which they lived. Madeline Kerr, in her analysis of five schools, points out that the subject matter was basically meaningless to the children. Central to the curriculum was the Bible, taught from a strictly fundamentalist point of view. Children memorized enormous passages of prose and poetry and learned to read by chanting passages from books. Discipline in the schools was often harsh, and although some teachers restricted the amount of lashing, beating was the rule, not the exception.[9]

Prior to independence (and even today), children attended elementary school up to the age of eleven when they were expected to pass a common entrance examination. The completion of this test entitled the child to enter an approved school until he or she passed the General Certificate of Education. This certificate admitted the child, in some cases, to a university.

One of the great problems of education in Jamaica is the lack of proper training of teachers, the majority of whom, until recently, reached a standard scarcely higher than the American high school.

With the coming of self-government there has been a remarkable increase in educational facilities. In 1944, primary school teachers numbered less than three thousand; by 1960, the figure had grown to over five thousand. School attendance figures are even more revealing. Whereas in 1944 there were only 171,455 elementary school pupils, by 1960 the figure had grown to 315,000. Great emphasis was also placed on secondary education. While there were only twenty-three secondary schools in 1944, by 1960 the number had reached forty-one. Recently, compulsory education has been instituted by the Peoples National party. Hundreds of new schools have been built and thousands of new pupils are now assured an education. Depending on the economic well-being of the island, the future of the educational system looks bright.[10]

The University College of the West Indies (now the University of the West Indies) was founded in 1948 at Mona, near Kingston, with an enrollment of thirty-three students. Current enrollment exceeds five thousand.[11] A number of vocational and technical schools have been constructed on the island to encourage and meet the demand for mechanical and technical skills in a developing nation. These upper-level educational institutions provide an excellent education but their number and capacity to meet the needs of an exploding population are grossly inadequate.

Jamaica's economy is basically agricultural, employing over 40 percent of the island's labor force.[12] Before the Second World War, agriculture accounted for 36 percent of the island's total exports in the form of sugar, bananas, and rum and comprised four-fifths of the island's export revenue. By 1961, however, agriculture provided only 13 percent of the total income. In the past ten years, rapid developments have taken place in mining, manufacturing, and tourism. All three industries presently are experiencing the uncertainties of worldwide inflation and recession. Thus the future of the Jamaican economy will demand courageous leadership and sound fiscal planning.

A striking characteristic of Jamaica's agriculture is the large number of small farmers. There are 159,000 small farmers, of whom 113,000 work less than five acres.[13] A recent report states that the agricultural pattern of Jamaican farmers has not changed in the last 100 years, largely due to lack of land and primitive techniques. The present government is dedicated to rectifying this imbalance, and new laws have been instituted to make unused lands available to the small farmers.

One of the largest known deposits of bauxite in the world was discovered in Jamaica in the early 1950s. This discovery promoted the establishment of a mining industry and boosted the general economy. Bauxite and aluminum currently account for 50 percent of the island's earning,[14] a figure expected to increase greatly in the next five years if the demand for bauxite-related goods continues to grow. The government recently moved to nationalize the bauxite industry which created a mini-international upheaval among the ranks of multinational cartels. Whether this move will prove dangerous to Jamaica is still uncertain, although at the moment, it seems certain that Jamaica will get the worst end of the bargain in the long run.

Industry has become a serious concern for the government. Its industrial development program has been implemented by the Industrial Development Corporation and included incentive legislation as well as promotional activities in the United States, United Kingdom, and Canada. As a result, the island now has a wider variety of manufactured products using both local and imported raw materials. Among these new products are clothing, footwear, textiles, paints, and building materials, including cement. Some of these are used locally, but most are exported.

This economic picture greatly affects the lives of Rastafarians. It is in response to this cultural and economic condition that the Rastafarians have emerged as a movement. The competence of most Rastas lies in the semiskilled or the marginally skilled occupations. They are mostly prepared to do farm labor, but possess no land. Some have taken up painting, masonry, or carpentry; others have become domestic servants, janitors, wood workers, or small shopkeepers. Wages for these occupations, when work is available, does not exceed twenty dollars per week. The labor problem in Jamaica is such that the number of unskilled laborers far exceeds the demand, and the population of unskilled laborers grows in geometric proportion yearly. The present situation demands the creation of new methods in the use of the island's manpower similar to the WPA scheme of the United States.

Living Conditions

The City of Kingston

The city of Kingston and its environs are a study in contrasts; beautiful suburban communities in the highlands overlook miles of slum dwellings in various stages of blight and decay as they swelter in the hot, putrid air which varies only a degree or two each night year-round. The ten-mile bus route from Tower Street to Cross Roads—on any of the many arteries leading north—is a jungle of dilapidated housing projects interspersed with new government office buildings which tower over what was once a thriving community of commercial and cultural enterprises. Now these areas seem deserted by the exodus of the more affluent population to the suburbs with new shopping malls in the greener pastures of St. Andrew.

Leaving the city and going north, one comes to an abrupt divide known as Cross Roads. This is indeed the crossroads between poverty and ostentation displayed by the middle- and upper-class Jamaicans who flaunt their manicured gardens and mansion-like houses, complete with quarters for the servants who attend them. Cross Roads was once a charming village town, containing one of Jamaica's most beautiful movie theaters, and pride of the city—Carib. Today, the theater stands blushing at the Jamaican omnibus terminal which spreads like an ulcer just past the Carib's entrance. As many as twenty-five buses filled with sweating passengers converge on this spot hourly.

The line of demarcation seen at Cross Roads typifies the division of wealth between the Jamaican upper-class and the masses from which the Rastafarian population is drawn. Slum conditions in Jamaican cities are probably the worst in the Caribbean, except for Haiti. The Rastafarian poet Sam Brown, in his unpublished poem "Slum Condition," depicts the existing situation in Kingston more eloquently than any other. The first verse describes the appearance of the slums of Jones Town and Trench Town where most cultists live:

Tin-can houses, old and young, meangy dogs, rats, inhuman
   stench,
Unthinkable conditions that cause the stoutest heart to wrench.
Tracks and little lanes like human veins, emaciated people,
Many giving up the ghost, their spirits broken, their gloom
   deepens.
Precocious boys and girls, yet adults, police, thieves,
   conglomerates,
Generally disjointed, sexually abandoned masters of their fate.

The next verse portrays what it is like to exist under these conditions:

Tribal warfares, rapings, inhumanity, police brutality, daily
    occurrence,
Yet, they are diamonds in the rough, who bites with this
    abhorence.
Like Alice, slums without pity, lacking love, each grim and screws,
Some ailing ones weaker than the rest, don't know what to do.

Sam Brown then shows that the cultists are aware of the
causes of their oppressions:

Some young desperates look to the hills, see the seat of their
    distress,
They see the dwellers of the hills as them that do oppress.
Churches wedged in among the hovels, squealing pigs, juke-boxes
    blaring,
Small land space, old cars and bars, Jesus could not get a hearing.

In the following lines he shows the callous attitude of the
elite to the poor:

Men, women and children stark naked, lunatics of wants,
    reformatory,
Milk powder, polio victims, rickity, medical infirmary.
Executives in horseless chariots sometimes pass through hold their
    noses,
Hapless poor look with vengeful eyes, for them no bed of roses.

Finally, the results of years of oppression—the gunmen who
now make life unbearable:

Better wanted, not worse, for him it can't be worse,
Conscience of man, humanity, civilization in reverse.
People in fear, bulldozer mashing, smashing, cannot save the
    situation,
Lift the ban, free the food, for peace reassemble the nation.
Corruption to achieve material, graft, bribes, high and low,
Official-mantled crooks, gunmen equal, the innocent have no place
    to go.[15]

The author of this poem has lived his entire life in the
slums of Jamaica. He was an occupant of the tin can houses
in that part of the city then known as "Back-O-Wall," before
the government destroyed it with a fleet of bulldozers. Since
then, the Rastafarians have moved into other tin can houses
in the heart of the city, or on the edges of it. The poem

touches on all of the sights, sounds, and smells of Kingston: the churches in the hovels, the blaring juke-boxes, the gunmen and their victims, and the ever-present police. The attitudes of the slum dwellers are clearly shown in the lines, "Some desperates look to the hills, see the seat of their distress," and "Hapless poor look with vengeful eyes, for them no bed of roses." The ratio of the haves to the have-nots in Jamaica was recently put at twenty to one. The narrowing of this gap is the declared goal of the present government. But for now, the result of the disparity in living conditions is hatred, fear, distrust, and anxiety among the wealthy, while the life of the poor grows only more unbearable.

The Rural Areas

Although great strides toward better living conditions have been made in the rural areas in the last decade, this has not changed the pitiful state of housing, cultivable lands, and economic wage differentials. In fact, the majority of rural Jamaican housing remains the same as that described by Martha Beckwith in her study of 1929.[16] Typical of these areas are the "wattle and daub" dwellings, houses built with sticks, covered with wattle, plastered with clay and a little cement, and then whitened with lime. Thatch palms cover the roof, though sheets of zinc are used by the more affluent. The average house is occasionally floored with boards, but more usually has only an earthen floor. Three of every four of these houses have no electricity or running water and most have only an outside pit-latrine. Cooking is done outside the house in a separate kitchen with wood or coal. One out of four rural houses that has an inside kitchen has a kerosene stove for cooking. About half of the rural dwellers rent their houses or lease their lands from large estate owners. It is not unheard of for families who have lived on a piece of land for generations to suddenly find themselves dispossessed by a neighboring landowner who, by fact or by fraud, can show that the land belongs to him.

In the last two years much attention has been given to the plight of the rural poor by the present government. One of

the most grievous problems in the countryside is the access
to cultivable lands. Prior to independence, about 60 percent
of the land was held by 1 percent of the population—largely
cane farmers who acted as absentee landowners. The rural
farmers had but a small piece of land, mostly on the hilly
slopes, on which to eke out a living. A large proportion of
the cultivable lands were either kept as grazing lands for the
very rich or left idle as private holdings. Recently, the government, under a very unpopular Land Acquisition Act, has
been laying claim to these lands and returning them under a
lease-hold arrangement to small farmers, hoping to improve
the conditions of the rural poor and to encourage able-bodied
persons in the city to return to the country.[17]

The wage differential in Jamaica is probably the most
alarming in the world. The few people who have a profession
or some skill receive as much as thirty times more than the
unskilled. In instituting the recent Minimum Wage Law of
1975, the prime minister, the Honorable Michael Manley,
startled the House of Parliament with the following revelations: twenty-eight thousand or more Jamaicans earn less
than ten dollars per week; sixty-four thousand earn less than
fifteen dollars per week; and one hundred one thousand earn
less than twenty dollars per week. The author is convinced
that about one half of all Jamaicans would fall under the category of ten dollars per week per capita.[18]

Unemployment and Crime

The legacy of colonialism now seen in the maldistribution
of land and wealth represents a growing problem which
must be remedied quickly if Jamaica is to survive. Eighty
percent of the common laborers who are unskilled earn
twenty dollars per week when they do get work. Add to this
the permanently underemployed and the unemployables,
and the situation is a sociopolitical headache for a new nation. The present government, which has followed a platform of democratic socialism since 1973, is feverishly im-
plementing crash programs to absorb some of the labor

force, but with inflation and recession, and few sources of revenues, its enthusiasm will remain stymied for some time to come.

In the meantime, the people who have no concept of the enormous difficulties facing the government are impatient. This impatience is mirrored in the rapid growth of crime on the island. Easy access to guns and their indiscriminate use is turning living conditions into a nightmare. The situation, though frightening, is understandable. The history of Jamaica is one long tale of exploitation by a few rich families whose privileges were never questioned. But with independence, Jamaica was thrust into the arena of the underdeveloped nations with little or no aid from those who benefited from the island. Many of these rich families continued to profit from their investments, spending little or nothing on the island. They were on the island but not of it. Most investors did not even keep their wealth in Jamaican banks, but stashed it in foreign banks. With the recent announcement of the government's new democratic socialism and the sudden awakening of social and cultural consciousness, the people of wealth have migrated from Jamaica, leaving the government and its people to simmer in a "stew" not of their own making.

With the passing of the old order, the oppressed masses have become bewildered by the rapid change which allows little time to learn the new symbols of socialism that remain in various stages of formulation. The result is mild chaos, mirrored in an ambivalent longing for the old, oppressive society, while groping uncertainly toward an untried future. The birth pangs of unrest shake the body. The criminal element is emerging from the people who have been consistently denied a share in the wealth of their homeland and who are now determined to get a piece of the pie by any possible means. The means now utilized is violence against the Black and White society. No one is excluded in this "war." The Jamaican gunman is a cold and systematic killer executing what he believes to be his duty. Gun crimes have become so pervasive that the government recently originated an internationally unique institution (probably the first in any democratic country)—the Gun Court—which is both a court of law and a detention camp.

The term is a pseudonym for a process of incarcerating apprehended gunmen and later trying them under the Jamaica Gun Court Act of 1974. Under this act, if a person is found guilty of possessing an unlicensed firearm, or even a few bullets, he receives a mandatory sentence of "detention for life with hard labor." A gunman can be released from this sentence only when deemed fit to live a wholesome life in the community, and that at the discretion of the governor general of Jamaica.

This social modification technique was designed to control the crime wave that drove Jamaicans to the brink of despair. The island is flooded with illegal firearms of largely unknown origin. As a crime control technique, the gun court was so unique in the Americas that it became a feature story on "Sixty Minutes" (CBS) in 1975. Despite the urgent need for the control of crime in Jamaica, some of the island's legal experts were convinced that a court set up outside the judicial provisions of the Jamaican constitution was illegal. As a consequence, in April of 1974, four men sentenced to indefinite detention for possession of firearms were encouraged to appeal their cases with the intention of testing the constitutionality of the Gun Court Act of 1974. The case was ultimately brought before the Privy Council Judicial Committee of Great Britain, which still operates as the court of last resort for Jamaican citizens. The Privy Council heard the case for six days; the final decision was that the Gun Court is constitutional, but a sentence of "indefinite detention is unlawful." Emboldened by this ruling, the gunmen opened a new campaign of violence. Shooting, burning, and other violent crimes spurred the government to rewrite the Gun Court Law of 1976. It demands a life term for firearm crimes, with no appeal; but under special privileges granted by the Jamaican Appeals Council, the act has also been widened to deal with violence of a political nature, which many observers believe to be at the heart of the Jamaican crime wave.

Early in 1976, violent crimes in Jamaica necessitated the government's call for "national emergency," which temporarily suspended certain freedoms of its citizens in order to deal with the criminal outbursts. Since then, the shootings have subsided considerably, but many Jamaicans feel that the objectives of the emergency have fallen short of the goal. Most of the gunmen have taken to the mountains and countrysides, awaiting the lifting of the emergency. Meanwhile, the Gun Court still exists on South Camp Road.

At the extreme end of Jamaican society stands another group who disagree with the tactics of the gunmen, but whose philosophy suggests that the remedy for Jamaicans' woes is total revolution similar to that of Cuba. Supported by the gunmen, this philosophy is advocated by intellectuals who are avid students of Marx and Lenin. Although sympathizing greatly with the declared democratic socialism of the government, the intellectuals feel that this halfway measure is not drastic enough to cure the ills of Jamaica. It will placate a few, but it will not cure the disease. To them socialism is a step in the right direction. But anything short of scientific socialism and a social revolution which will dislodge the privileged and destroy the strangle hold of multinational corporations will be but salve on a deep wound.

At present, then, Jamaica is experiencing a situation in which the government is trying—through democratic socialism—to eradicate the repressive colonial past, a past based on the privilege of the landed gentry and the financiers of goods and services which bring exorbitant prices and profits. These businesses are staffed by a middle class who depended on their monied masters for their existence. On the bottom stood the hungry masses, effectively kept at a distance by the arm of the law, whose duty it was to protect capital. With independence and the awakening consciousness of the masses—a climate which now pervades all Third World nations—there emerges a militant avant-garde who cannot wait for the government's step-by-step socialistic program but feel it their duty to bring about the millenium by forcible means. The middle-class intellectuals, although sympathetic to socialism, feel that the problems demand revolution now. In the meantime, the once beautiful island of paradise now exists with an overgrown serpent coiled around its center. The frustration of this situation was expressed by the columnist of the *Sunday Gleaner* on June 29, 1975, who wrote under the heading "Paradise Lost":

More and more criminals appear to possess guns and to use them on victims with or without provocations; people's houses are being broken into and the inmates killed, wounded or raped; residents are being chased away and their houses burned or broken down; shops, betting places and payrolls are being robbed right and left; complaints and witnesses are disappearing so that accused have to be let off for lack of evidences, and physical evidences have been destroyed; by bombing a police station; criminals are escaping after conviction; courthouses have been invaded and the police attacked to free prisoners; organized gangs of young thugs have taken over meetings; praedial larceny is more prevalent than ever.

Despite this long litany of woe, the writer has left out many more problems that could have been included. One that comes to mind is the desecration of holy places, a problem previously unheard of in Jamaica.

Religion:

To enter into a discussion of Jamaican religiosity, one must first deal with a short historical background of the island's inhabitants, the earliest being the Arawak Indians, who were finally destroyed under Spanish rule between 1502 and 1655. When the British conquered the Spanish in 1655, not a trace of these Arawak people could be found. As a result, the Spanish substituted African slaves in small numbers until, under the British, thousands of West African slaves were brought to Jamaica.

The West Africans brought to the island were mostly from the Gold Coast and Nigeria. The British Planters insisted on

these people above all others because of their sturdiness. It
was the Ashanti, however, that left the greatest cultural imprint on Jamaica, noticeable to this day. Consequently, the
language of the Jamaican peasants still carries hundreds of
words that need no translation from the original Ashanti
tongue—Twi. But the area most dominated by Ashanti influence was the folk religion, still practiced today under the
name of *Kumina*.[19] The word comes from two Twi words:
Akom—"to be possessed," and *Ana*—"by an ancestor." This
ancestor-possession cult became the medium of religious
expression for all Africans during the slave period. Throughout most of the Caribbean, this kind of African religious
syncretism seems to have taken place. Examples can be
found in Haiti where all the tribes taken there seem to have
fused their religious rituals under the Dahomean rubric
known as *Vodun*.[20] The same thing happened in Trinidad
where the Nigerian influence dominated, fusing the disparate elements into a cult known as *Shango*.[21] A similar process also occurred in Cuba under the name *Santeria*.[22]

Slave Religion in Jamaica

Unlike Haiti, where the slaves were commanded if not
forced to be members of the Catholic church, the English
Planters in Jamaica adamantly refused to share their religion
with the slave population. The Church of England and its
high liturgy was considered too sophisticated for people of
"lesser breed" and, further, the masters feared that the
preachers—in their unguarded inspirational moments—
would stretch the equality of humanity before God a little
too far. The slaves, left to themselves, developed elements of
the remembered religious systems from their homeland.
This was not difficult to do because among the slave population were African religious functionaries who had been indiscriminately carried to the island. According to Herbert
DeLisser, one of Jamaica's historians on slavery:

Both witches and wizards, priests and priestesses, were brought to
Jamaica in the days of the slave trade, and, the slaves recognised the

distinction between the former and the latter. Even the masters saw that the two classes were not identical, and they called the latter "myal-men and myal-women" . . . [these were] the people who cured . . . .[23]

DeLisser goes on to say that the legitimate slave priests and priestesses of African religion were unable to function in their customary roles and therefore turned to sorcery—practicing witchcraft as ritual aggression against the slave system. They became what is known in Jamaica as *obeah*-men and *obeah*-women. The word *obeah* is known throughout the English slave regions, and is derived from two Ashanti words *oba*—"a child," and *yi*—"to take." The idea of taking a child was the final test of a sorcerer, a deed giving the status of Ph.D. in witchcraft.[24] *Obeah*, then, became the most dreadful form of Caribbean witchcraft, plaguing both Black and White in the days of slavery and continuing to haunt Jamaicans today.

Although the legitimate priests and priestesses were unable to do their work under slavery, they did not wholly forget their roles. They remained capable of casting and exorcising spells. Exorcism became the function by which they were best known and in this role became known as *myal*-men and *myal*-women. The word *myal* has come to mean "being in a state of possession," and the ritual which accompanied it was a rigorous dance now known as *Kumina*. *Kumina* soon caught on among the slaves and later became the slave religion.

The earliest eyewitness of this cult-behavior was the Moravian missionary, J. H. Buchner, who was in Jamaica in the late eighteenth century:

As soon as darkness of evening set in, they assembled in crowds in open pastures, most frequently under large cotton trees, which they worship, and counted holy; after sacrificing some fowls, the leader began an extempore song, in a wild strain, which was answered in chorus; the dance followed, grew wilder and wilder, until they were in a state of excitement bordering on madness. Some would perform incredible revolutions while in this state, until, nearly exhausted, they fell senseless to the

ground, when every word they uttered was received as divine revelation. At other times *obeah* was discovered or a *shadow* was
caught; a little coffin being prepared in which it was enclosed
and buried.[25]

Buchner's observations were very accurate. The details hold
true even today. A *Kumina* is called on special occasions,
especially for ceremonies surrounding the rites of passage
(birth, puberty, marriage, and death). But other calamities,
such as sickness and other natural or unnatural occasions,
may necessitate a *Kumina* service. This service is accompanied by drumming and dancing. A sacrifice is always
necessary; alcoholic spirits are always present; and the dancing continues until spirit possession is achieved. These
spirits are always the ancestors of the dancers or of the person who calls the *Kumina.* Under spirit possession a revelation is given by the ancestors concerning the occasion for
which the *Kumina* is called. This revelation is considered
very important and is heeded in every detail. It may consist
of the reason for the sickness or the death, suggest the cure
for the illness, or warn of coming calamities. Under possession, the evil spirit that may have caused the person's illness
may be captured. It might be a ghost sent by an *obeah*-man
or woman to haunt the house. Under *Kumina* possession,
the revelation is sometimes given in an unknown tongue,
very often in an African language, now forgotten, but known
to the possessed.

Missionary Religion

Brief mention must be made of the entrance of missionary
religions into the island. The Spaniards brought Roman
Catholicism to Jamaica in 1509; few documents survive to
describe the Spanish slaves. When we meet the remnants of
these Africans, known as Maroons, who served the Spanish
in the mountains, they were still worshipping their Ashanti
God—*Nyankopong.*[26] The Catholics did not lift a finger to
help the Arawak Indians found on the island before the arrival of the Blacks. When the British finally drove out the

Spaniards between 1509 and 1655, the Arawaks were extinct. Their number was estimated to have been sixty thousand.[27]

When the English came, the Church of England followed, but they paid no attention to the African population. One hundred and sixty-one years after England took over Jamaica and established the slave trade, no attempt had been made to Christianize the slaves. All this time the slaves continued to serve their African dieties. It was not until 1816 that the Jamaica House of Assembly passed an act to "consider the state of religion among the slaves, and to carefully investigate the means of diffusing the light of genuine Christianity among them." This act was not heeded. The resistance of the Planters to teaching Christianity to the slaves was so strong that no clergyman would dare risk his benefits to do so. According to historian Edward Long, however, the Anglican ministers of that period were so deficient in morals that they were incapable of preaching the gospel to anybody; as he said, "Some were better qualified to be retailers of salt-fish or boatswain to privateers than ministers of the Gospel."[28]

The urge to consider the state of religion among the slaves was brought about by the entrance of the Moravians in 1734, the Methodists in 1736, the Baptists in 1783, and the Presbyterians in 1823.[29] These nonconformist denominations were a real threat to the establishment, finding ready ears among the slaves and winning over large numbers to their cause. The loose rituals of these churches—especially the early Methodists and Baptists with their spirit-filled enthusiasm—fit beautifully the exuberant religion of the slaves and brought about an early syncretism between Christianity and various African religions. The slave masters saw, in this amalgamation of the "doctrine of Methodism combined with African superstition,"[30] an imminent danger to the community. Every effort, legal and illegal, was utilized to arrest the spread of the nonconformists.

Despite resistance and persecution by the established

church, the spread of Christianity continued *unabated* until
the emancipation of the slaves in 1835. In that year the
slaves celebrated the occasion as the Great Jubilee. Recog-
nizing the considerable effort of the nonconformist churches
on their behalf, the slaves flocked to these denominations in
great numbers. But as the nonconformist churches gained
recognition as a result of emancipation, their spirituality
diminished, and they began to establish themselves as real
denominations with rules, rituals, and structures far removed from the interests of their newly emancipated members. The slaves, sensing a new regimentation of their lives
by the Europeans, were not satisfied with the new order. The
churches were little prepared for what was soon to develop
in Jamaican religion.

The Great Revival of 1860–61

About 1860–61, just over two decades after the emancipation, the missionary religions were in the process of con-
solidating their religious efforts when a revival similar to
the Great Awakening in the United States swept the island.
The enthusiasm was so powerful that the missionaries were
unable to cope with the demand. Thousands of slaves
flocked to the churches day and night—men, women, and
children. The behavior patterns of this revival were similar
to those observed in New England by Jonathan Edwards,
with much singing, crying, dancing, spirit possession, and
loud prayers. W. J. Gardner, a Congregationalist minister of
that time who evidently relished a more sedate approach to
God, described it as follows:

In 1861, there had been a very remarkable religious movement
known as "the great revival." Like a mountain stream, clear and
transparent as it sprung from the rock, but which becomes foul and
repulsive as impurities are mingled with it in its onward course, so
with this most extraordinary movement. In many of the central
districts of the island the hearts of the thoughtful and good men
were gladdened by what they witnessed in changed lives and
characters of people for whom they long seemed to have laboured

in vain; but in too many districts there was much of wild extravagance and almost blasphemous fanaticism. This was especially the case where the Native Baptists had any considerable influence. Among these, the manifestations occasioned by the influence of the *myal-men* were common. To the present time what are called revival meetings are common among these people.[31]

Gardner was correct in his observation. He saw practices which were not those of the sedate Congregational church: to him they were repulsive and extravagant, even blasphemous and fanatic. He saw in these behaviors the influence of *Kumina.*

P. D. Curtain, in his book *The Two Jamaicas,* referred to this Great Revival as the parting of the ways between the missionary churches in Jamaica and the present Afro-Christian sects. As he noted, "What appeared to have been a missionary hope, turned out to be a missionary's despair."[32]

The Great Revival allowed the African religious dynamic—long repressed—to assert itself in a Christian guise and capture what might have been a missionary victory. Since then, Christianity has been a handmaiden to a revitalized African movement known as *Revival religion.*

Afro-Christian Syncretism

At present there are three types of Afro-Christian sects in Jamaica: *Pukumina,* which is mostly African in its rituals and beliefs; the Revival cult, which is partly African and partly Christian; and Revival Zion, which is mostly Christian and the least African in its rituals and beliefs. I place these Revival cults under the broad heading of Afro-Christian religions because all have adopted some aspects of Christianity in their rites, and prefer to be called Christian. All have general characteristics by which they can be analyzed. For example, the leaders of these cults are known as the "shepherd" or "shepherdess," the leader of a *band.* A *band* is a collection of believers from twenty to two hundred members who occupy a *yard,* or a ritual center where meetings and other rituals are held. The *yard* may be an elaborate

commune where members build their homes and live together, or just a tabernacle where cult-members of the
community visit on holy days. Each band possesses a hierarchy of leaders known as shepherds in a graded order. The
first or leading shepherd (or shepherdess) can be identified by
his (or her) elaborate turban. He (or she) is generally the
founder of the *band* and considered to be a person of high
spiritual attainment. A shepherd is commonly a *seer* with
great clairvoyant powers who serves as preacher, healer,
judge, and diviner. If a male shepherd is married, his wife is
sometimes known as "the mother" and is as highly respected as her husband in most cases. Below the head
shepherd is the warrior shepherd who protects the *band*
from the intervention of evil spirits. The water shepherd
presides at baptism and sees that water is placed in the
tabernacle at all times—water is the avenue through which
good spirits enter the service. The wheeling shepherd works
around the *yard* counterclockwise to detect any evil, such as
witchcraft, which might be present. Many other
functionaries operate in a *band*, each distinguishable by
dress and role.

Services are called for various occasions, such as birth,
death, and illness. Regular services take place on Sundays
and weekdays for fasting and especially for healings. A typical service includes singing, drumming, preaching, and holy
communion. The rituals of the services vary from one *band*
to another. Some use the rituals of the Anglican church, including the *Book of Common Prayer*. These services integrate high church ritual, dancing, and drumming in which
spirit possession, speaking in tongues, and prophecy are tied
together. Visitors are amazed at the level of integration that
has been achieved. Other *bands* resemble the Baptists with
their more free and spontaneous service. All *bands* engage in
a special ritual known as "trumping and/or travailing" in
the spirit. This consists of dancing counterclockwise in a
circle to the beating of drums and chanting. The peak is
reached when the singing stops and a peculiar guttural
sound begins caused by inhaling and exhaling air while mov-

ing the body forward and backward, allowing the air to explode through the lips. It is during this rite that spirit possession is most generally achieved and when many of the dancers attain altered states of consciousness, becoming mouthpieces for gods and spirits. It is often in this same state that members give warnings of imminent dangers such as approaching hurricanes, earthquakes, dangers surrounding births, deaths by accidents—or by revealing to spectators problems which could prove dangerous to them. Such warnings are spoken in English or in "unknown tongues," and are interpreted by other members or by the leader of the *band*. The spectators take these revelations seriously and usually seek the advice of the leaders.

The mountain-top experience of a Revival service is generally followed by a healing service for those who are sick or who need advice on matters which were revealed to them during spirit possession. Usually this service continues late into the night. In some *yards*, healing continues as an ongoing ritual throughout the week. Over 90 percent of the Jamaican peasants depend upon healing centers for their medical needs. Healing and curing involves herbal remedies, baths in herbal mixtures, oils, incense, drinking water blessed by the healers and, in recent days, the use of patent medicines.

Revival and Revival Zion sects are closer to Christianity than *Pukumina*. It is believed that the *Pukumina* sect engages in witchcraft and casting spells, while the Revival groups counteract witchcraft and neutralize spells. Many patients observed at Revival services by the author suffered from mental and psychosomatic complaints. Such people generally seek the help of the Revival healers, who are believed to have gifts of clairvoyance and prognosticate psychic problems in a remarkable way. Incidently, these healers are not only popular with the poorer class; the elite also seek their services, though secretly. In my research, I discovered that people from the highest levels of the society frequent these healers in time of psychic distress, either to be cured of illness or to ensure that the jobs they hold are not easily taken from them. Native spiritualists and herbal healers in Jamaica form an integral part of the medical profession and will continue to for years to come. One major reason for this is the scarcity of trained physicians in the rural areas. At present, 50 percent of the over-the-counter pharmaceutical drugs purchased are prescriptions written by native healers.

Pentecostalism and Revivalism: A Comparison

As Jamaica experiences rapid social change, its native religions are also undergoing dramatic changes. North America is taking deep root on the island, especially since the advent of the jet age. Beginning about 1929, the native religion received a fresh challenge from the United States of America in the form of high-voltage–eight-cylinder-type Pentecostal sects. First to appear on the island was the Church of God, headquartered in Cleveland, Tennessee. Then followed the Church of God in Christ and the Apostolic Faith, and finally almost all the Pentecostal churches known in America. These sects have made great headway on the island and have, in some cases, greatly depleted the membership of the missionary denominations. The impact of Pentecostals on Revival sects has been less severe. The similarities and differences between the two movements are complementary, giving advantages to both. Similarities in ritual behavior and organizational structure have probably kept the Pentecostals from completely displacing the Revival sects.

Some other obvious similarities might be mentioned here. The leaders of the Pentecostals are generally charismatic men and women. Like the Revivalist shepherd and shepherdess, they are able to hold an audience spellbound under the most adverse physical setting—whether a crude shack, a storefront, or a street corner. In both sects, healing plays a prominent part in their rituals. Some Pentecostals make use of oils for anointing the sick, and the laying-on-of-hands for exorcisms—practices common to the Revivalists. Both lay great stress on the baptism in the Spirit with the evidence of speaking in tongues. They both believe in baptism by water and place little emphasis on the Lord's Supper.

Oriented toward the lower strata of society, the Revivalists and Pentecostals alike share strong feelings against established denominations and the ruling class. The use of various musical folk instruments—including drums, guitar, cymbals, handclapping—and a worship service with a high emotional overtone is important to both sects. And surprisingly enough, there are close similarities between the native religion of Jamaica and the new charismatic movements imported from America, thereby heightening the religious prestige of the Revivalists who can see their White counterparts in America behaving in the same manner. The result has been a new wave of religious groups, a syncretistic offshoot of Revivalists and Pentecostals on the island. These are identified by the long dress common among American fundamentalists, the clapping of hands, and the ritual ejaculations of the words "Amen," "Hallelujah," and "Praise the Lord."

But with these similarities, we must also speak of the differences between these two sects—differences largely of ideology rather than structure or organization. While the Pentecostals emphasize the baptism in the Holy Ghost, the Revivalists do not limit spirit possession to the Holy Spirit of Acts 2. Myriad spirits may possess the believer. Among these are the ancestors, angels of the New Testament variety, and other spirits of unknown origins—good and bad. For Pentecostals the Bible is central; to the Revivalists, it is peripheral. Their emphasis lies on dreams and visions. The working of miracles and their interpretation are more meaningful as symbols of divine manifestations than biblical words. The great figures of the Bible become spiritual manifestations who often appear in their services; for example Jeremiah and Ezekiel, and angels such as Michael and Gabriel, and other archangels often appear in their services as real figures.

True Revivalists are nonfundamentalists; that is, the forbidden things taught by Pentecostalists seem very strange to them. Abstention from liquor and tobacco, and such things as dancing and a little romancing now and then are very wholesome practices for Revivalists. Sin to them is not what you do, but the spirit in which you do things. So, in a sense, the Revivalists are far more integrated and open to life and living than the Pentecostals. This is not to say they are loose in their spiritual lives, but that they find life more positive than negative.

This short description of Jamaican religions may sound like a chaos of cults running wild on the island. But acquaintance with the island and its people will show that, despite the seeming confusion, a real function is being carried out in the various religious expressions. As I have tried to show historically, the African religious mold, firmly rooted during slavery, has not been dislodged by missionary religions for many reasons. African religious traditions take into consideration not only one's intellect, but also one's emotions, the mental and the visceral. African religion is not a Sunday-go-to-church religion, but one that participates with all of nature—both the living and the dead. An awareness is found not only of the gods and the spirits, but also of demons and powers who can harm the living.

The majority of Jamaicans retain this level of belief. Religion is a total involvement for them, not a mental exercise. Within one's religion one lives, moves, and has one's being. As recently as fifteen years ago, only about a third of the people could read or write; consequently, only a few of the Jamaican masses were able to receive any benefits from the sophisticated liturgies of the missionary churches, which demanded a higher level of literacy to fulfill catechetical requirements for membership. Only the privileged elite became members of the larger denominations and attended these churches with pomp and pride, looking down at the masses who flocked to the Revival *yards*. But, it is in these Revival *yards* that the real Jamaican folk tradition was nourished and preserved. From this folk religion came the charismatic leaders to take over the political leadership of the island before the educated elite succeeded them: from these *yards* folk painters, sculptors, and musicians emerged. The educated Jamaican elite has remained static and uncreative in most fields of cultural dynamics.

At present, there is an increased availability of education, but most young Jamaicans are choosing to associate with the Revivalists and the Pentecostals, and a large body have opted for the Rastafarian religious expressions. They are finding these religious groups considerably more satisfying and relevant to their spiritual needs. In the last election, the present prime minister—born to the elite—took on the role of a Revival shepherd, calling himself Joshua and carrying a shepherd's staff. He won a landslide victory!

Anyone visiting Jamaica should take the time to go to the prestigious churches in the day, and at night visit the *yard* tabernacles to see the differences. The effervescence of these traditional gatherings confirms that the day of pasteurized religion is over, at least in Jamaica.

The Rastafarian movement of Jamaica is the most recent religious expression of a people who have experienced a bitter history of exploitation and oppression. Its emergence comes as a reaction not only to the native religions which the Rastas see as unreal in the presence of formidable sociopolitical forces, but also against the missionary religions which they view as the religious arm of colonial oppression. The next chapter will trace the development of this phenomenon in Jamaican history.

Domination and Resistance in Jamaican History

Jamaicans are by nature some of the most fun loving, hardworking, and gregarious people in the Caribbean. Treated with kindness and respect, they are likely to remain the most confident and dependable friends on earth. But if treated with impunity and disrespect, all the rage of a deep psychic revenge may surface with unpredictable consequences. This calm-and-storm personality of contemporary Jamaicans is a direct inheritance from that group of Africans who suffered the most frustrating and oppressive slavery ever experienced in a British colony.

The early history of Jamaica is one long tale of sad intrigue, human suffering, lawlessness, and immoral profit, at the center of which were the African slaves—the ancestors of present-day Jamaicans.[1] Slavery in Jamaica lacked any vestige of humanity. A handful of greedy planters held absolute power over thousands of slaves. Only through violence could such complete domination by a minority be initiated and perpetuated. So in Jamaica, as in North America, the psychology of slave control was highly developed, and in Frederick Douglass's words, "Fear, awe, and obedience became interwoven into the very nature of the slaves."[2]

Under such complete domination two reactions were provoked: fight and flight. This chapter will study these two reactions in an attempt to analyze how these survival techniques aided in breaking the chains of their ancestors and descendants. I shall also show that these behavior patterns (and their consequences) are directly responsible for the independent Jamaica of today, and that these patterns still remain a part of the Jamaican's psychic reactions to life. Beginning with the emergence of the Maroons, we shall review the prominent freedom movements from the seventeenth century to the emergence of the Rastafarian movement during the twentieth century.

The Jamaican Maroon: A Study of Fight and Flight

The evidence is now well documented that the Africans who were carried to the Caribbean resisted their enslavement and continued to resist their bondage both passively and violently up until the abolition of slavery and beyond. The classic example of this resistance is the presence of Maroon communities all over the New World.[3] It is only recently that Maroon history has become accessible, but the historical events of the Jamaican Maroons were probably some of the earliest to be recorded. Their fame as freedom fighters and their elusiveness (assisted by the mountain fastness of the Jamaican hill country) forced the British to sue for peace as early as 1738. In this way, the Jamaica Maroon communities existed as a free people sixty-six years before the independence of Haiti and ninety-six years before slavery was abolished on the island.

The story of the Jamaican Maroons begins with the English defeat of Spain in 1655.[4] The Spaniards, finding themselves outclassed by the British, sailed from the north coast of Jamaica for Cuba and left their slaves to the British. But the slaves had ideas of their own. Although we have no true records of the treatment of Spanish slaves in Jamaica up to 1655, we may assume from the behavior of the Spanish slaves that they were discontent with slavery, for they soon sought freedom in the hill country where they fought a grueling war to the death. These Spanish slaves came to be called "Maroons." The origin of the word derives from both French and Spanish and carries the same connotation in both; that is, as hunters of wild animals—probably the wild pigs and wild cattle native to the mountains on the island. Later, the word took on the connotations of *wildness* and *fierceness* and soon the Maroons were themselves known as the *wild and fierce ones*. The first Maroons were under the leadership of Juan de Bolas (immortalized by a village bearing his name near the borders of St. Catherine and Clarendon). In 1663, after eight years of harassing the British, an attempt was made to pacify them. Juan de Bolas was made a colonel by the British and was sent to his followers to sue for peace. The Maroons correctly perceived the whole matter as a deception to re-enslave them: they ambushed their chief and, according to Bryan Edwards, "He was cut to pieces."

Other pockets of runaway slaves began to develop in the eastern and northern parts of the island, most of them new recruits from Africa, especially from the Gold Coast. These were called *Coromantees*—slaves shipped from the Koromantyn slave castle situated near Elmina on the Cape coast of present-day Ghana. They were mostly mixtures of Ashanti and Fanti and sold into slavery during the development of the Ashanti Federation. Since most were prisoners of war, they were well trained in guerrilla fighting which was to become an important part of their lives. Many of these runaway slaves took refuge in the hills and joined forces with the original Maroons. The Planter historian Edward Long states:

With the importation of slaves by the English, almost from the start irrepressible spirits among the Koromantyn fled to the mountains and found refuge with the Maroons in such numbers that they soon gained control of the entire body.[5]

Among the "irrepressible spirits" was an Ashanti family who was carried to Jamaica. The family members were Cudjoe, Johnny (who seemed to have adopted an English name quite early), Accompong, Cofi (spelled Cuffee in Jamaican documents), and Quaco. All appear to have been fighters in

Africa. According to Long, Cudjoe had exemplified himself as a leader as early as 1693[6] and had organized most of the Maroons under his leadership. The life or death struggle for freedom had begun. There seems to have been little difference between the Spanish Maroons and the Koromantyns in manners and language, and even the other tribal groups who joined them soon overcame their differences and adopted the Ashanti language. R. C. Dallas, who wrote the first full-length history of the Maroons, observed: "The Coromantee language, however, superseded the others, and became in time the general one used."[7]

Cudjoe, on assuming his command, appointed his brothers Accompong and Johnny to be leaders under him, and named Cuffee and Quaco subordinate captains. The brunt of the Maroon campaign was carried on under these five men and were assisted by others, mainly in the northern and southern parts of Jamaica. On the east side of the island, another sizable group of Maroons formed under the leadership of the legendary Acheampong Nanny who was said to be either the wife or the sister of Cudjoe. Not much is known of her, but there is a town named in her honor in that point of the island, and her fame has been so great in Jamaican folk tradition that the legislature has posthumously named her the first woman to receive the distinction of National Hero in the year 1975. But if nothing is known of Nanny, much is known of her colleague in command, Captain Quaco,[8] who later supervised the signing of the treaty with the English for that group of Maroons in 1739.

Fighting Method

The terror the Maroons caused the English in the seventeenth and eighteenth centuries was far greater than what the Maroons could have commanded in size alone. (It is believed that at no time did their number exceed one thousand five hundred.[9]) But the deployment of small groups by Cudjoe in sudden and savage attack and swift withdrawal kept the English completely disoriented about their strength. Their ability to use the rugged mountain terrain provided another effective strategy. Their excellent intelligence network allowed them to know well in advance when a mission was being sent against them. Dallas, speaking of their guerrilla tactics, observed:

Such are the natural fortifications in which the Maroons secured themselves in times of danger, and from which it has been ever found difficult to dislodge them. [Their camps were always situated at the mouth of a rock] which look like a great fissure made through some extraordinary convulsion of nature, and through which men can pass only in a single file, the Maroons, whenever they expect an attack, disposed of themselves on the ledges of the rocks on both sides. Sometimes they advanced a party beyond the entrance of the defile, frequently in a line on each side, if the ground would admit; and lay covered by the underwood, and behind rocks and roots of trees, waiting in silent ambush for their pursuers, of whose approach they had always information from their scouts.[10]

Such strategies at this period were unkown to the English army whose philosophy of warfare was that of the gentleman soldier. One historian of the period contrasted the English soldiers with the Maroons as follows:

The [British] troops marched in their proper regimentals, as if they were going to fight a regular and *civilized* enemy, and sometimes had even the absurdity to traverse the mountainous roads with drums beating. The customary accoutrements were too clumsy and burdensome for traversing the woods and clambering over rocks, and the red coats were too conspicuous an object to the Maroon marksmen, who seldom missed their aim.[11]

After nearly forty-five years of fighting a losing battle and after nearly a quarter of a million pounds and hundreds of lives taken, Governor Trelawny was urged to offer peace to the Maroons. This advice was politically fruitful for the English, and it later destroyed the image of the Maroons as a symbol of freedom.

The Peace Treaty of March 1, 1738

Leaving out all the drama surrounding the signing of the treaty,[12] I shall present only the main articles of this historical document, beginning with the preamble about the king, and God's displeasure over the shedding of blood. The treaty contains fifteen articles:

First, That all hostilities shall cease on both sides forever.

Second, That the said Captain Cudjoe, the rest of his captains, adherents, and men, shall be forever hereafter in a perfect state of freedom and liberty, excepting those who have been taken by them, within two years last past, if such are willing to return to their said masters and owners, with full pardon and indemnity . . . provided always, that, if they are not willing to return, they shall remain in subject to Captain Cudjoe and in friendship with us, according to the form and tenor of this treaty.

Third, That they shall enjoy and possess, for themselves and posterity forever, all the lands situated and lying between Trelawny Town and the Cockpits, to the amount of fifteen hundred acres, bearing North-West from the said Trelawny Town.

Fourth, That they shall have liberty to plant the said lands with coffee, cocoa, ginger, tobacco, and cotton, and to breed cattle, hogs, goats, or any other flock, and dispose of the produce or increase of the said commodities to the inhabitants of this island; provided always, that when they bring the said commodities to market, they shall apply first to the custos, or any other magistrate of the respective parishes where they expose their goods to sale, for license to sell the same.

Fifth, That Captain Cudjoe, and all the Captain's adherents, and people now in subjection to him, shall all live together within the bounds of Trelawny Town, and that they shall have liberty to hunt where they shall think fit, except within three miles of any settlement, crawl, or pen; provided always, that in case of the hunters of Captain Cudjoe, and those of other settlements meet, then the hogs are to be equally divided between both parties.

Sixth, That the said Captain Cudjoe, and his successors, do use their best endeavours to take, kill, suppress, or destroy, either by themselves, or jointly with any other number of men, commanded on that service by His Excellency the Governor, or Commander-in-Chief for the time being, all rebels wheresoever they be, throughout this island, unless they submit to the same terms of accommodation granted to Captain Cudjoe, and his successors.

Seventh, That in case this island be invaded by any foreign enemy, the said Captain Cudjoe, and his successors hereinafter named or to be appointed, shall then, upon notice given, immediately repair to any place the Governor for the time being shall appoint, in order to repel the said invaders with his or their utmost force, and to submit to the orders of the Commander-in-Chief on that occasion.

Eighth, That if any white man shall do any manner of injury to Captain Cudjoe, his successors, or any of his or their people, they shall apply to any commanding officer or magistrate in the neighbourhood for justice; *and in case Captain Cudjoe, or any of his people shall do any injury to any white person he shall submit himself, or deliver up such person to justice.*

Ninth, That if any negroes shall hereafter run away from their masters or owners, and fall in Captain Cudjoe's hands, they shall immediately be sent back to the chief magistrate of the next parish where they are taken; and those that bring them are to be satisfied for their trouble, as the legislature shall appoint.

Tenth, That all negroes taken, since the raising of this party by Captain Cudjoe's people, shall immediately be returned.

Eleventh, That Captain Cudjoe and his successors, shall wait on His Excellency, or the Commander-in-Chief for the time being every year, if thereunto required.

Twelfth, That Captain Cudjoe, during his life, and the Captains succeeding him, shall have full power to inflict any punishment they think proper for crimes committed by their men among themselves, death only excepted; in which case, if the Captain thinks they deserve death, he shall be obliged to bring them before any justice of the peace, who shall order proceedings on their trial equal to those of any other negroes.

Thirteenth, That Captain Cudjoe with his people, shall cut, clear, and keep open, large and convenient roads from Trelawny Town to Westmoreland and St. James's, and if possible, to St. Elizabeth's.

Fourteenth, That two white men, to be nominated by His Excellency, or the Commander-in-Chief for the time being, shall constantly live and reside with Captain Cudjoe, and his successors, in order to maintain a friendly correspondence with the inhabitants of this island.

Fifteenth, That Captain Cudjoe shall, during his life, be chief Commander in Trelawny Town; after his decease the command to devolve on his brother Captain Accompong; and in case of his decease, on his next brother Captain Johnny; and, failing him, Captain Cuffee shall succeed; who is to be succeeded by Captain Quaco; and after their demise, the Governor or Commander-in-Chief for the time being, shall appoint, from time to time, whom he thinks fit for that command.

The Effects of the Treaty

The treaty brought an end to hostilities between the Planters and the fighting Maroons. It made them a free people with their own lands and leaders and created for them a mystical sophistication which has continued to the present day. But a careful reading of the treaty shows quite clearly that for the Maroons it was a Pyrrhic victory, the greatest advantages falling into the hands of the English settlers. The treaty reduced the fighting Maroons from gallant freedom fighters to an unpaid army of English Planters and a permanent police force, a duty which they willingly performed up to the Rebellion of 1865.

The effects of the treaty on the plantation slaves were devastating. The sixth and ninth articles of the treaty were supported by the Maroons to the letter and, on the basis of this loyalty, every bid for freedom by the slaves and free Jamaicans—even after the emancipation—was successfully crushed by the Maroons. As the following events prove, of the thousands of Blacks whose blood was spilled for freedom in Jamaica after the signing of this treaty, the Maroons far outdid the British militia, who depended on them to do the dirty work while praising and damning their savagery at the same time. Jamaican history should record that the gallantry of the Trelawny Maroons ceased with the signing of the Peace Treaty of March 1, 1738, and that of the Leeward Maroons of July 23, 1739. The history of the Maroons, thereafter, has been a sad tale of atrocities perpetuated against their countrymen. After the signing of the treaties, the Maroons

became traitors to freedom and have contributed very little
to the development of the island. For the most part, they
have remained secluded from the rest of the society in their
haunted mountains, living on the recollection of a dead past.

On my recent visit to Accompong in 1973, I saw what appeared to be a conscious awareness of a crippling stagnation,
especially among the young Maroons. They were very critical of the leadership of their people and showed their resentment by disrupting the rituals of their most cherished
festival by throwing away the meat that had been painstak-
ingly cooked for the traditional feast. The Rastafarians often
praise the Maroons, but are also selective in their praise.
Cudjoe, Quaco, and Nanny receive their honor. The
Rastafarians—avid readers of Jamaican history—seem
clearly to understand that the Maroons (after Cudjoe and his
generals) sold out to the British and failed to set an example
for movements of liberation to follow. It is no wonder that
the Rastas to this day have resisted any prominent leadership. They have repeatedly expressed to me that they are
afraid that leaders of the movement would only "sell us
out." I have no doubt in my mind that the Maroon experience lingers in their memory.

Despite the treaties of 1738–39, very little was done to
see that the provisions of the Maroons were carried out.
The English, having disposed of an immediate problem, applied themselves to making money on their plantations.
Lulled into complacency, the Maroons went about their
business, trying as best they could to exist on the worst
pieces of lands in Jamaica. It was only a matter of time before the peace of 1738 was to turn against the Trelawny Maroons; by 1795, they had been reduced to humble peasants.
The white superintendent placed among them saw no threat
to the government by the Maroons and so he spent long
periods away from his post. The Maroon lands had become
so overcrowded and fruitless that the Trelawnys were actually starving. Their white resident captain, Mr. James, was
finally replaced by Captain Craskell, whom the Maroons
disliked. Insubordination mounted daily until finally in

mid-July of that year, Captain Craskell was driven out. But the coup de grâce of the whole episode was the beating of two Maroons (in Montego Bay), as sentenced by a regularly constituted court, for having stolen two pigs. Although the penalty was a regular one, the flogging was done by a runaway slave: both an affront and grave insult to the proud Maroons. All of this led to a renewal of war between the Trelawny Maroons and the colonial government. By this time however, the Maroons had neither the united front nor the gallantry of past years. Forty-six years had passed since the peace treaty had been signed. A section of the Maroons under Captain Accompong had settled in the Nassau Mountains in a town that now bears his name. They refused to support the Trelawnys on account of some differences that had developed. Instead, the Accompongs joined forces with the colonialists, and the fate of the Trelawnys was sealed. After a short but vigorous battle they surrendered and six hundred of them were transported to Halifax on June 6, 1796; finding the place unsuitable for Blacks, however, the colonial government—in agreement with Sierra Leone—removed them to Freetown, West Africa.[13] I will return to the subject of the Maroons who remained in Jamaica, but for now I will discuss one of the most important attempts at freedom in Jamaica—made by the regular estate slaves rather than by the Maroons.

The Sam Sharpe Rebellion: 1831–32

Chattel slavery was enormously profitable. In the seventeenth and eighteenth centuries the epithet, "as wealthy as a West Indian,"[14] was given to a body of English Planters who grew rich and powerful through their enormous profits on Caribbean investments in slaves and sugar. But if slaveholding was profitable, it was always at the expense of peace of mind, deep forebodings, and an unpredictable future, because the slaves were always a "troublesome property." In Jamaica, as the record will show, not a year passed between the seventeenth and the nineteenth centuries without a re-

bellion or at least the threat of one. Even when no overt rebellion (that demanded the militia) took place, the covert or
passive rebellion was equally disruptive and always present.

The dawning of the nineteenth century saw the twilight
of "the peculiar institution"—slavery. The French Revolution had just taken place and commoners everywhere in
Europe saw the citadels of privilege suddenly coming to
ruin. In the Caribbean, the Haitian slaves had freed themselves from their long night of slavery, proving to the army
of Napoleon that they not only desired freedom, but were
also willing to die for it. In England, the Anti-Slavery Society
would soon put an end to the commerce in human flesh. In
the West Indies the mighty Planters suddenly saw the
handwriting on the wall. This sudden change in the social,
political, and economic arena of Europe and the Caribbean
threatened to ruin those who invested heavily in the slave
trade. As a result, the Planters began to muster all their
weapons against what they considered to be the irrational
sentiments of the humanitarians and missionaries. Between
the proslavery and the antislavery camp, the slaves bided
their time. The proslavery propagandists opened the
nineteenth century with a scurrilous attack on the senti-
mentality of the humanitarians, the rationality of slavery,
and the gross inferiority of Africans whose only hope of redemption from savagery was by way of servitude.[15]

The Jamaican slaves in the nineteenth century were not
entirely ignorant of these developments. Many of them were
able to follow the controversy in the local papers and com-
municate it to their illiterate brethren. Many servants also
overheard the heated discussions on their fate as their unguarded and enraged masters poured out their vitriol against
their pending demise.

Samuel Sharpe was one slave who was well-equipped both
mentally and emotionally to follow the controversy;[16] in
1831, he inspired one of the most extensive rebellions on the
island of Jamaica. Partly because of this rebellion, the King
of England hastened the emancipation of the slaves in
Jamaica in 1834. According to Henry Bleby, an eyewitness to

this insurrection, evidence taken by the Royal Commission after the rebellion "demonstrated to the Imperial Legislature, that among the negroes themselves the spirit of freedom had been so widely diffused as to render it most perilous to postpone the settlement of the important question of emancipation to a later period."[17] This widespread spirit of freedom resulted from a variety of sources; for example, a large number of the slaves had become Christians and literate enough to assume lay leadership, most of them of the Methodist and Baptist faith. Of the Baptists, there were two varieties: those of the London Baptist Missions, staffed by White missionaries; and the Native Baptists, the older variety, founded by George Liele. Liele—an American Baptist slave-preacher taken to Jamaica after the American Revolution—started a thriving Baptist mission on the island. The Native Baptists grafted Christianity to the African ethos of the slaves and took on a messianic-millenarian fervor. This spiritual combination became the energizing force behind the slaves in their demand for freedom as a command from God.

Sam Sharpe was said to be a member of the London Baptist Mission of Montego Bay, but the author believes that he was also a leader in the Native Baptist church. It appears that the groundwork for the rebellion was laid in a prayer meeting. Henry Bleby, who interviewed the prisoners after the insurrection for the Rebellion Committee, is our only source on this matter. One of the men he interviewed was Edward Hylton, whom he referred to as "one of the original conspirators." According to Hylton, sometime during 1831 (he could not remember the month), he received an invitation from Sam Sharpe—a slave at the Retrieve Estates near Montego Bay—to attend a meeting at the home of Mr. Johnson on the same estate. The first part of the rendezvous consisted of a prayer meeting. After prayer, most of the members left the house leaving only Sharpe, Johnson, and Hylton. Soon these three were joined by others who approached "under extreme caution." According to Hylton,

Sharpe was expecting these people. After they had safely assembled, Sharpe rose to address them, speaking in soft tones
"so that his voice was not heard beyond the building." According to Hylton:

He [Sam Sharpe] then proceeded with a long address to those
around him on various topics relating to the *great subject* he had
on his heart, and with an eloquence which kept all his hearers fas-
cinated and spell-bound from the beginning to the end of his
speech. He referred to the manifold evils and injustice of slavery;
asserted the natural equality of man with regard to freedom; and,
referring to the Holy Scriptures as his authority, denied that the
white man had any more right to hold the blacks in bondage than
the blacks had to enslave the white.[18]

Although the style of the above quotation may differ from
what Hylton repeated to Bleby, there is no doubt that the essence of Hylton's confession is authentically recorded.
Another participant of the 1831 rebellion was Captain
Gardner, one of Sharpe's commanders in the field. In his
confession to Bleby, he told of another meeting where
Sharpe spoke to his followers. He states that on that occasion:

Sam Sharpe spoke for a long time on the subject of slavery and told
us what he had read in the papers concerning it; and he addressed
us in such a manner that he [Gardner] was wrought up almost to a
state of madness. After this speech he entered in the freedom
fighting with all his soul.[19]

The above quotations show that Sam Sharpe was not just
an ordinary slave, but a man of extraordinary authority over
his fellow slaves—a man of charisma, a religious leader, and
an orator who commanded the attention of his audiences.
Bleby's description of Sam Sharpe shortly before his death is
even more enlightening. He wrote:

Samuel Sharpe was a man whose active brain devised the project;
and he had sufficient authority with those around him to carry it
into effect having acquired an extraordinary degree of influence
amongst his fellow-slaves.[20]

Bleby went on to say, "He was the most intelligent and re-markable slave I ever met with." He described Sam Sharpe as follows:

Middle in size—fine sinewy frame—handsomely molded—his nose and lips exhibited the usual characteristics of the negro race. He had teeth whose regularity and pearly whiteness, a court-beauty might have envied—and an eye whose brilliancy was almost daz-zling. He possessed intellectual and oratorical powers above the common order.[21]

And this, said Bleby, "was the secret of the extensive influ-ence which he exercised."[22]

An insight into Sharpe's charismatic powers (also ren-dered by Bleby) goes to the heart of the character of this free-dom fighter:

I heard him [Sam Sharpe] two or three times deliver a brief extem-poraneous address to his fellow-prisoners on religious topics, many of them being confined together in the same cell; and I was amazed both at the power and freedom with which he spoke, and at the ef-fect which was produced upon his auditory. *He appeared to have the feelings and passions of his hearers completely at his com-mand;* and when I listened to him once, I ceased to be surprised at what Gardner had told me, "that when Sharpe spoke to him and others on the subject of slavery," he, Gardner, was "wrought up almost to a state of madness."[23]

The sentence in Bleby's description of Sam Sharpe which is most interesting from a theoretical viewpoint reads: "He appeared to have the feelings and passions of his hearers completely at his command." This peculiar ability to com-mand is the exclusive gift of the charismatic leader. Robert C. Tucker, in his analysis of charismatic leadership, states.:

Charismatic movements for change arise and spread at times when painful forms of distress are prevalent in a society or in some par-ticular stratum of a society. The unique personal authority of the leader and the rapturous response of many of his followers grow out of their feeling that he, by virtue of his special powers as a leader, embodies the movement's salvational promise, hence that which may be of supreme significance to them. Since he ministers to their most pressing need—the need to believe in the real possibility of escape from an oppressive life predicament—they not only follow voluntarily and without thought of material recompense, but they tend to revere him and surround him with that spontaneous cult of personality which appears to be one of the symptomatic marks of the charismatic leader-follower relationship. . . . Wherever, and whenever human beings in serious numbers live in desperation or despair or similar states, charismatic leaders and movements are likely to appear.[24]

The central cause of this rebellion (sometimes called the Baptist War) evolved from Sharpe's assertion that the slaves' free papers had arrived and were being withheld by the Planters' pressure on the governor of Jamaica. This idea was circulated among the estates of St. James, Hanover, Westmoreland, and St. Elizabeth. Sam Sharpe, it was reported, sent messengers to the estates to "spread the news." This idea of free papers took on eschatological significance similar to the messianic "day of the Lord" concept among the Jews. The prophet who was in touch with the source of the message—England—was Sam Sharpe.

It may be helpful to consider what precipitates revolution, such as the one in Jamaica. One of the major causes of revolution is the presence of what the social scientists call relative deprivation;[25] that is, when a segment of the society is deprived of the wealth and status enjoyed by another segment of society because of race, religion, or sexual inferiority imposed by the privileged class. In the Jamaica of the 1800s, this type of social inequity might easily be considered a cause of the rebellion, but the peculiar status of slaves prescribed by law and the force of law would seem to preclude such an analysis. A more appropriate theory (which fits rather uniquely with the Sam Sharpe rebellion) is one that has received little attention: it posits that revolution is brought about by a *feeling of heightened expectation.*

Whether this *feeling of heightened expectation* was created by Sam Sharpe, or through the preaching of the Native Baptist Church, or through the behavior of the Planters is now difficult to pinpoint. A fair evaluation would suggest a combination of all these factors. Whatever the reason, most of the slaves in the county of Cornwall had mentally, psychologically, and eschatologically ceased being slaves. The decision was made by a large body of slaves not to return to work on any plantation after the Christmas holidays of December, 1831. On December 26, 1831, Bleby (the missionary) reported that he visited Ramble, a village in Westmoreland, and learned there that the slaves had a plan to cease work. As a typical Methodist minister, Bleby implored his members "not to give heed to the unfounded and mischievous reports that were in circulation about their freedom having been given by the King, and to have nothing to do with those persons who were disposed to create mischief and lead them astray."[26] He reported that all the slaves present stood up and pledged themselves to act upon his advice. If we may believe the records, it is generally agreed that the Methodist slaves never participated in the Sam Sharpe rebellion. This is an awful commentary on the Jamaican Methodists when compared with the freedom-fighting Methodists of the United States. A very different attitude was shown by the Baptists on the same day—December 26—when the Baptist Chapel at Slater's Hill near Montego Bay was dedicated. The speaker was the Reverend William Knibbs[27] who, alluding to the gossip of impending freedom which he sensed in the congregation, reported it as false. Bleby recalled:

His remarks were met with evident dissatisfaction by many of the slaves present, several of whom left the chapel offended, and others remarked that "the man," meaning Mr. Knibbs, "must be mad to tell we such things."[28]

Bleby concluded:

The spirit and conduct of these negroes created no small alarm, and the missionaries who were present on the occasion left the place with gloom and painful foreboding.[29]

What is suggested here is that "the spirit of heightened expectation" cannot be satisfied with meaningless words, even if these words are facts. Given the psychological state of the slaves, not even the governor of Jamaica could convince them that they were not to be freed. This was their faith, and faith needs no proof. Freedom is not a thing given; it is a state of mind, and, as this book will show, many of the slaves went to their death in freedom, even without the "free papers."

The War

According to Bleby, Sam Sharpe's strategy was to start not a violent but a nonviolent revolution.[30] Life was not to be taken except in self-defense, but once the wrath of oppressed peoples was set loose, it was not to be contained until, quoting Bleby's words, "one of the fairest portions of this beautiful island was laid to ruins."

So secretive were the preparations for the revolt that not even the keen eyes of Bleby nor the suspicious Planters (who used every cunning to reveal the plot) were able to discern any signs of the impending upheaval. Bleby reported that after the Ramble meeting and the dedication of the Slater's Hill Baptist Church,

Mr. Murray [a missionary colleague of his] proceeding to Montego Bay, I to Lucea. Our way lay though in different directions, through the country which was destined so soon to be laid waste; but at that time the most perfect quiet prevailed. There was not visible the slightest indication of the storm which was about to burst over our heads with such appalling and desolatory violence.[31]

Sam Sharpe and his men had done their homework thoroughly, but only to a point. If Sam Sharpe had intended only a nonviolent demonstration of solidarity against slavery, some of his lieutenants did not get the message. As Bleby puts it:

In the evening (of the same day) as it grew dark, the first indication of the actual revolt was given, by the burning of the houses and sugar-works on a large plantation called "Kensington" the property of a Mr. Morris. And soon after, the example was followed on other estates: so that all through the night the heavens were lighted up by the burning properties in all directions.[32]

It is believed that Kensington, situated on a hill, was used to signal the slaves that the insurrection had begun. What had been intended as a nonviolent protest was now on the way to being one of the most violent slave uprisings in Jamaican history.

Needless to say, the inhabitants of Montego Bay were seized with fear. For them, the long-awaited day of judgment had come. With the example of Haiti fresh in their minds, the White Planters took flight to the sea using every available ship in port to escape with their women and children. The principal figure on whom the Whites depended was one Mr. Grignon, an attorney, who acted as manager of many estates whose owners lived in England. According to Bleby, he was one of the most inhuman characters in the history of Jamaican slavery, with a habit of using his slaves in such a way as to "discredit" the system! Bleby believed that such behavior by an overseer was a primary abuse of the slave system which finally brought disgrace to all! This rather mild rebuke, however, showed the insensitivity of Bleby himself. At the opening of the rebellion, Grignon assumed the role of colonel and hastily organized what was called the Western Interior Regiment, composed entirely of White Planters.[33] This mustering of White Planters was a slave tradition in which able-bodied Planters formed their own regiment to defend their properties. They had two barracks for this occasion—one at Belvidere Estate in Montego Bay and one at Shettlewood Estate between the borders of St. James, St. Elizabeth, and Westmoreland. Initially, two hundred fifty of these men formed into an army. But for some unknown reason, Colonel Grignon retreated with his White Companions to Montpelier Estate (about thirty miles from Montego Bay) instead of protecting the estates around Montego Bay. Here, on December 28, he was joined by the seventh Regiment of St. James—a company made up entirely of Black soldiers— leaving Montego Bay and the valuable plantations without protection. The slaves immediately proceeded to wreak vengeance on the symbols of their oppression. On the evening of the twenty-eighth, Sam Sharpe's army attacked Montpelier. Reporting on this confrontation, Bleby stated that the slaves' attack was accompanied by the blowing of horns and shells, the noise of which so unnerved Colonel Grignon and his fellow Planter-soldiers that they were petrified. Had it not been for the Black soldiers, the slaves would have probably achieved their most dramatic victory.

The attack by the slaves was led by two Black colonels: Johnson and Campbell. In the fighting, Johnson was killed and Campbell was mortally wounded. On the Planter's side, all the fighting was done by the Black soldiers who alone were brave enough to battle the insurgents. Bleby reported that, during the battle,

Colonel Grignon and his entire regiment remained inactive, drawn up in a hallow square leaving the Coloured Company to fight it out with the Negroes as best they could.[34]

Unable to stand up against superior weapons, the slaves retreated. The Coloured Company who wanted to pursue the slaves into the interior—a plan which would have crushed the resistance early—was overruled by Colonel Grignon who decided to play it safe and hastily retreated to Montego Bay. The retreat was so hasty that the one White soldier who had been killed was left unburied. That same night the slaves returned to burn down Montpelier; they took the White soldier out of the hastily made coffin, committed him to the flames, and buried their leader—Colonel Johnson—in it. Colonel Grignon later reported to the Governor that he and his men were attacked by ten thousand men, who came down upon him in four columns, but that he succeeded in repulsing them. Bleby, who investigated the matter, was satisfied that there were only five hundred slaves at most.

The Montpelier setback was a great blow to the rebellion, but the quick retreat of the militia inflamed the slaves, and a renewed desire for freedom mounted. Thousands of slaves joined the ranks of the insurgents. All communications between the principal towns were cut off and the entire county of Cornwell was in the hands of the slaves who set fire to all the estates in the parishes of St. James, Hanover, Westmoreland, and St. Elizabeth. Bleby reported that not one white man was to be seen from Montego Bay to Savanna la Mar, and from Black River to Lucea. The militia was confined to the coastal towns of the north coast.

The day of reckoning, however, was approaching. As soon as news of the insurrection had reached the governor in Spanish Town, martial law was declared; this meant vengeance on the Blacks, both slaves and freed. The arrival of General Sir Willoughby Cotton as commander in chief of the campaign, with the combined force of the seventy-fourth, seventy-seventh, and eighty-fourth regiments, demonstrated the seriousness of the conflict. Sensing the danger of a campaign against an army of slaves whose spirits were high (and probably recalling the futility of fighting against the Maroons who knew the rugged mountains), Sir Willoughby issued a pardon to all slaves willing to lay down arms and return to their former owners; only the ringleaders were to be punished. The leniency of the commander in chief reinforced the slaves' belief that the king's army would do them no harm, and that slavery had indeed been abolished. Bleby reported that the slaves greeted the English ships with joy, believing that the soldiers had come to protect them. This misconception was to be the doom of many who, upon hearing General Cotton's proclamation, tried to return to their former masters. Bleby reported sadly: "The proclamation leniency was aborted by the gross revenge of the masters who used it as a lure to delude unsuspecting slaves to their death." The worst was yet to come.

As soon as Sir Willoughby Cotton had left the scene of the conflict, slaves returning to their masters were slaughtered indiscriminately. The bloodthirsty repression on the part of the soldiers only caused the rebellion to be prolonged, but now, the tide was turned against the slave population. This disadvantage, as might be expected, was brought about by the slaves' lack of military equipment. Their primary weapons were cutlasses, stones, homemade spears, and a few old guns. They had no mutual plan of action, nor did they have the military training to stand against the disciplined veterans of the British Army.

Some of those who returned to the estates were killed; others were severely flogged and reviled. But the larger number of the insurgents fled to the mountains. These were hunted by small bands of soldiers who wreaked vengeance on them. Most were hunted by the Maroons who were paid to kill the fugitives and bring their victims' ears as proof. So thoroughly did the Maroons perform their jobs that Bleby referred to them as "demi-savages." The insurrection was effectively over.

The Aftermath

During and after the period of martial law, the revenge of the landed gentry was unremitting. Thousands of slaves were put to death after trial by court-martial, first by the bullets of the firing squad, and later by the gallows which was erected in the town square of Montego Bay. Bleby, an eyewitness of these atrocities, told of crowds of condemned slaves who were hanged: half an hour elapsed between sentencing and death. Bleby's sensitive conscience was disturbed by this unusual haste to snuff out the lives of the insurrectionists. He asked rhetorically:

What was the motive of this indecent and inhuman haste, I do not pretend to determine. The only reason I can suggest apart from a thirst for blood, which it was horrible to witness, is this—that, after the military began at last to move, such multitudes of prisoners were sent in from the country, that there was no place in which to secure them: the gaols became over-crowded to excess, and perhaps it was considered necessary to make room for the new arrivals by putting as many as possible out of the way.[35]

But the real reason was a "thirst for blood." As Bleby rightly observed, the officers of the militia and the members of the court-martial—those who captured and sentenced the slaves to death—were the very men who regarded the insurrectionists the culprits of their ruin. For weeks, the gallows were seldom empty. Generally, four hung at once; their bodies remained stiffening in the breeze until the court-martial board supplied another batch of victims for the hands of Bacchus—the name of the Black slave who acted as executioner.

Bleby made some important notes on the mental and emotional attitudes of the condemned:

The undaunted bravery and fortitude with which many of the insurgents met their fate formed a very remarkable feature in the transactions of the period: and strikingly indicated the difficulty attendant upon the maintenance of slavery, now that the spirit of freedom had gone abroad, and many of the negroes had learnt to prefer death to bondage.[36]

Bleby was moved by the bravery and calmness with which many met their death:

Not even a muscle was seen to quiver and the dignified bearing with which many met their death showed clearly that they were untroubled with any misgivings as to the justice of their cause.[37]

No real figure of the carnage was ever disclosed. After martial law was lifted and killing was forbidden in the public square, the slaughter continued unabated on the estates, where condemned slaves were sent to their death in secret. The last man to die was Samuel Sharpe. He was executed in Montego Bay on May 23, 1832. According to Bleby who spoke with him, Sharpe was, until the last, rather regretful of the death and destruction his plans had caused, but "he was not however, to be convinced that he had done wrong in endeavoring to assert his claim to freedom."

Bleby, who witnessed Sharpe's death along with hundreds of others, recounted the scene:

He marched to the spot where so many had been sacrificed to the demon of slavery, with a firm and even dignified step—clothed in a suit of new white clothes. He seemed to be unmoved by the near approach of death. In a few moments the executioner had done his work, and the noble-minded originator of this unhappy revolt ceased to exist.[38]

As a footnote, Bleby added "He was such a man, too, as was likely, nay, certain, had he been set free, to commence another struggle for freedom."[39]

The spirit of freedom could only be contained briefly, for Sam Sharpe's image continued to inspire Jamaicans from that day to the present. Today, this spirit is seen in the Rastafarian movement and in the Manley government which has renamed the square in which Sam Sharpe was executed as Sam Sharpe Square, thus giving dignity to one of Jamaica's martyrs for freedom. But the honor paid him was only anticlimatic in view of the real victory which his death brought about. Soon after the death of Sam Sharpe, slavery itself was dead. Within two years of his death, the abolition of slavery was proclaimed throughout the British colonies and a new era in Jamaican history was begun. The chains were now loose from the feet of the sons of Africa and their search for a place in the sun commenced—a search which was to encounter more obstacles, as the rest of the story will reveal.

The Morant Bay Rebellion, 1865

The abolition of slavery in 1834 left Jamaica in a state of chaos. The transition envisaged for slaves, based on an apprenticeship system intended to displace slave labor with a wage-earning economy, was an ideal based on the good will of the Planters and the slaves' willingness to work. The nature of society proffered this dream without the means to implement it. For one thing, the Planters, though heavily reimbursed for the loss of their slaves, still held a deep resentment toward the Imperial Government for upsetting their way of life through the emancipation, and they resented all instructions from England. On the other hand, the freed slaves resented all aspects of forced labor, the Planters, and the plantations. Their primary interest was to keep alive by working their small provision grounds and to enjoy their newly-won freedom as long as possible. On top of it all, religious and political rivalry made Jamaica into a churning caldron of hate. On the one side, the Church of England and the masters were deeply resentful of the Methodists and Baptists who championed the welfare of the slaves, most of the freed Blacks, and the rising colored elites. To these was added a marginal group of religionists known as the Native Baptists and the Revivalists whose revolutionary tendency threatened the status quo.[40] As indicated in the previous discussion of the Sam Sharpe Rebellion, it was within this marginal group that the spirit of revolution was nurtured, and from this group the dynamics of the Morant Bay Rebellion would find expression and support. The attitude toward the Native Baptists was expressed by a contemporary of the period as:

[A] place in which ignorance and superstition are enthroned—the hot-bed in which Obeahism and Myalism and other heathen practices attain their most vigorous growth and where the grossest impurity and vice are found in strange and unnatural alliance with a profession of the pure religion of Christ.[41]

We need no other documentation of the attitude of the establishment toward the Native Baptists, but it will be useful to keep in mind that both G. William Gordon and Paul Bogle, the two heroes of the Morant Bay Rebellion, were ministers of the Native Baptist Church of Jamaica.

The Setting

The three main figures around whom the Morant Bay Rebellion was played out were the English Governor Edward John Eyre, the Jamaican mulatto elitist George William Gordon, and the Black Baptist deacon-preacher Paul Bogle. These men represented three different worlds in nineteenth-century Jamaica. Governor Eyre (after years of mediocre work which included exploring in Australia, sheep raising in New Zealand, and a lieutenant governorship in St. Vincent) was sent to Jamaica in March, 1862, as a temporary replacement for Governor Darling—a position which became permanent when Governor Darling was appointed to another post. Eyre, the son of an Anglican minister and a man of rather modest attainment, came to Jamaica—as the record showed—"in hope to distinguish himself."[42] Whether this hope was ever fulfilled is a matter of interpretation. If murdering human beings is a distinguishing characteristic, he has, without question, highly distinguished himself in this accomplishment. But the historical opinion of him in Jamaica, and his long and agonizing trials in England for his acts in Jamaica, leave no doubt in the minds of his English contemporaries and the world that his appointment to Jamaica was one of the more regrettable episodes in British colonial history.

As governor, he was placed in an ill-fitting situation. In the second half of the nineteenth century, Jamaica was one of the most difficult islands to administer. Governor Eyre's appointment, being temporary, carried no real power for decision making at a time when strong and firm leadership was desperately needed to cope with the powerful conflicts which existed. His salary—a mere pittance—placed him in an odd position amid a snobbish, though waning, aristocracy of Planters and an affluent colored middle class of merchants and lawyers. As a high church Anglican, he had little respect for the sectarians and absolutely disdained the native cults. These elements were later to emerge in a fatal combination for the Black Jamaicans to whom Eyre was by nature unable to relate. It is in this light that we must see the unfolding of the Morant Bay debacle.

One of the men with whom Eyre was forced to deal was a radical politician, a self-ordained minister of the Native Baptist Church, and a wealthy landowner named George William Gordon.[43] Gordon was born in 1818, the son of Joseph Gordon, a White attorney, and a slave mother. His father—a politician and one time custos of St. Andrew—was the owner of the Cherry Gardens Estate, now a beautiful suburb in the foothills overlooking Kingston. Gordon was one of seven illegitimate children who was freed with his mother by his father. Young Gordon was brought up in Black River with his godfather, James Daley. He received no formal education but was able to pick up a great knowledge of business in Daley's store where he worked. At eighteen, he was back in Kingston in a business of his own where he prospered so well that, in 1843, he was reported to have been worth ten thousand pounds.[44] In 1848, he was proprietor of four estates, one being Cherry Gardens which he bought from his father. It is said that although he was never allowed to enter his father's house, he was always kind to the old man who, in his old age and having fallen on bad days, had his passage back to England paid by young Gordon.

Depending on the sources one reads, Gordon was reported to be a crooked man; an owner of slaves, whom he treated badly; a hypocrite; an obeahman; and a shylock. Others saw him as man of unbounded benevolence and a champion of the dispossessed, a brilliant orator, and deeply religious. We may now easily ignore the negative descriptions of the man—in those days to be a member of the Native Baptist Church and a champion of the dispossessed were enough to brand anyone a revolutionary. Socially, Gordon was highly placed among the colored merchants of his day and was wealthy enough to be elected to the House of Assembly in 1850 as a member of the Town Party. Originally, he seems to have been a member of the Presbyterian Church, but later became a Native Baptist in the mass conversion of the 1861 revival. He married Lucy Shannon, the daughter of a White school principal and appears to have had a good marriage before his untimely end. We are also told that he established a tabernacle in Kingston and ordained various deacons there, among whom was Paul Bogle of Stony Gut of St. Thomas-in-the-East. The connection between these two men will soon become clear.

As politician and champion of the dispossessed, it was not long before Gordon began to attack the leadership of Governor Eyre. Gordon felt Eyre was insensitive to the needs of the poor. His open attack of the governor and the House of Assembly—in what would still be called unguarded speech—won him no friends among his White colleagues with whom the governor had become quite friendly. The governor and the House of Assembly taxed the poor beyond their capacity, thereby forcing them to return to the estates.

Gordon's political downfall began with an incident in St. Thomas where, because of his vast holdings in real estate, he was made a magistrate of that parish. In 1862, he sent an open letter to the governor complaining about the abnormal conditions of poverty and official neglect of the Blacks in that parish. This letter was taken as an insult to the established church, whose rector was head of the vestry[45]—a body empowered to look after the welfare of the people, and a body of which Gordon himself was a member. This attack on the established church and the White Planters gave Eyre his chance to revenge his accuser. Gordon was summarily dismissed from his post as magistrate. This dismissal came as a blow to Gordon's pride. His tirades against the governor became increasingly vitriolic. Hated by the governor, the Planters, and the church Gordon asserted himself as the messianic leader of the Blacks and colored with one intention—self-government by Blacks.

An example of Gordon's forcefulness is preserved in the biography of Edward John Eyre by Hamilton Hume. In a parliamentary debate on conditions in Jamaica in 1865, Gordon actually prophesied the coming rebellion in a rebuttal of his opponents. The following is an excerpt:

Mr. Gordon: It does not seem that his Excellency's natural endowments qualify him for the government of this country. (Cries of "Order!") I desire to give honour to whom honour is due, and I respect every man in authority; but if a ruler does not sway the sword with justice, he becomes distasteful, and instead of having the love and respect of the people, he becomes despised and hated. All the privileges, all the rights, and all the purposes of the constitution should be maintained in their highest integrity and purity, by the gentlemen who may from time to time be entrusted with the government of this country. So soon as he digresses from this, so soon does he descend from his high position, and become grovelling, portentous [sic] and prevaricating.

Mr. Speaker: Order! The language of the honourable member cannot be allowed. The honourable gentleman must know that he is out of order.

Mr. Gordon: I regret, Mr. Speaker, that I am out of order, but when every day we witness the mal-administration of the law by the Lieutenant-Governor, we must speak out. You are en-

deavouring to suppress public opinion, to pen up the expression
of public indignation; but I tell you that it will soon burst forth
like a flood, and sweep everything before it. There must be a
limit to everything: a limit to oppression—a limit to
transgression—and a limit to illegality! These proceedings remind me of the time of Herod—they remind me of a tyrannical
period of history! I do not think that any Governor has ever acted
so before. While he justifies himself in one case, he uses the
police force to accomplish another illegality. What an example to
the prisoners who are confined in prison! If the Lieutenant-
Governor is to go on in this way, what can you expect from the
populace?

Mr. Lewis: Insurrection (Laughter)

Mr. Gordon: Ay! *that will be the result* . . .[46]

This small sample of Gordon's proclamations demonstrates
his bold attacks on the status quo and clearly suggests the
burden he felt for his country. It also suggests that things
were not going well with the populace. The clear warning in
this parliamentary discussion would soon break loose in
Jamaica. His use of the word "portentous" instead of "pre-
tentious" was rather prophetic as we now review the tragic
outcome of Eyre's governorship.

We need to know a little more about the social and economic conditions in the year 1865, and for this we must turn
to a letter written by Mr. Edward B. Underhill; Mr. Underhill visited Jamaica shortly before the rebellion. This letter
was addressed to the Honorable Mr. Edward Cardwell, M.P.,
England's Secretary of State for the Colonies during the governorship of Eyre.[47] The letter is commonly believed to be
one of the documents that encouraged the rebellion. After
his usual salutation to the colonial secretary, he began:

I venture to ask your kind consideration to a few observations on
the present condition of the Island of Jamaica . . . Crime has fear-
fully increased. The number of prisoners in the penitentiary and
gaols is considerably more than double the average, and nearly
all for one crime—larceny. Summons for petty debts disclose an
amount of pecuniary difficulty which has never before been experienced; and application for parochial and private relief prove

that multitudes are suffering from want, a little removed from starvation.[48]

Mr. Underhill then went on to describe the naked conditions of the people who, accustomed to dressing modestly, walked around in rags scarcely sufficient to cover their private parts. Even though he saw this condition resulting from the steep rise in cotton, he attributed it to the gross mismanagement of the island's economy and, more specifically, to the lack of employment; on an island of four hundred thousand people, only thirty thousand were employed on the sugar estates. Then pointing directly to what he thought to be the source of the problems he wrote:

I shall say nothing of the course taken by the Jamaica Legislature; of their abortive immigration bills; of their unjust taxation of the coloured population; of their refusal of just tribunals; of their denial of political rights to the emancipated negroes.[49]

He then proceeded to suggest a sweeping inquiry into the Jamaica legislature since emancipation, the need for the development of native products, and new ways of utilizing the land for agriculture other than cane and sugar. For example, he saw such minor products as spices, tobacco, farinaceous foods, coffee, and cotton as excellent possibilities for Jamaica, if the proper incentive were given by the government. (This suggestion, incidently, remains a prime need for present-day Jamaica.) Mr. Underhill closed with a warning:

It is more than time that the unwisdom (to use the gentlest term) that has governed Jamaica since emancipation should be brought to an end—a course of action which, while it incalculably aggravates the misery arising from natural, and, therefore, unavoidable causes, renders certain the ultimate ruin of every class, planter and peasant, European and Creole.[50]

This letter was forwarded to Governor Eyre in Jamaica, who circulated it to the custodes and heads of religious denominations. As a member of the legislature, G. W. Gordon was probably the first to get a copy of it. As expected, almost all the leading men in Jamaica denied that conditions were as bad as the letter described them. A sweeping defense of the establishment was launched by those who controlled the power. But for G. W. Gordon, this only confirmed his assessment of the island situation, and, armed with the support of this letter from an Englishman who told it like it was, he began to urge the common people to resist their domination. His burning zeal for a better Jamaica caused him to use insurrectionary language, which could do little but inflame the oppressed. His speeches were later to be the cause of his death. But we must now introduce the other hero of the rebellion.

Paul Bogle

In a bill of description published for the capture of Bogle after the Morant Bay Rebellion, he was described as "very black, shiney of skin, heavy marks of smallpox on face, especially on nose; good teeth—large mouth, red thick lips; about five feet eight inches tall, broad shoulders; carries himself indolently, with no whiskers."[51] I found no information about his place of birth or the circumstances surrounding his childhood. But it is reported that he was the owner of a large piece of land in the hill country of St. Thomas, in a village named Stony Gut, six miles from Morant Bay. He was closely connected with G. W. Gordon, who was reported to have baptized him in his Kingston Tabernacle, where he was ordained either as a preacher or a deacon in the year of the rebellion, 1865. Records of Bogle's involvement with Gordon are rather scarce, but there is no doubt that they both had close religious ties and that both were champions of the dispossessed. Gordon was a man of words and, like Sam Sharpe, could stir his audience to a state of madness; Paul Bogle was a man of action who was not afraid to confront the establishment with a show of strength.

It now appears that in September, 1865, Bogle had made up his mind to cross the Rubican of Jamaica's long years of oppression, and to risk his life in an attack on Morant Bay.

But he feared the Maroons. In that same month he was reported to have met with Major Sterling of the Windward
Maroons who received him but gave him no definite answer.
However, the ambiguity of the Maroons' answer led Bogle to
believe that if a campaign were launched, he could depend
on them. This was a gross mistake—the history of Jamaican
revolts should have been too fresh in Bogle's mind for him to
have been so duped. It also appears that the Maroons were
well aware of the plans for the rebellion and that they had already given their allegiance to the government.[52] Meanwhile, at his Baptist Chapel at Stony Gut, Bogle began to
make his not-so-secret preparation by drilling his mountain
recruits in military operations. His plan was to march on
Morant Bay with an army of men to show his strength. On
October 7 (a market day), he marched into town at the head
of two hundred men, with fife and drum and an assortment
of weapons.

What took place that day in Morant Bay could not have
been the only reason for his long march with two hundred
men. The demonstration, however, provided the real spark
for the historic rebellion which followed. On reaching the
court house, it is said, Bogle left his soldiers in the public
square and entered the court house where two minor cases
were being tried. The case or cases must have been of some
interest to Bogle, or perhaps it was simply a coincidence.
The eventual incident was triggered by a young man who
became mildly abusive to the magistrate when a convict
was charged for crimes committed on a woman. His conduct
would have caused him to be apprehended by the police as
he attempted to leave the court, had it not been for Bogle's
intervention. Poorly documented, this very insignificant
skirmish is about all that took place, although there is some
indication that Bogle's men did "rough-up" a few policemen. Bogle thus was technically guilty of obstructing the
police from performing their duty. He could also have been
charged with disorderly conduct.

To get a clearer picture of Morant Bay, it might be of some
interest to introduce the leading men who served the colo-

nial government in St. Thomas. One of the men closely connected with the Gordon and Bogle controversy was the Reverend Stephen Cooke, Anglican rector of Morant Bay and president of the vestry (a sort of parochial council). Another man, the custos of the parish, the Honorable Maximilian Augustus, Baron von Ketelhodt, had come to Jamaica in the 1830s and became a Jamaican citizen in 1839 after marrying a rich widow; he owned five plantations, mostly in St. Thomas. He and Mr. Gordon were avowed enemies. Baron von Ketelhodt was to play a prime role in the whole episode. The third man was the Reverend V. Herschell, curator of Bath in St. Thomas. Many others made important contributions to the rebellion, but these three were G. W. Gordon's companions on the vestry, and all were to become key figures in the historical drama.

Soon after Bogle and his men returned to their homes in the hills, warrants were issued for the arrest of Bogle, his brother, and twenty-five other men on charges of rioting and of assaulting the police. Eight police were dispatched to Stony Gut to apprehend them. It is now easy to surmise what took place over one hundred years ago, but the idea of sending eight police to an area from which two hundred armed men had come was either conceived by an inexperienced civil servant, or the episode was designed to have Bogle commit himself. The fate of this apprehending party can easily be imagined. They were severely beaten, and, had they been White soldiers, they would have been killed. The police were forced to take an oath on the Bible that they would fight on the side of the Blacks; after this they were set free.

While in Stony Gut, the police overheard that Bogle's army had planned to march on the town the following day, October 10, 1865. On learning of the planned march, Baron von Ketelhodt dispatched a message to Governor Eyre and alerted the Morant Bay police. In the letter he added the following postscript: "The shells are at this moment blowing to collect men all through St. John's." (This blowing of shells and horns was a practice of the Maroons in time of war.) Then he added, "Gordon's inflammatory speeches had borne fruit earlier than I at least anticipated." On the 10th, Paul Bogle, at the head of several hundred men, marched into town and attacked the vestry. Eighteen persons were killed, mostly White, among whom were Baron von Ketelhodt and the Reverend Herschell. Thirty-one were wounded and fifty-one prisoners were freed from jail. Bogle and his men took the prisoners to Stony Gut, where Bogle held a prayer meeting to thank God for his victory.

By the time Baron von Ketelhodt's letter had reached Governor Eyre, the Baron was already dead. Preparations were made to dispatch men to Morant Bay on the H.M.S. *Wolverine* and the *Onyx*—both anchored on Port Royal. Late on October 10, Governor Eyre heard that the massacre had taken place and he sailed from Port Royal on the French ship *Caravelle* to survey the situation in person. On his way to Morant Bay he met the *Wolverine* returning with a cargo of refugees and got a firsthand report of the dimensions of the war. Meanwhile, Paul Bogle and his men were on the move. The town of Bath was taken on the twelfth of October, but this move was the beginning of the end for the Bogle rebellion. At the request of the magistrate of Bath, the Maroons joined the conflict against Bogle. This was a mortal blow. On October thirteenth, martial law was declared for the county of Surrey which included St. Thomas, Portland, and St. George. Kingston was excluded. On the fourteenth, court-martial was instituted at Morant Bay and the British military mill of martial law began its day-by-day extinction of human life. Dutton states that the aim of martial law was the restoration of law and order, but the method used to achieve this goal was terror. It was a license to flog and kill subjected citizens of the colonies. Eyre's martial law was a monster that he was unable to control. The 1831 rebellion in the county of Cornwall was a model for Surrey. Martial law continued for thirty days and with the help of the Maroons, whose loyalty for the Crown never waivered, the militia (numbering nearly fifteen hundred, most of whom were experienced in the historical campaigns of Great Britain's far-flung empire) brutally crushed the rebellion. As many as a thousand people were killed, including George William Gordon and Paul Bogle; over a thousand cottages owned by rebels were burned and, in all this, there is no evidence that any sailors or soldiers were killed after the initial eighteen at Morant Bay.

Governor Eyre blamed the cause of the rebellion on Gordon and ordered his arrest. Dutton reported Eyre as saying:

There is one very important point to be decided upon. Throughout my tour in the *Wolverine* and the *Onyx* I found everywhere the most unmistakable evidence that Mr. Geo. Wm. Gordon, a coloured member of the House of Assembly, had not only been mixed up in the matter, but was himself, through his own misrepresentation and seditious language addressed to the ignorant black people, the chief cause and origin of the whole rebellion.[53]

Gordon was not in Morant Bay on the day of the rebellion (he was sick at home), but his speeches had implicated him and, as Eyre stated,

Having obtained a deposition on oath that certain seditious printed notices (Gordon's proclamation "STATE OF THE ISLAND") had been sent through the Post Office directed, in his handwriting, to parties who have been leaders in the rebellion, I at once called upon the Custos to issue a warrant and capture him.[54]

Gordon, learning of the arrest warrant, turned himself in to the officials in Kingston. He should have been tried in a civil court because he was not arrested in an area where martial law was declared, but Eyre himself accompanied Gordon in the *Wolverine* to Morant Bay where there was no law, fearing he would have won his case in Kingston. Here he was tried by three junior officers and found guilty of high treason and complicity in a rebellion. This case was to be Eyre's downfall. This farce of justice was so illegal that it brought a hurricane of legal entanglements on the governor, involving some of the greatest legal minds in England. On October 22, 1865, George William Gordon was hanged at the Morant Bay Court House. He denied his complicity in the rebellion to the last.

Paul Bogle was captured on the same day by the Maroons at Stony Gut. In his trial he refused to implicate Gordon and, at 5 P.M. on the twenty-fourth of October, he was hanged from the yardarm of the H.M.S. *Wolverine*. With the deaths of Gordon and Bogle, two more freedom fighters in the Jamaican liberation struggle had left their indelible marks on history.

The rebellion was not at all in vain. The fear it brought about was so overpowering and portentous of future troubles that the Planters, the most obstreperous and loggerheaded individuals of the British colonies, finally submitted to the end of their privileges. On December 22, 1865, "the 202-year-old representative institution of Jamaica ended, and became a Crown Colony." The privileges of the oligarchy were put to an end, thanks to Gordon and Bogle. It was another two centuries before moderate independence was accorded to Black Jamaicans, but the rule of tyranny was overthrown by the Morant Bay rebellion.

Crown Colony to Independence: 1865–1962

This section will give only an outline of the social, political, and economic developments from 1865 to 1962, when Jamaica became an independent nation of the British Commonwealth.

Faced with a society it could no longer dominate, the Jamaican Assembly surrendered the old constitution and became a crown colony. Under the new constitution the real power of decision-making now rested with the governor advised by a cabinet which controlled the legislative council. In this council the governor enjoyed a permanent majority of nominated officials over elected members. By 1884, the members of the legislative council were elected, of which the overwhelming majority were White. However, this new constitution had built-in guidelines which anticipated the inevitable hour when the Black majority would seize power. It stipulated that the success of the government would depend on a maintenance of reasonable economic and social

conditions. If, however, the governor and the members of
the legislative council failed to maintain friendly working
relations, and, if the economic life of Jamaica were to suffer
from acute depression, leading perhaps to labor violence, or
if the overwhelmingly large Black element in the population
should become conscious of its inferior position and find capable leaders with a positive democratic program—then the
political constitution might have to be amended or
abolished to meet the new conditions.[55]

Despite the new constitution, the political climate from
1884 on remained as lethargic as before, perpetuated by
apathy and disdain toward the Black population. Not until
1920 to 1921, under the leadership of Marcus Mosiah Garvey, did the Black population begin to show some political
consciousness.

Encouraged by the awakening consciousness brought on
by Garvey, Jamaican expatriates in New York, who were
members of the Jamaica Progressive League under the leadership of Mr. W. Adolphe Roberts, began to exhort
Jamaicans to:

... begin to act as people within the framework of the Empire and
cease speaking—or even thinking—as apathetic subjects under a
Crown Colony system which has long outlived its time. The inhabitants of Jamaica are, in fact, a people. The awakening of a consciousness of nationality is what is needed today.[56]

The exhortation to sense a "consciousness of nationality"
met with genuine response. Definite interest now began to
develop in political matters, with citizens' associations
forming in the Kingston area to organize discussions on public matters. But the turning point in Jamaica's political development came in 1938—violence again acting as stage
director—when labor unrest came to a head in the parish of
Westmoreland at the Tate and Lyle sugar factory, followed
by labor unrest in Spanish Town and Kingston. Serious violence, put down by an armed constabulary with the loss of
many lives, brought Jamaican conditions to the attention of
the imperial government, which appointed a Royal Com-

mission under the leadership of Lord Moyne. The colonial mentality is peculiarly myopic; it can act only by violence or the threat of it on the part of the Blacks. Lord Moyne's report recommended the need for a new constitution as a basis of the future development of self-government. Jamaican independence was a direct result of that far-reaching report.

The 1938 rebellion saw the emergence of the learned barrister-politician, Norman W. Manley, and the flamboyant Alexander Bustamante, who set in motion the two political parties which have steered Jamaica to its present status. Sir Alexander Bustamante, at this writing, is still alive and revered by all Jamaicans. The Honorable Norman Manley is now dead, but the mantle of Jamaican leadership is today worn by his charismatic son, Michael Manley, whose dedication to the dispossessed and whose dislike for those who sit in the citadels of privilege is well known. In no other politician has the spirit of G. W. Gordon been so thoroughly reincarnated as it is in Michael Manley, except possibly the national hero, Marcus Mosiah Garvey.

Garvey and the Rastafarians

We shall conclude this chapter with a short analysis of the influence of the Back-to-Africa movement inspired by Marcus Garvey in Jamaica, and see what connections exist between the demise of the Universal Negro Improvement Association and the rise of the present-day Rastafarians.

Marcus Mosiah Garvey, one of the world's most renowned Black leaders, was born in the parish of St. Ann in 1887, just twenty-two years after the Morant Bay rebellion.[57] His childhood and early manhood coincided with that period of Jamaican history in which political apathy in the Black population—due to restrictions on Black expression by the ruling class—was at its highest. Social and economic stagnation was widespread. The yoke of colonialism was secure on the island and in Africa as well. Every aspect of Jamaican life was dominated by the Europeans, and there was very little hope for native Jamaicans to improve their position. Despite this context, Garvey was no ordinary man, but one of those rare creatures of history whose fate it is to be seized with the social and economic oppression of a people and who see this oppression as his or her own spiritual mission. His middle name, Mosiah or Moses, was a portentous appellation—to deliver his people from the yoke of colonialism was to be his lifelong struggle. No other Black man in history was able to understand so clearly the worldwide oppressions of Black people, and no other was in turn perceived by so many Blacks as the one person with the solution to their problems.

Garvey's personality took on messianic proportions to Blacks in Jamaica, the United States, and Africa, resulting in the formation of a movement around him. In 1914 he organized the Universal Negro Improvement Association in Kingston, a movement that was to change the self-image of Blacks all over the world. But since "A prophet is not without honour, but in his own country,"[58] Marcus Garvey had to leave Jamaica in order to pursue his dreams. First, he wanted a worldwide confraternity of the Black race; second, he wished to see the development of Africa from a backward, colonial enclave to a self-supporting giant of which all Blacks could be proud; third, he wanted to see Africa as a developed Negro nation, a force in world power, and a place to which all Blacks could return; he envisioned a Black nation from which Black representatives were to be sent to all the principal countries and cities of the world; fifth, he wanted to see the development of Black educational institutions for the teaching of Black cultures; and last, he wanted to work for the uplifting of the Black race anywhere it was to be found.[59]

In Jamaica, Garvey's dreams were unaccepted. Though he developed a large following, official opposition to his program came from both Blacks and Whites. The Whites viewed him as a threat to Pax Britannica and the Blacks, especially those of the middle class, felt themselves beyond the class of a man like Garvey. His success as a leader was to come in the United States. His demonstrated ability as a leader in a foreign country later gave him legitimacy in his homeland. Jamaica has since made him a national hero.

The ethos of the Garvey movement did not wane with his death. His philosophy—"Africa for the African at home and abroad"—was to be taken up by various Black movements after him; one of these is the Jamaican Rastafarians.[60] It is often repeated among the Rastafarians that, just before Marcus Garvey left for the United States in 1916, he is reported to have said in his farewell address, "Look to Africa for the crowning of a Black King, he shall be the Redeemer." To the Rastafarians this king was Haile Selassie. Today, all Rastafarians revere Marcus Garvey as their inspirer; his picture is prominent in all homes and cult houses. His speeches are avidly read; songs and poems are written in his honor and, in the pantheon of the Rastafarians, Marcus Garvey is second only to Haile Selassie.

We have followed the long and bloody road that Jamaica and its people have traveled from the seventeenth century to the present. Despite the great price in death and suffering Jamaicans underwent in this struggle, their resistance to domination has never faltered. The fight or flight syndrome of the Jamaican personality represents a cultural experience which has become a permanent part of the people's psyche. The Rastafarian movement is the most recent expression of this national character.

Ethiopianism in Jamaica

The emergence of the Rastafarians will remain a puzzle unless seen as a continuation of the concept of Ethiopianism which began in Jamaica as early as the eighteenth century. The enchantment with the land and people of Ethiopia has had a long and interesting history. From biblical writings through Herodotus to the medieval fantasy with the mythic King Prester John right down to our day, Ethiopia has had a hypnotic influence on history, which has been retained by the imagination of Blacks in Diaspora. In the nineteenth century, when the defenders of slavery tried to divest Blacks of every dignity of humanity and civilization, Blacks appealed to the fabled glory of Ethiopia. When confronted by stalwarts of religion, philosophy, and science who sought to falsify history in the service of Western slavery, Black preachers—though for the most part unlearned—discovered in the only book to which they had access (the Bible) that Egypt and Ethiopia were in Africa, and that these countries figured very importantly in the history of civilization. They evidently read and pondered the meaning of Psalm 68:31—"Princes shall come out of Egypt; Ethiopia shall soon stretch out her hands unto God"; and with some reflection they must have read Jeremiah 13:23—"Can the Ethiopian change his skin, or the leopard his spots?" They no doubt figured

"Not Far Away" by Ras Daniel Heartman, representing a Rastaman as Ethiopian warrior, the lion of Ethiopia, and the ganja plant.

-NOT FAR AWAY-
By Daniel Hazeltine
-CHURCH TRIUMPHANT-

out that Simon of Cyrene, who helped Christ to bear his cross on the day of the crucifixion, was an African and that the Ethiopian eunuch of the Acts of the Apostles was a man of great authority. Such references to a Black race in the Bible were probably the key to the dynamic mythology which became known as "Ethiopianism" and which energized Black religion in slavery. From South Africa to the Caribbean to North America, the concept of Ethiopianism has remained a part of Black religious thought.

Because few writers have connected Ethiopianism with the rise of Rastafarianism, in this chapter first we will explore the concept of Ethiopia in ancient history; second, the concept as used in Black religious reaction to proslavery propaganda; and third, the term as used by Black leaders such as Marcus Garvey, who inspired the Rastafarians. Then we will look at the beginning of the Rastafarians and how they adopted the concept as a model for social transformation in Jamaica.

Ethiopia in Ancient Thought

Rivers of ink have been spilled trying to obscure the identity of the Egyptians and the Ethiopians. This became especially necessary as it grew fashionable to foster a "sociology of knowledge" in the nineteenth century which claimed that Blacks were by nature uncivilized and have remained so throughout written history. At all costs, it became necessary to prove that all areas of highly developed civilization, in which Blacks were numerous, were originated by the White race. If White origin was impossible to prove, it was necessary to de-negrify the Blacks in these civilizations by calling the inhabitants White, even if such a description denied scientific objectivity. To "scientifically" prove these notions, nineteenth-century scholars divided the Black race into various categories of skin color; thus the people of West Africa were true Negroes—based on the melanin in their pigmentation. Under such categories, the people of Egypt and

Ethiopia, who were of lighter color through centuries of miscegenation, were not Negroes but Hamites. Others who were less mixed but obviously too Black to be called Hamites were designated Nilotics. Even today, Africa and its people suffer from these confusing racial classifications, though modern scholarship has long since destroyed their credibility.[1]

But who are the Hamites? Today, this question is very controversial and might best be left unanswered. But many Black scholars are becoming restless to answer the question, and would like to see some new discussion. If the true history of the Black race is to be written, the dogmatic statements of the nineteenth-century scholars need to be challenged. Despite the avoidance of the question and the emotion surrounding it, great emphasis is placed on the mythical origin of the Hamites by fundamentalist Christianity and racist bigots. It is therefore of interest to millions of Blacks that this question be reconsidered.

The first mention of the name Ham occurs in the Christian Bible; here the myth of the origin of human races is recorded and their place of habitation allotted to them. Although learned scholars interpret the myth as the total assertion of ancients' minds which gain meaning only through interpretation, naive and unlearned minds believe them to be truths at face value. And they are true to the extent that mythical statements make total assertions of the world in "beginning" time, and even more so when we consider that the book of Genesis is considered by some to be the revelation of God.

Most Hebrew dictionaries agree that "Ham" or "Cham" mean "heat" or "hot," a designation that fits well into the climatic theory that is supposed to cause blackness. In Hebrew, "Cush" is the word for "Black" and wherever "Cushite" is used it refers to people of Black Africa. "Mizraim" is still used in the Near East for Egypt, whose people were described by the ancient texts as Black. "Phut" or "Put" is a reference to Ethiopians. From biblical references, then, one may conclude that the Hamites or Cushites were Black and that both Egypt and Ethiopia were inhabited by Cushites or the Black race. One can further conclude that Blacks, contrary to the attempts of Western writers to deny the evidence, were the founders of one of the greatest civilizations history has recorded.

To discuss Ethiopia without discussing Egypt is impossible. The author believes that they were both inhabited by one and the same people. The word "Ethiopia" as we now know it is a Greek translation of the Hebrew word for the Blacks. In Greek, "Ethiop" means "burnt" or "black;" when the old Testament was translated from Hebrew to Greek, "Cush" was changed to "Ethiop." The flowering of Black civilization arose in Nubia on the banks of the Upper Nile and has come down to us as the Meroitic civilization, from which both the Egyptians and the Ethiopians drew their cultural dynamics. An early eyewitness of the Egyptians and Ethiopians was Herodotus, according to whom "the natives of the country [Egypt] were black with the heat." On another occasion he states "they are black-skinned and have wooly hair." On comparing a tribe of India with the Ethiopians he said, "they all, also have the same tint of skin which approaches that of the Ethiopians."[2] Numerous sources from ancient history exist which testify to the fact that the Ethiopians and the Egyptians were one and the same people. Both were of the Black race and the forerunners of one of the world's great civilizations. It may be argued that the present people of Egypt and Ethiopia do not qualify as Blacks. This cannot be denied, but when Herodotus met the Egyptians in the fifth century B.C., a lot of miscegenation had already taken place. The Persian blood had been added to the stock, followed by the Greeks under Alexander, the Romans, and finally the Arabs.

Nowhere was Dionysus more favoured, nowhere was he worshipped more adoringly and more elaboratedly than by the Ptolemies, who recognized his cult as an especially effective means of promoting the assimilation of the conquering Greeks and their fusion with the native Egyptians.[3]

In time, the conquering armies of Eurasia would modify the African stock, but our history of creativity went back ten thousand years before that, and even at this Herodotus was not misled—unlike the writers of history and our modern-day anthropologists. Count Constantin de Volney (1747–1820) spoke about the race of Egyptians that produced the Pharaohs and later paid tribute to Herodotus' discovery when he said:

... the ancient Egyptians were true Negroes of the same type as all native-born Africans. That being so, we can see how their blood, mixed for several centuries with that of the Romans and Greeks, must have lost the intensity of its original color, while retaining nonetheless the imprint of its original mold. We can even state as a general principle that the face [this is the Sphinx] is a kind of monument able, in many cases, to attest or shed light on historical evidence on the origins of the people.[4]

The Egyptian monument depicting the fact of the African race caused Volney to reflect:

What a subject for meditation . . . . Just think that the race of black men, today our slave and the object of our scorn, is the very race to which we owe our arts, science, and even the use of our speech.[5]

Needless to say, many scholars later disputed Volney's observation. One of these was the brother of the decipherer of the Rosetta Stone, Champollion-Figeac, who declared that black skin and wooly hair are not sufficient characteristics to designate a man Black. Since that time, proponents of this kind of doubletalk have come and gone.

But to conclude this short review of the ancients, we must quote Diodorus of Sicily who gave us an important view of the Ethiopians:

The Ethiopians call themselves the first of all men and cite proofs they consider evident. It is generally agreed that born in a country and not having come from elsewhere, they must be judged indigenous. For it is likely that located directly under the course of the sun, combining with the humidity of the soil, produces life, those sites nearest the Equator must have produced living beings earlier than any others. The Ethiopians also say that they instituted the cults of the Gods, festivals, solemn assembles, sacrifice, in short, all the practices by which we honor the gods. For that reason they are deemed the most religious of all men, and they believe their sacrifices to be the most pleasing to the gods.

They claim that the gods have rewarded their piety by important blessings, such as never having been dominated by any foreign Prince. In fact, thanks to the great unity that has always existed among them, they have always kept their freedom.[6]

Here we may observe that, even before the findings of modern archeologists, the ancients expressed the belief that humanity originated in Africa and that all religion began there. The ancient enchantment with Ethiopia is addictive, but this short discussion must suffice. We have tried to show that Egypt and Ethiopia figured greatly in the building of civilization, and that the earliest and the most creative peoples of this civilization were Black Africans. The testimony of the ancients and many Egyptologists have confirmed that this Black civilization, however, was unable to withstand the barbaric hordes which surrounded the Mediterranean basin. By 814 B.C., with the Roman victory over Carthage, the Black civilization lost its power. Thereafter, they were oppressed by all races. Oppression by strangers no doubt sparked migration of Blacks south and west from the Nile basin to be regrouped in empires west of Egypt. Meanwhile, Egypt and Ethiopia were to undergo radical change, but despite the vicissitudes of history, they remain a part of Africa. Although there have been various attempts to Europeanize these people, Blacks all over the world still find the origins of their ancestral creativity in these two great civilizations. And although Egyptologists have attempted to emphasize Egyptian civilization as the greatest civilization in history, in Black tradition, the word "Ethiopia" has come to designate all of Africa including Egypt.

Ethiopianism and the Black Struggle

It is now impossible to know with certainty when Ethiopianism emerged in American Black religion. But it is

certain that all American Blacks knew themselves as Africans before and after the emancipation. Thus, when the first
Black churches began to emerge in the ante-bellum period,
almost all placed their nationality ahead of the various denominations with which they became affiliated. The first
Baptist church organized by Blacks in the South was named
the First African Baptist Church in Savannah, Georgia
(1788). This appellation became the norm throughout the
United States, whatever the denomination. The Blacks in
America saw themselves as a nation entirely separate from
other Americans until long after emancipation.

By the time of the emergence of the Black churches, Africa
(as a geographical entity) was just about obliterated from
their minds. Their only vision of a homeland was the biblical Ethiopia. It was the vision of a golden past—and the
promise that Ethiopia should once more stretch forth its
hands to God—that revitalized the hope of an oppressed
people. Ethiopia to the Blacks in America was like Zion or
Jerusalem to the Jews. It began to take on an eschatological
dimension. As the Black church developed in America, the
spirit of missions developed. This course was part and parcel
of the denomination to which they belonged, but for the
Black church, the mission grew increasingly concerned with
the Blacks in the New World, of which Haiti was the first,
and Africa the second and more important.[7]

As a result of the missionary outreach, Ethiopianism
began to take on a more realistic dimension. Pioneered by
the Rev. Edward Wilmot Blyden, who was sent to Liberia as
a missionary by the American Colonization Society, the
new dimension began to take shape.[8] His wide training gave
him a grasp of African culture far beyond that of his contemporaries. He saw the Pan-African dimension of the Black
race worldwide, and began to structure it in a series of books
and articles. The eyes of Blacks in both America and Africa
began to open. For a knowledge of Africa he went to the classical sources of the Greeks, the Romans, and the Arabs
where he discovered that Africa was not the barbaric, inferior culture projected by whites, but the founder of all
civilizations. From Ethiopia the Blacks had penetrated the

desert westward to find the great West African civilization and it was from these great civilizations of the West that slaves were taken in the sixteenth century to the New World. Although a Christian missionary, Blyden believed that Christianity was a destroyer of the dignity of Blacks. He even advocated Islam as a better religion for the Africans.

Ethiopianism did not take on any really revolutionary dimension in the United States. It merely existed as a mild ideology, forceful but unstructured. Then, toward the close of the nineteenth century this ideology assumed a revolutionary aspect in Africa and carved out a new Ethiopian church movement from the missionary churches. This reaction to missionary Christianity was a direct rejection of the European orientation of Christianity and a search for an African Christianity which would more adequately answer the needs and aspiration of their people. This Ethiopian ideology set off a tidal wave of independent movements in Africa. The last estimate of these movements amounted to six thousand different schisms.

Ethiopianism in Jamaica

Long before Ethiopianism came to America, the term had been adopted in Jamaica by George Liele, the American Baptist slave preacher who founded the first Baptist church in the island in 1784—which he named the Ethiopian Baptist Church. This church (discussed in Chapter 2) grafted itself onto the African religion of Jamaican slaves and developed outside of the Christian missions, exhibiting a pure native flavor. It has continued to do so under various names and is still the church most acceptable to the masses because it was the religious expression most suitable for the political and social aspirations of the slaves. From it came the grassroots resistance to oppression.

But the movement that was to embody the Ethiopian ideology par excellence was the Back-to-Africa Movement of Marcus Garvey. It was in Garvey—the prophet of African redemption—that the spirit of Ethiopianism came into full blossom. Through his writings and speeches, the glory of Ethiopia-Africa became the glory of things to come. We must look at some of his most inspired words. Speaking on the image of God, he wrote:

We, as Negroes, have found a new ideal. Whilst our God has no colour, yet it is human to see everything through one's own spectacles, and since the white people have seen their God through white spectacles, we have only now started out (late though it be) to see our God through our own spectacles. The God of Isaac and the God of Jacob let him exist for the race that believe in the God of Isaac and the God of Jacob. We Negroes believe in the God of Ethiopia, the everlasting God—God the Son, God the Holy Ghost, the one God of all ages. That is the God in whom we believe, but we shall worship him through the spectacles of Ethiopia.[9]

From this statement by Garvey most Black God movements have drawn their origin. Among these are the Church of the Black Madonna in Detroit, the Black Muslims of America, and the Rastafarians.

Marcus Garvey was bold and virulent about the defense of African history. He, like Blyden, saw African civilization as anterior to all others, and he seemed to have been well versed in the ancient references to Ethiopia. In one of his strongest speeches he asserted:

But when we come to consider the history of man, was not the Negro a power, was he not great once? Yet, honest students of history can recall the day when Egypt, Ethiopia and Timbuctoo towered in their civilization, towered above Europe, towered above Asia. When Europe was inhabited by a race of Cannibals, a race of savages, naked men, heathens and pagans, Africa was peopled with a race of cultured black men, who were cultured and refined; men who, it is said, were like the gods.[10]

Marcus Garvey returned to this theme of the superiority of the ancient Black race time and again. There was no equivocation in his belief about the dignity of the Black race; this dignity was only to be ignited for the Blacks to assume the true leadership of the world as they had in times past. He realized that the Western world was so demoralized that there was no need to appeal to its conscience.

When reflecting on the nature of twentieth-century man, Garvey stated:

As by the action of the world, as by the conduct of all the races and nations it is apparent that not one of them has the sense of justice, the sense of love, the sense of equity, the sense of charity, that would make men happy, and God satisfied. It is apparent that it is left to the Negro to play such a part in human affairs—for when we look at the Anglo-Saxon we see him full of greed, avarice, no mercy, no love, no charity. We go from the white man to the yellow man, and see the same unenviable characteristics in the Japanese. Therefore we must believe that the Psalmist had great hopes of this race of ours when he prophesied "Princes shall come out of Egypt and Ethiopia shall stretch forth his hands unto God."[11]

The importance of this verse of Psalm 68 cannot be overestimated. It was the theme of the Garvey movement and has remained the most quoted text in the Rastafarian movement. The style and ardor of Garvey's speeches and writings were those of a prophet of Israel. His clarity of speech and his reiteration techniques were such that he could bring the spirit of an audience to boil. No wonder he became the inspirer of such men like Kwame Nkrumah of Ghana and numerous other African leaders.

The messianic dimension of Garvey's movement has not only a revolutionary thrust, but indeed a high ethical force. His movement was designed to restructure a fallen race and, like a prophet, he was impatient for its accomplishment. In his address *Who and What Is a Negro?*, we can feel this impatience:

The power and sway we once held passed away, but now in the twentieth century we are about to see the return of it in the rebuilding of Africa; yes, a new civilization, a new culture, shall spring up from among our people, and the Nile shall once more flow through the land of science, of art, and of literature, wherein will live blackmen of the highest learning and the highest accomplishments.[12]

Here is the language of a prophet. Notice the reference to the Nile. No accuracy of geography exists here; the emphasis is

on racial uplift, not scientific precision. Garvey never
visited Africa. His knowledge of the continent was biblically
oriented. Despite this, his followers both in the New World
and in Africa perceived the meaning of his message. The
fulfillment of this quotation in our day cannot be denied.

The movement he organized worldwide was known as the
Universal Negro Improvement Association. In a speech delivered at Madison Square Garden in New York, March 16,
1924, he described the movement in these words:

The Universal Negro Improvement Association represents the
hopes and aspirations of the awakened Negro. Our desire is for a
place in the world; not to disturb the tranquility of other men, but
to lay down our burden and rest our weary backs and feet by the
banks of the Niger and sing our songs and chant our hymns to the
God of Ethiopia.[13]

Here again we find the Ethiopian theme: not heaven with its
rivers of milk and honey, but by the banks of the Niger. Here
the Niger replaces the Nile, but that makes no difference.
The songs and chants shall be sung to the God of Ethiopia. In
this same vein we shall be able to understand the ideology of
the Rastafarians who also use the term Ethiopia in what
seems to be a contradiction. This is religious language—a
language aimed at inspiration, not information.

In Marcus Garvey, Ethiopianism reached its highest development. From ideology, it became a movement. In this
movement Ethiopianism was a lived experience. Its leader
was named the Provisional President of Africa. The god worshipped was the God of Ethiopia, and all structures and
orientation were aimed toward African redemption. Finally,
even the national anthem of the Garvey movement—which
has been adopted by the Rastafarians—expresses the mythic
dimension of this ideology in military fervor. In the Fortieth
Article of the "Declaration of Rights of the Negro Peoples of
the World" (adopted in New York in 1920), one can find the
original anthem in the following reference and context:
"Resolved, that the anthem 'Ethiopia, Thou Land of Our

Fathers' etc. shall be the anthem of the Negro Race." Entitled "The Universal Ethiopian Anthem," it was based on a poem by Burrel and Ford. The words are as follows:

> Ethiopia, thou land of our fathers,
> Thou land where the Gods loved to be,
> As the storm cloud at night suddenly gathers
> Our armies come rushing to thee.
> We must in the fight be victorious
> When swords are thrust outward to gleam;
> For us will the victory be glorious
> When led by the red, black and green.

> **Chorus**

> Advance, advance to victory,
> Let Africa be free;
> Advance to meet the foe
> With the might
> Of the red, the black and the green.

> Ethiopia, the tyrants falling,
> Who smote thee upon thy knees,
> And thy children are lustily calling
> From over the distant seas.
> Jehovah, the great one has heard us,
> Has noted our sighs and our tears,
> With his spirit of Love he has stirred us
> To be one through the coming years.[14]

Leaving the history of Marcus Garvey, we move to a discussion on the emergence of the Rastafarian movement in which the ideology and inspiration of Garvey have been retained as in no other organization, and where Ethiopianism has now become a full-fledged doctrinal base of the movement. This recognition prompted the Ethiopian Orthodox church to establish a mission in Jamaica in 1968 (more on this topic in Chapter 7).

The Birth of the Rastafarian Movement

When Marcus Garvey left Jamaica for the United States in 1916, his followers in Jamaica fell into disarray. Although the movement continued to exist with local leadership, no one could fill his void. Particularly due to the headstrong nature of the Jamaican personality, the movement needed a strong charismatic leader. In the course of time, many small movements professing to be Garveyites emerged. This situation existed until 1930 when Ras Tafari, great grandson of King Saheka Selassie of Shoa, was crowned Negus of Ethiopia. He took the name Haile Selassie (Might of the Trinity), to which was added "King of Kings" and the "Lion of the Tribe of Judah," placing himself in the legendary line of King Solomon. His coronation in St. George's Cathedral, Addis Ababa, in November of that year brought representatives of all the great powers as well as journalists and correspondents from every part of the world. The crowning of a young Ethiopian king, with this Biblical title, together with the pomp and grandeur of the fabled empire, was more than a secular occasion.[15] For the people of Marcus Garvey's leaning, this came as a revelation from God. In Jamaica, an almost forgotten statement of Garvey who, on the eve of his departure to the United States was supposed to have said "Look to Africa for the crowning of a Black King; he shall be the Redeemer," came echoing like the voice of God. Possessed by the spirit of this new development, many Jamaicans now saw the coronation as a fulfillment of Biblical prophesy and Haile Selassie as the Messiah of African redemption.

Among those who took this crowning seriously were Leonard Howell, Joseph Hibbert, Archibald Dunkley, and Robert Hinds. All four may have been original Garveyites and at least three of them had traveled outside of Jamaica. It could be expected that they had become acquainted with other cultures, witnessed social and economic developments of other countries and, as a result, most likely had reasons for becoming frustrated with the colonial stranglehold which existed in Jamaica.

We have very little information on the history of these men. Had they not figured so prominently in the founding of the Rastafarian movement, no one would have heard about them. In a monograph written by three university professors in 1960, we learned that Leonard Howell was a world traveler who had served in the Ashanti War of 1896 and during that time had learned several African languages. He also visited the United States where he encountered severe racial discrimination. Finally, sometime before 1930, he returned to Jamaica. Joseph N. Hibbert was born in 1894. At age 17 he migrated to Costa Rica where he lived for twenty years. While in Costa Rica he became a member of the Ancient Order of Ethiopia, a Masonic Lodge, and returned to Jamaica in 1931. We do not have the early history of the two other members of this quartet. All four were ministers and founders of separate groups claiming to have received the revelation that the newly crowned King of Ethiopia was the Messiah of Black people.

Leonard Howell—later to become the leading figure in the early development of the movement—began his ministry in the dilapidated slums in West Kingston where he immediately developed a following. Hibbert started his mission in St. Andrew, in a district called Benoah, but later moved to Kingston where he found Howell expounding the same doctrine; Robert Hinds was his deputy. Archibald Dunkley, a seaman employed by the United Fruit Company, started his mission in Port Antonio and later came to Kingston as a minister. It was in Kingston, then, that the movement had its period of incubation, and from this point of inception that the movement gradually spread throughout the island. Recruiting members from the various splintered cells of old Garveyites, it appeared by 1934 that under the leadership of Howell, Dunkley, and Hinds a solid nucleus of Rastafarians had been established in Kingston.

No one knows how the name "Ras Tafari" was adopted over the title "Haile Selassie." The name "Ras" in Amharic is the title given to Ethiopian royalties, comparable to the English title "Duke." "Tafari" is the family name of the King. Whatever the reason, this name has become not only a holy appellation and a ritual invocation, but also the name of the movement itself. The name "Rastafarians" is a Jamaican rendering of "Ras Tafari" and is the name given to the

members of the movement. The name "Haile Selassie" is
used mostly in prayers and songs. The other name rever-
enced in the movement is "Jah," used frequently in the
combination, "Jah-Ras-Tafari." The "Jah" seems to be the
shortened version of the Biblical "Jehovah" which does appear in their prayer.

The inception of the movement is grounded in some key
verses of the Old and New Testament. First and probably
most convincing of these is Revelation 5:2-5:

And I saw a strong angel proclaiming with a loud voice: Who is
worthy to open the book, and to loose the seals thereof? And no
man in heaven, nor in earth, . . . was able to open the book, neither
to look thereon. . . . And one of the elders saith unto me, Weep not:
behold the Lion of the tribe of Juda, the Root of David, hath prevailed to open the book, and to loose the seven seals thereof.

A collaborating scriptural revelation is also found in Revelation 19:16—"And he hath on his vesture and on his thigh a
name written: KING OF KINGS, AND LORD OF LORDS." To
these Jamaican seers the similarity of these verses to the
title of the newly crowned King was far from mere coincidence. The titles of the King as found in the Bible were
God's revelations to the religious mind. Therefore they
searched the scriptures to find more assurances of their new
revelation. To their surprise more and more verses seemed
to answer their questions. In Psalm 68:4, they found one of
the ritual names: "Sing unto God, sing praises unto his
name: extol him that rideth upon the heavens by his name
JAH, and rejoice before him."

In the prophesy of Daniel they believed to have established not only the longevity of the Ethiopian Kingship, but
also the color of the King. In Daniel 7:9,

And I beheld till the thrones were cast down and the Ancient of
days did sit, whose garment was white as snow, and the hair of his
head like pure wool: his throne was like the fiery flame, and his
wheels as burning fire.

In this verse, the Rastafarian exegetes find not only that the
King was of the Black race (compare Herodotus' description

of the Negroes), but that fire is synonymous with blackness. Many more scriptures pertaining to the Rastafarian beliefs will be discussed in the chapter on their beliefs and practices in order to understand Jamaican religious philosophy. The doctrine does not matter; so long as the preacher can document it with the scriptural text, the truth of the doctrine is "sealed and signed."

It is necessary to understand that movements of this type are not interested in empirical truths, but rather in the certitude of the doctrine. That is, if it fulfills an emotional need it can succeed. In this case the inception of Rastafarianism came, as the scripture would say, "at the fullness of time." Jamaica in 1930 was at low tide economically and socially. Socially, people experienced the brunt of the Depression as well as disaster due to a devastating hurricane. Politically, colonialism gripped the country and the future of the masses looked hopeless. Any doctrine that promised a better hope and a better day was ripe for a hearing.

Armed with this situation and possessed by a new messianic message, Leonard Howell and his men set out to make the "crooked path straight and the rough places plain." Haile Selassie was now given divine status. The God of Ethiopia, of whom Marcus Garvey spoke, had appeared in the flesh, and all who needed redemption could now receive it from the most powerful ruler on earth before whom all kings had bowed. Black people throughout the world needed only to call on his name and the Lion of Judah would break all chains. Armed with this unique power, early Rastafarian leaders set out to preach the glad tidings. But this new wave of enthusiasm was not to be overlooked by His Majesty's representatives in Jamaica, and the spread of Rastafarianism was soon to run contrary to the "Law and Order Code of the British Empire."

The Struggle

The incubation period of the movement occurred in the slums of Kingston between 1930 and 1933. Satisfied with

the success of the new movement and having set up a nucleus in the capitol, Howell decided to evangelize its members throughout the island. To finance his project, he is reported to have made photographs of the newly crowned
King, Haile Selassie, and sold them at a shilling each as
passports to Ethiopia. Sources say he sold five thousand
copies in a very short time. His most successful area was St.
Thomas, the neighboring parish to Kingston. This had been
the scene of the 1865 Morant Bay Rebellion, thus a ripe area
for revolutionary doctrine. On January 5, 1934, the *Daily
Gleaner* of Jamaica reported the arrest of Leonard Howell in
St. Thomas, for it was reported that the movement had
taken on a radical revolutionary stance. The arrest resulted
from an open-air meeting held in the village of Trinityville,
St. Thomas, on December 16, 1933. At that time Howell had
advocated six principles: (1) hatred for the White race; (2) the
complete superiority of the Black race; (3) revenge on Whites
for their wickedness; (4) the negation, persecution, and
humiliation of the government and legal bodies of Jamaica;
(5) preparation to go back to Africa; and (6) acknowledging
Emperor Haile Selassie as the Supreme Being and only ruler
of Black people. This first glimpse of the new doctrine that
launched the Rastafarian movement has not changed significantly over the years. Needless to say, Howell's conviction for seditious activities followed and the Rastafarians received their first island publicity.

The *Daily Gleaner* reported that crowds of people
gathered in Court House Square at Morant Bay for a glimpse
of the alleged seditionists and their followers charged with
less serious offenses. Among the charged were Robert Hinds
and Leonard Howell. Howell, who was reported to be the
representative of Ras Tafari, King of the Ethiopians on the
island, was charged with uttering a seditious speech in
which he abused the government of both Great Britain and
the island. He intended to excite hatred and contempt for
His Majesty the King and those responsible for the government of the island, to create dissatisfaction among the subject of His Majesty, and for disturbing the public peace and

tranquility. Howell pleaded not guilty, but the jury wasted very little time in reaching a guilty verdict. The case was tried before the Acting Resident Magistrate for the parish of St. Thomas, Ansel O. Thompson. The magistrate called Howell a fraud and sentenced him to two years imprisonment; Hinds, his deputy, was given a sentence of one year. The government, sensing that a new and dangerous movement was beginning, quickly arrested Archibald Dunkley and Joseph Hibbert, the other two founders of the movement. With the sudden arrest and imprisonment of the leaders of the Rastafarians, both the government and the concerned citizens of the island suspected that they had silenced the potential seeds of violence in His Majesty's domain. But, to the cultists, the setback was temporary. Trusted lieutenants assumed the activities of the movement and matters continued in secret.[16]

Following the release of Howell and Hinds from prison, Howell organized what was known as the "Ethiopian Salvation Society" and quietly recruited a large following and by the year 1940 he was the leader of a cult commune deep in the hills of St. Catherine overlooking the city of Kingston.

Rastafarians Turned Maroons

In his continued effort to avoid the harassment of the police, Howell headed for the privacy of the hills and, like his Maroon ancestors, either purchased or captured a piece of the hill country near Sligoville (about twenty miles from Kingston). The name of the commune was Pinnacle. Followers were estimated to number from five hundred to as many as sixteen hundred. The entrance was known only to members and could be reached only by foot, at great hazard. Life in the commune was strictly patterned after the Maroon communities of Jamaica. Howell served as chief (African style), and was reported to have taken thirteen wives for himself. For a living, they planted native cash crops, among them the famous ganja (marijuana) herb that has remained the center of the movement's ritual practice. This early phase of Ras-

tafarian wilderness life was rudely destroyed when
neighbors in the community, harassed by the cultists who
demanded that taxes should not be paid to the Jamaican
government but to them in the name of Haile Selassie,
tipped the police to their existence. About July 1941, police
raided the commune and arrested seventy Rastas, charging
them for acts of violence and for the cultivation of a dangerous drug. Twenty-eight Rastas were sent to prison, but
Howell, their leader, evaded the police—a feat which was
considered miraculous and enhanced his power, but he was
finally apprehended and sent to prison for another two-year
term.[17]

As with a dedicated prophet, opposition to Howell merely
reinforced dedication; in 1953, news reached the public that
Pinnacle was again in operation with little change, except
for greater security. In this second phase of Pinnacle, the
male members began to grow their hair in locks—a custom
that distinguishes the Rastaman to the present. They were
called "locksmen," now known as "dreadlocks" or "natty-
dread," but in their early period they were known as Ethiopian warriors. Ferocious dogs were used for security. To
enter the commune one made one's presence known by
sounding a gong at the gate.

However, success evaded this second phase of the Pinnacle as it had the first. Early in 1954, the police again raided
the cultists and 163 members were arrested. Howell and his
lieutenants were also apprehended and tried, but by this
time the government had become tired of sending them to
prison. The judge acquitted them as nuisances—but the
Pinnacle experience did not end here. The commune was
destroyed by the police who then turned the members and
their leaders loose in the slums of Kingston. The long struggle with the police seemed to have taken its toll on Howell,
by now advanced in age. Impressed by his powers or because
of senility, he began to claim divinity for himself. With that
claim, his followers deserted him and it is said that in 1960
he was committed to the Kingston Mental Hospital, where
he must have died.

The Pinnacle commune is an important phase of the early development of the Rastafarians because it established several facets of the movement. It began a communal pattern of living which has continued among a large segment of the cultists. (Today, an example of the Pinnacle experience is being carried out in the group headed by Prince Edward in St. Thomas.) The use of ganja may have been adopted as a ritual practice in the hills where it was easily grown in abundance and the freedom to indulge was unimpeded. Pinnacle, then, was the wilderness experience which became the "bridge-burning act," solidifying the movement around certain rites and practices with which they are now identified. The university team of professors who made a report on the movement in 1960 said of Pinnacle:

By all accounts, Pinnacle seemed to have been rather more like an old maroon settlement than a part of Jamaica. Its internal administration was Howell's business, not Government's. It is therefore understandable that the unit could have persisted as a state within a state for several years without the people or the government of Jamaica being aware of it.[18]

With the destruction of Pinnacle, the followers of Howell returned to Kingston to settle in that part of the town where the dispossessed of the city always found a place where they could feel at home. The area was then known as "Back-O-Wall" or "Shanty-Town" (the descriptions of which are given in Chapter 1). Here the most industrious began a new life in what the Kingstonians called "skuffling," which means making the best of life by any means possible. Among the displaced were the semiskilled who earned their livelihood by making brooms (an occupation still carried on by some cultists), cutting and selling wood, fruits, and fish—any occupation to keep life going. But the lieutenants of Howell did not sit idly by; many took to the sidewalk and began to harangue the passers-by about their social conditions, spreading the glad tidings of the King of Kings and Lord of Lords who could bring a better day.

The period between the destruction of Pinnacle and 1959 was one of regrouping. It was a time of intense hatred for the establishment and especially for the police. The name *Baby-lon* was now given to the establishment, and Rastafarians with their dreadlocks roamed the street like madmen calling down fire and brimstone on Babylon, using the most profane language to shock the conservative establishment. Their wild behavior attracted large audiences and their Rastafarian rhetoric of defiance made their presence felt in Kingston. Although many were shocked by their appearance and behavior, hundreds of the dispossessed began to receive their message and soon several small camps had sprouted in Shanty-Town.

A Message from the King of Kings

New impetus was injected into the early development of the movement in Jamaica through the Ethiopian World Federation, Inc., of New York, established in 1937 as a lobbying organization to solicit aid and goodwill for Ethiopian struggles against Italian colonialism. It was said to have been organized under the direct authority of Haile Selassie. As early as 1938, a branch of this organization was established in Jamaica. The aim of the EWF, as its preamble proclaimed, was to unify, solidify, liberate, and free the Black people of the world in order to achieve self-determination, justice, and to maintain the integrity of Ethiopia—which is the divine heritage of the Black race. We do not know whether the Rastafarian leaders knew of this movement, but it is quite possible that Howell might have been connected with it and that his Pinnacle enterprise (the Ethiopian Salvation Society) might have been aided by this movement. Our sources suggest that the success of the Jamaican EWF led to many schisms, each claiming to be the true organization. To this day, the Rastafarians are in close touch with the EWF group, sometimes combining efforts in their enterprises.

The great impetus came in 1955, when a leading official of the Ethiopian World Federation, Inc., visited Jamaica with an important message which was to energize the flagging Rastafarian movement. The *Daily Gleaner* of September 30,

1955, headlined the event as "Large Audience Hears Message from Ethiopia." Among the statements is the following, attributed to Mrs. Mamie Richardson:

The Emperor [Haile Selassie] is now engaged in building up a Merchant Navy . . . and the time was not far distant when ships from Addis Ababa would sail to American ports. There was the possibility too that ships would one day call here [Jamaica].

But better news was just around the bend for the Rastafarians—news that was to develop their doctrine of inevitable repatriation. Soon after Mrs. Richardson's return to New York, the Ethiopian World Federation of that city informed the various branches in Jamaica that the Emperor had granted 500 acres of land to the Black people of the West who, through the EWF, aided Ethiopia in its time of distress. The rich and fertile land was the personal property of the Emperor and was being given on a trial basis. If used successfully, additional grants would follow. The letter stipulated the types of people who would best profit from the land grant were farmers, carpenters, plumbers, masons, electricians, and other skilled persons including nurses and doctors. The vision of ships and now land in Ethiopia created what might literally be called a religious revival among the Rastafarians. "Repatriation now!" was the cry of cultists. With the news of imminent repatriation in Ethiopia in His Majesty's ships and with royal lands awaiting the pilgrims, recruitment for both the Ethiopian World Federation and Rastafarians was easy. The movement doubled its membership almost overnight. This news of an African return came at the time when thousands of Jamaicans were leaving to seek a living in Great Britain, a land which for them was strange, cold, and unknown. At this time the Rastafarians developed the phrase, "Ethiopia! Yes! England! No! Let my people go!"

All the ingredients for our framework have now fallen into place. Therefore, at this point, we should reflect on the early stages of the movement because—from this point on—the movement and its beliefs and rituals will only be-

come more firmly routinized in the society. We have seen
that Jamaica has never rid itself of social upheavals, most of
which were occasioned by dispossessed groups at the fringes
of the established society. Whereas in the earlier days, upheavals were caused by the religious dynamics of the Native
Baptist church, the dynamics of the present day are a revival
of the same, only in this case the fuel comes from a newly
awakened doctrine—Ethiopianism. The new movement
also reinforces the theory that it is in the religious teaching
which exists outside the established churches that political
pressures are brought on behalf of social change.

The dynamics of movements of social transformation
may come from various incidents which, to established
segments of society seem purely secular, but to the dispossessed, who often perceive events in supernatural perspec-
tives, may seem cues for actions of redemption. Thus the
founders of the Rastafarian movement accepted the crowning of Haile Selassie as an important sign toward the day of
redemption. Seemingly secular events in world history became signs for the masses. The embodiment of this event as
an ideology for social upliftment was powerful enough to
generate a sudden wave of opposition and a vigorous reaction from the establishment. But this opposition and reaction also brought valuable publicity to the movement,
which in turn yielded a following. The leaders of revolutionary movements are generally the first to meet the brunt of
the establishment's reaction, but the success of revolutionary movements is made on the blood of martyrs; in the case
of the Rastafarians, Howell, although now almost forgotten,
was the real hero of the establishment of Rastafarianism.
The harassment of Howell by the police might have been
the reason why Rastafarians, since the destruction of Pinnacle, have decided to remain leaderless—a decision which has
strengthened the movement. The abortive attempt of
Claudius Henry, which we shall discuss shortly, probably
sealed this decision. The sustained activity of the police
against the cultists after Pinnacle was to create a boldness in
the cultists which finally led to serious reactions. Instead of

a flight to the mountains, they now decided to stand up and fight.

The First Nyabingi

The growing popularity of the Rastafarians in the city of Kingston and elsewhere in the island suggested to some of the leading brethren that it was now time to assess their strength and, if possible, to seek to unify the various cells and camps into an organized whole. This decision led to what the Jamaican news media called a convention, but it was known to the Rastafarians as *Grounation:* today it is called *Nyabingi.* The Rastafarian "Universal Convention" took place in March of 1958. The gathering of the "bearded brethren" was unprecedented and an equally unprecedented outpouring of Rastafarian effervescence emerged under the influence of the herb, because they soon attracted attention of the press which gave sensational coverage to their activities. The Jamaican evening paper first reported this meeting as follows:

For the first time in local history members of the Rastafari Cult are having what they call a "Universal Convention" at their headquarters known as the Coptic Theorcratic Temple in Kingston Pen. Some 300 cultists of both sexes from all over the island have assembled at Back-O-Wall headquarters since Saturday, March 1. The convention is scheduled to last until April 1. The convention was said to be "the first and the last" in that they were expected to migrate to Africa their homeland.[19]

This convention not only revealed to the public some of the little known rituals of the Rastafarians; it also gave them much publicity. The meetings consisted of drumming, dancing, and smoking the herb around a bonfire of old car tires which gave the otherwise drab living condition of Back-O-Wall a festive air. The press reported that with this festive air came a great amount of abusive language directed at the police, and that one of the items on the list of their agenda was the decapitation of a police officer as a peace offering. Except for routine surveillance by the police, the government paid very little attention to the Rastafarian assembly. But as the days went by, the headlines became more lurid, and police vigilance was increased. Failing to provoke a confrontation with the police, which some cultists might have expected to do for strategic reasons, more militant Rastas tried to capture the city of Kingston in the name of Haile Selassie. The *Star* of March 24, 1958, reported this incident as follows:

The City of Kingston was "captured" near dawn on Saturday by some 300 bearded men of the Rastafarian cult along with their women and children. About 3:30 a.m. early market-goers saw members of the Rastafarian movement gathered in the center of Victoria Park, with towering poles, atop of which, fluttered black, green, and red banners, and loudly proclaiming that they had captured the city. . . . When the police moved toward them, a leader of the group with his hands raised issued a warning to the police: "touch not the Lord's anointed." . . . The police finally moved them.[20]

This new militancy of the cult was to continue during this period, including many clashes with the police. Later in that same year, they attempted to capture Old King's House of Spanish Town in the name of Negus, the King of Ethiopia. The government's reaction was immediate. Under the Jamaican Dangerous Drug Law, cultists were arrested for the possession and use of ganja, and were subject to search and various harassments, such as shaving their heads and beards. The 1958 convention gave the cultists both positive and negative publicity in the eyes of the government and the public, but out of this convention was to come a most alarming incident. More on that shortly.

Following the convention, many voices were raised among both the intellectuals and the middle-class community, beseeching the government to take a realistic look at the grievances of the common people. A sociologist from the University of the West Indies wrote: "The aspirations of a social group are not to be disregarded by an attitude of angry contempt for its personal and private habits. . . . For in the long run the type of Prince Emanuel (a Rastafarian leader) may have more to do with the West Indian future than the type of Lord Hailes,"[21] the then Governor General of the aborted West Indian Federation. Another columnist of the *Daily Gleaner* wrote: "If the problem of the Rastas is not faced now, it is liable to get so big that no one can deal with it and it then becomes, perhaps very unpleasantly, yours and mine and the ministers."[22]

The reference to Prince Emanuel by the university professor enables us to introduce two figures who loom quite large in the unfolding of the Rastafarian story: Prince Edward Emanuel and the Reverend Claudius Henry. It was under the auspices and leadership of Prince Emanuel that the 1958 convention was called. One of the oldest Rastafarian leaders since the days of Leonard Howell, the Prince's leadership is still the strongest and his group the most organized on the island. It was his invitation that brought the Reverend Claudius Henry, the mastermind of the abortive repatriation scheme, to Jamaica to visit the 1958 convention. The Prince, as he is called by his followers, had been one of the most prominent Rastafarian leaders of Back-O-Wall since 1953, and has been in almost every confrontation with the government on behalf of African repatriation. In an interview he reported that he appeared on earth in the Parish of St. Elizabeth in 1915, and, like Melchizedek, is without father or mother; he came to Kingston in 1930, and was fortunate enough to see Marcus Garvey. When I met him in 1963, he was still residing at Back-O-Wall with his members. The Prince is the picture of an Ethiopian patriarch—six-foot-four-inches tall and now sixty-two years old.

The reference to the Prince by the university professor was occasioned by the severe harassment he received following the 1958 convention. In that year, his camp was raided by the police who arrested him and burned his settlement to the ground. His trial was highly publicized in the city mainly because of the fame of his lawyer, Barrister Evans, who was said to have defended members of the Mau Mau movement in Kenya. Prince Edward and his men were finally released—a great victory to the Rastafarian cause. The Prince remained at his camp at Back-O-Wall until 1966, when the government carried out a "scrape-the-earth campaign" and drove the various Rastafarian groups from that part of the city.

The Aborted Repatriation

All urgings for the government to face the Rastafarian problem before it was too late were indeed prophetic. In 1959, the problem became very unpleasant not only for the average Jamaican citizen, but also for the government ministers. The aftermath of it was to lead to a national emergency. The actor in this drama was Claudius Henry, who gave himself the title, "The Repairer of the Breach." According to Prince Edward Emanuel, Claudius Henry was a Jamaican who lived for some time in New York City, and who was in Jamaica during the 1958 convention on the Prince's invitation. Other sources said Henry was a member of the Ethiopian World Federation, and on his return was connected to that movement in Jamaica, but resigned because of differences in leadership. No evidence exists that the Reverend Henry was ever a member of the Rastafarian movement. In 1959, he founded an organization called the African Reformed Church in the western part of Kingston, where he attracted a heterogenous membership of many former Rastafarians. He seemed to possess dynamic leadership ability, for he was soon able to take control of a large segment of the Rasta movement, setting himself up as the "Moses of the Blacks," who would lead them to the Promised Land.

The drama began when he distributed thousands of cards bearing the following statement:

Pioneering Israel's scattered children of African Origin "back home to Africa." This year 1959, deadline date—Oct. 5th; this new government is God's Righteous Kingdom of Everlasting Peace on Earth. "Creations Second Birth." Holder of this Certificate is requested to visit the Headquarters at 18 Rosalie Avenue . . . August 1st, 1959, for our Emancipation Jubilee, commencing 9 A.M. sharp. Please reserve this Certificate for removal. No passport will be necessary for those returning to Africa, etc. We sincerely, "The Seventh Emanuel's Brethren" gathering Israel's scattered and anointed prophet, Rev. C. V. Henry, R.B.

Given this 2nd day of March 1959, in the year of the reign of His Imperial Majesty, 1st Emperor of Ethiopia, "God's Elect" Haile Selassie, King of Kings and Lord of Lords, Israel's Returned Messiah.[23]

Sold at a shilling each, many hundreds of these cards were acquired by the hopeful masses. The symbols contained in it could not fail to appeal to various sect and cult members. It was tailored to appeal to a wide audience. First, the card aimed at a segment of people accustomed to celebrate the emancipation of slavery on August 1st each year—a custom recently discontinued on the island. Second, the word "Israel" would not fail to bring a segment of Jamaicans who claimed to be Black Jews; and the imminent repatriation themes were sure to draw hundreds of Rastafarians and EWF members. The selling of the cards for a shilling each recalled the similar incident with Leonard Howell in St. Thomas. It seems that the jubilee celebration was to be a briefing for the day of repatriation—October 5. Apparently, thousands of Rastafarians and other hopeful Jamaicans believed the announcement of the "Repairer of the Breach" and swarmed to his banners.

On October 5, 1959, people from all over Jamaica flocked to Rosalie Avenue ready to depart to Africa. The *Daily Gleaner* carried the following report:

Hundreds of Rastafarians gathered at Headquarters of the African Reformed Church, 78 Rosalie Avenue, following the report that members of the cult wishing to join the Back-to-Africa movement would leave the island by ship yesterday. No ships or plane had come for them, no passport arranged, nor passages booked but they were going to Africa. The cultists who came from all parts of the Island, started arriving at Rosalie Avenue from Sunday afternoon and up to yesterday afternoon were still trickling in taxicabs, trucks, and afoot. Some with their belongings said that they were ready to leave for the trip. It was learned that many of them especially from

the country parts, had sold out their belongings and were planning
to leave for Africa yesterday. Many more were expected to arrive
especially from Montego Bay area last night.[24]

The Reverend Henry now found himself in a very large
"ditch" indeed. With thousands ready to depart, the atmosphere was charged with expectation similar to that experienced at Mona near the present university when Bedward of
the Native Baptist church gathered his followers to ascend
to heaven in December, 1921. At the appointed hour of the
ascension, the liftoff was put forward a day, and then
another day, until the Prophet finally landed in the Kingston
jail. The same fate was soon to befall the Reverend Henry.

A representative from the *Daily Gleaner* visited Henry,
who painfully explained that the October 5 deadline had
never been intended as the day of a departure for Africa, but
the day on which he expected the government to explain
how it would meet the demands of Jamaica's African
peoples. Here may be seen a classic example of what is
known in social movement theory as "revolutionary judo,"
that is, the contradiction between symbolic declaration and
real intention. Much of what is said by leaders of revolutionary movements is mostly "word magic" to jolt the society out of its complacency. But sometimes true believers do
not understand parables, and in this case irresponsible pronouncements created a fiasco. The *Daily Gleaner* of October
7, 1959, reported:

Hundreds with no place to go lingered at 78 Rosalie Avenue;
among these were women and children. Many from Kingston and
St. Andrew, and St. Mary left for their homes, but others were
ashamed to go home because they had sold their houses and lands.
They lingered on the premises until they could stay no longer.[25]

The excitement created by this Henry fiasco was given little attention by the government for many days. Several days
after the aborted repatriation scheme, Henry was finally arrested but the court freed him and ordered him to keep the
peace for one year with a fine of £100, a very lenient sentence compared with the suffering his irresponsible acts had

cost his faithful followers. But this was not to be the end. Crushed in pride and possibly misjudging the government's leniency toward him, Henry became increasingly hostile to the government. His previously religious stance became radically revolutionary and militant. News began to leak to the police that Henry was planning a military takeover of the island. Ridiculous as the information seemed, the police decided it best to investigate. What they found was close to the gossip for, early in April, the *Jamaican Gleaner* carried the following story:

PASTOR AND NINE OTHERS ARRESTED

A police raiding party in an early morning raid yesterday seized over 2,500 electrical detonators, 1,300 detonators, a shotgun, a 32-caliber revolver, a large quantity of machetes sharpened both sides like swords, placed in sheaths, cartridges, several sticks of dynamite and other articles at headquarters of the African Reformed Church, 78 Rosalie Avenue.[26]

The other articles were discovered to be conch shells filled with marijuana. Other raids were carried out at Clarendon where the movement had branches. The author is unable to verify any of this account, but the Reverend Claudius Henry was indicted for a breach of the treason laws and sent to prison for six years. Others of his party received lighter sentences.

The Henry escapade took a new twist when, soon after his imprisonment, his son Ronald was reported to be in the Red Hills overlooking Kingston training a guerrilla band of Rastafarians with high powered rifles reportedly brought secretly into the island from New York, the city from which Ronald had come. No one now knows for certain if the operations of father and son were the same, but many Rastafarians interviewed by the author agree that they were. News of this operation reached the ears of the Jamaican police, and a combined force of police and soldiers of the Royal Hampshire Regiment, which formed a part of the British command in Jamaica, moved against the rebels in the hills. Two of the British soldiers were killed from ambush, and Ronald and

his men made their escape. A national emergency was declared and a manhunt undertaken. Days of running soon
took its toll on the rebels who were caught while sound
asleep in the Parish of St. Catherine. Ronald Henry and four
of his men were tried and sentenced to death. Later search
in the hills discovered three bodies of Ronald Henry's men
buried in shallow graves. It was later revealed that these
men had probably been shot by the rebels because of disloy-
alty to the cause of liberation.

The news of these tragic happenings related to the Rastafarian cult aroused Jamaican society from its slumber.
Even the *New York Times* dispatched a correspondent to
cover this news. Upper-class Jamaicans, who once saw the
Rastafarians as a set of unscrubbed bums, now lived in fear
of them. But most of all, the confrontation of the cultist
with the powers-that-be brought the need for a closer examination of the grievances of the poor of which the Rastafarians were only the cutting edge. At the request of the leading Rasta brethren, Dr. Arthur Lewis, head of the University
of the West Indies, authorized three of his best scholars to
study the doctrines and special conditions of the Rastafarians and to make recommendations to the Premier of
Jamaica on their behalf. The summary of this document will
close this chapter.

The Rastafarians Get a National Hearing

The study carried out by the three university professors was
a landmark in the history of the movement. Although less
than a month was spent in gathering the materials, the intensity, dedication, and urgency with which the scholars
tackled the problem and the expertise of the men who carried out the research resulted in one of the finest pieces of
scholarly, objective reporting ever carried out by the university on behalf of the community. The study not only revealed the socioeconomic conditions of the movement to
the general public, but also, for the first time, articulated the
history and doctrine of the movement. At the same time,

the study presented to the Rastafarians a mirror in which they could view themselves in relation to the community. Ten recommendations were presented to the government:

The government of Jamaica should send a mission to African countries to arrange for immigration of Jamaicans. Representatives of Ras Tafari brethren should be included in the mission.

Preparations for the mission should be discussed immediately with representatives of the Ras Tafari brethren.

The general public should recognize that the great majority of Ras Tafari brethren are peaceful citizens, willing to do an honest day's work.

The police should complete their security enquiries rapidly, and cease to persecute peaceful Ras Tafari brethren.

The building of low-rent houses should be accelerated, and provision made for self-help cooperative building.

Government should acquire the principle areas where squatting is now taking place, and arrange for water, light, sewage disposal and collection of rubbish.

Civic centers should be built with facilities for technical classes, youth clubs, child clinics, etc. The churches and the University College of the West Indies should collaborate.

The Ethiopian Orthodox Coptic Church should be invited to establish a branch in the West Indies.

Ras Tafari brethren should be assisted to establish cooperative workshops.

Presses and radio facilities should be accorded to leading members of the movement.[27]

In the Jamaica of 1960, these recommendations were considered the radical dreams of a set of ivy tower intellectuals out of touch with reality. But acceptance of the recommendation by the Honorable Norman Manley and his bold attempts at carrying them out demonstrated a sense of maturity and vision on the part of the government to act decisively in an area of social action that demanded immediate attention. Of the ten recommendations, the first article created the greatest controversy, but the government considered it the most crucial and immediately adopted it and the mission to Africa was carried out with great thoroughness.[28] Though no large-scale immigration to Africa by

Jamaicans was achieved, the sending of some Rastafarian leaders to Africa resulted in the movement's enhanced knowledge of African realities, and probably diffused the movement's enthusiasm for immediate repatriation. Almost all of the recommendations have been carried out to some extent over the years, the last being the establishment of a branch of the Ethiopian Orthodox Church on the island. Also, the present freedom of the Rastafarian movement on the island may to some extent be attributed to the far-reaching insights of these recommendations.

Except for the "Holy Thursday Massacre" in the parish of St. James, near Montego Bay in 1963, in which several police and others including Rastafarians were killed, the progress of the movement has had an uneven but steady growth up to the present. The work of the university professors, issuing from the most prestigious institution of the island, gave high visibility to the Rastafarians in the public eye, and people of the community began to take the movement more seriously, many seeing the cultists as the vanguard of social transformation. Their ideology was soon to affect the economy, politics, social relations, and the educational system, but their struggle had only just begun.

In this chapter we have discussed the rise and struggle of the Rastafarian movement from its inception to the first phase of its recognition by the government and people of Jamaica as a legitimate social movement of reform. We have shown that this movement, like other movements of its type, rose out of stressful social situations by adopting an ideology—Ethiopianism—which had already existed in the society, but which was given new meaning to spark a revolution for social transformation in a society that had grown insensitive to the needs of the masses.

We have proved a point that a social movement of transformation is most likely to succeed when that movement attaches itself, even though unconsciously, to traditional elements in the cultural milieu, and that, if this traditional residue is sufficiently grounded, its power to threaten the status quo often triggers a negative response from the privileged classes of the society. In this overreaction, the privileged classes often create a climate of growth and acceptance for the movement from the oppressed class. If a social movement such as the Rastafarians is able to refine its ideology and sustain a viable opposition, maintaining its independence from cooptation, its possibility for bringing about social change in the society may be achieved. We shall now see how the further development of the movement has maintained this pressure.

Beliefs, Rituals, and Symbols

Beliefs

Systems of belief provide cult movements with a major source of power. This power, as we have seen, derives not from a body of systematic or logical truths but rather from the psychological, emotional content of the ideology. This is especially true of Rastafarian beliefs. To the outsider much of Rastafarian rhetoric appears to be meaningless babbling yet, on the deeper level of communication, it appears to project the message to the native hearers despite the seeming madness. As the university report sums up: "What people believe or assert emphatically represents a social force which cannot be disposed of merely by denial."[1] By their very nature, myths remain outside the realm of truth or falsehood, being subject neither to the rules of logic nor to the techniques of scientific investigation. A religious myth such as Rastafarianism, then, claims for itself an immunity from logic not granted to any other kind of knowledge system, demanding commitment and action. On this point, it was the thirteenth-century philosopher Bonaventure who once said that an eternal gulf exists between conviction based on religious grounds and conviction based upon mere scientific or rational argument. He observed that history has given preponderant evidence that humans will die more frequently for religious beliefs than will the scientist for so-called "truth."[2]

The Rastafarians have developed for themselves a body of myths and rituals which, although not yet written down, can be summarized in a systematic form. In this chapter, only the central ideas will be discussed, along with some of the important rituals of the movement. Beliefs and rituals may change from one group to the next. Those included in this chapter have been laboriously gleaned from public addresses, interviews, and short articles written by the leading brethren, and from personal observations of the cult over a ten year period.

At least six basic beliefs can be identified as uniquely Rastafarian:

—Haile Selassie is the living god.
—The Black person is the reincarnation of ancient Israel, who, at the hand of the White person, has been in exile in Jamaica.
—The White person is inferior to the Black person.
—The Jamaican situation is a hopeless hell; Ethiopia is heaven.
—The Invincible Emperor of Ethiopia is now arranging for expatriated persons of African origin to return to Ethiopia.
—In the near future Blacks shall rule the world.[3]

Haile Selassie Is the Living God

All true Rastafarians believe that Haile Selassie, Emperor of Ethiopia, is the true and living god, at least of the Black race. A member of the Rastafarian Repatriation Association explained it this way:

We know before that when a King should be crowned in the land of David's throne, that individual would be Shiloh, the anointed one, the Messiah, the Christ returned in the personification of Rastafari. (On his vesture and on his thigh is a name written, "King of Kings and Lord of Lords.") He (Ras Tafari) is the "Ancient of Days" (the bearded God). The scripture declares that "the hair of whose head was like wool (matted hair), whose feet were like unto burning brass" (i.e., Black skin). The scripture declares that God hangs in motionless space surrounded with thick darkness (hence a Black man).[4]

In his *Treatise on the Rastafarian Movement*, Samuel Brown incorporated the idea as follows:

Gods are the creation of the inner consciousness of nations' deification of an individual. Elders and parents beget progenies who in turn carry on the perpetuation of such culture.

Unlike all orders of religion, the culture of Rastafari was not handed down from father to son as the people of Christendom. We who have perused the volumes of history know that in this 20th century a king would arise out of Jesse's root, who should be a God (Almighty) for his people, and a liberator to all the oppressed of earth. We the Rastafarians who are the true prophets of this age, the reincarnated Moseses, Joshuas, Isaiahs, Jeremiahs who are the battle-axes and weapons of war (a Jihad), we are those who are destined to free not only the scattered Ethiopians (Black man) but all people, animals, herbs and all life forms.

We are vanguard of 144,000 celestial selectees who shall in turn free 468,000 millions particularly, and the world at large. We are the disciples of Rastafari, who have walked with God from the time when the foundation of creation was laid through 71 bodies, to behold the 72nd house of power which shall reign forever. We now stand as the fulfillers of prophecy; we knew before that when a king should be crowned in the land of David's throne, that individual would be Shiloh, the anointed One, the Messiah, the Christ returned in the personification of Rastafari (on his vesture and on his thigh is a name written, "King of Kings and Lord of Lords"). We also know the significance of Daniel, declaring from that time to this time, for I behold until all the thrones of Babylon were cast down and the ancient of whose head was like unto wool, whose feet were like unto burning brass, and he treadeth the fierceness of the winepress of his wrath, to execute Justice and Judgment on the Gentiles. The scriptures declare God hangs in motionless space surrounded by thick darkness; hence a black man.

God came in many bodies to reign forever in Rastafari the holy one of Israel whose ray of light shall finally dim the eyes of the dragon, and through whose power all those of many nations who embrace the faith and uphold its laws shall live forevermore with God. We are those who shall fight all wrongs and bring ease to the suffering bodies and peace to all people.[5]

We can see a syncretism of Old Testament prophecy. Gnostic mysticism and Christian theology fuse into a revolutionary rhetoric typical of the movement's unique form of expression. It is a symbolic language spun from hallucinogenic experiences which befuddles the mind of the average Jamaican. But the cultists have not developed this notion of their King's divinity from ganja experience alone; they believe that numerous biblical texts support the doctrine. From Jeremiah 8:21 they are convinced that God is Black: "For the hurt of the daughter of my people am I hurt; I am black; astonishment hath taken hold of me." A Black god to the Rastafarians is of the greatest importance, because "Blackness is synonymous with holiness." The distinctiveness of Haile Selassie for the movement lies therefore in the authority of the scriptures of his divinity and in the fact that he is Black. His Ethiopian birth further strengthens the belief, for the Bible clearly states that their god would be born in that country. So, according to cultists, Psalm 87:3–4 is unquestionable proof:

Glorious things are spoken of thee,
O city of God. Selah.
I will make mention of Rahab and Babylon to them that know me: behold Philistia, and Tyre, with *Ethiopia*; this *man* was born there.

The book of Revelation, containing the holy prophecy about the Emperor, has become the central text for the cultist. In this book the great titles of the King are found, "King of Kings and Lord of Lords, Conquering Lion of the tribe of Judah, Elect of God and Light of the world."

The Rastafarians also believe that the Jesus spoken of in the Bible is Haile Selassie. But the White slave masters and the missionaries present him as European in order to hide from their Black slaves their true dignity.

Consequently, the White person's god is a different god

Rasta priest with picture of Haile Selassie.

from that of the Rastafarians. The Whites' god is actually the devil, the instigator of all evils that have come upon the world, the god of hate, blood, oppression, and war; the Black god is a god of "Peace and Love."[6] It follows that the Christian preachers of the White god, especially Black clergy, are the greatest deceivers and represent the greatest evil to the Black Jamaican, because they continue to deny Blacks their true dignity by daily presenting to them a god who expects one to be humble and to bear suffering and shame in this life for an imaginary heaven somewhere in the sky after death. To the Rastafarians who believe in life eternal in the here and now, this doctrine is a total farce. Eternal life in Ethiopia is imminently possible, and will be enjoyed under the leadership of a Black god among Black people.

How does Haile Selassie see this development? And how does he respond to the idea of being called God? No comment from his majesty has ever appeared on this subject. However, Dr. M. B. Douglas, a delegate to Ethiopia in the mission of 1961, offered the writer this interesting report. On the mission's arrival in Addis Ababa, the delegates were met by the Abuna, Archbishop of the Ethiopian Orthodox Church, and upon learning that the cult worshipped the Emperor as God, advised them not to make this known to the King because such information would cause him great displeasure. He informed them that the Emperor was a devout Christian and a regular worshipper at the cathedral. Dr. Douglas recalled that this in no way discouraged the Rastafarians; to the contrary, it only strengthened their belief. Their reply to the Abuna was, "If he does not believe he is god, we know that he is god;" they informed the Abuna that the King would never display his divinity for "he that humbleth himself shall be exalted, and he that exalteth himself shall be abased." "The Rastafarians left Ethiopia," observed Dr. Douglas, "more convinced than ever, that Haile Selassie is God."[7]

The minority report on the mission to the Government written by the Rastafarian delegates reflected this belief and served to strengthen the brethren in Jamaica. Haile Selassie's visit to Jamaica in 1966 did not diminish the belief in his divinity; many felt that the visit had served to strengthen their faith, an observation supported by statements from both Rastafarians and leading Jamaicans.

So the Rastafarians continue in this belief as they daily pray: "So we hail our God, Selassie I, Eternal God, Rastafari; hear us and help us, and cause thy face to shine upon us thy children."

Some questions have been raised as to whether the Rastafarian movement is a genuine messianic cult. Dr. Donald Hogg, professor of sociology at the University of Puerto Rico, Rio Piedras, who reviewed my first monograph sees this cult as a millenarian movement. He argued that millenarian movements emphasize the move to a golden age in the future here on earth, where all problems will be solved while, in the messianic movement, the messiah shares bodily in shaping and leading the movement. Dr. Hogg's idea is correct and agrees with A. F. Wallace, who sees the messiah as "a divine savior in human flesh in mazeway transformation."[8] However, Wallace further states that: "The parallel terms do not denote mutually exclusive categories, for a given revitalization movement may be nativistic, millenarian, messianic, and revivalistic all at once."[9]

The Rastafarian movement, although fitting in the millenarian category, has such prominent messianic tendencies that designating it "messianic" allows for a greater range of interpretation of its ideology. It is also interesting to note that the move to a golden place—Ethiopia—was probably not one of the earlier tenets of the movement, but a later addition. The Rastafarians saw Haile Selassie as a real messiah in the flesh until August, 1975, but in the spiritual body since his death. His spiritual presence is with them in all they do. He is the supreme being of the cult to whom prayers are made, hymns are sung, and around whom a sizeable body of myth is developed. They had their ambassadors visit him in Ethiopia, and welcomed him in Jamaica, although his

visit was not occasioned by them. His Kingship is the dominant inspiration of the movement and, at present, at least 50
percent of the movement's members reject repatriation.
From this the author feels it safe to call the movement
messianic-millenarian.

The Rastafarian movement, as with most messianic-
millenarian movements, is a reaction to the grinding poverty experienced by the peasant class. Some of the creative
minds of this society perceived that the only way out of
their stress and distress was by the strong hand of a god or
messiah. This messiah they perceived to be Haile Selassie
who, for them, is the Returned Messiah.

The movement was born in colonial oppression and structured itself in the slums. By the time of independence in
1962, it was the only voice of a powerless peasant class
whose numbers are still multiplying in the island. The
movement has institutionalized poverty and, as such, has
become the symbol of the poor people's search for a place in
their homeland. It is a symbol of the establishment's neglect
of the poor.

The movement is a symbol of the neglect of an educational system which failed to inculcate in the youth a pride
in their homeland, their African heritage, and their identity
as a unique people—who by an historical accident became a
mixture of many races. The movement has become a symbol of correction to this system which saw no good in the
variety of teaching materials at hand, but sought to bring in
alien materials from England to substitute for the living
Jamaican experience. The result has been a calamity. The
movement is a symbol of religious neglect, exposing the established church which, for centuries, was the citadel of the
status quo and the preservation of irrelevant religion. The
church, therefore, failed significantly to reach out to the
poor and needy and catered to the rich and the progressive in
its liturgy and its teaching institutions. Only recently has
the church been forced to become Jamaicanized. Until recently, a White minister in Jamaican pulpits was the most

acceptable and, unless the Black minister was White in all aspects but skin color (which could be overlooked if all other mannerisms were Europeanized), the Blacks would not be accepted by certain congregations. Unfortunately, this tension still prevails in established Jamaican churches. In this light the Rastafarian movement can be seen as a symbolic representation of a people whose self-identity has been suppressed by dominant alien symbols from the outside.

The Black Person Is the Reincarnation of Ancient Israel

Deeply influenced by the Judaeo-Christian religion through the use of the Bible, the cultists have been unable to break away from the word "Israel." To them "Israelite" and "Ethiopian" are one and the same name—simply referring to a holy people. According to the Rastafarians, they, the true Israelites, have been punished for their sins by god their father through slavery under Whites. This sin led to their exile in Jamaica. They have long since been pardoned and should have returned to Ethiopia long ago, but because of the slavemasters' trickery have been unable to return. As true Israelites, though, they observe strict dietetic and hygienic laws based on the Old Testament. As Samuel Brown has expressed it:

The Rastafarian is he who bows the knee to God above, we are those who obey strict moral and divine laws based on the Mosaic tenet. (1) We strongly object sharp implements used in the desecration of the figure of Man, e.g., trimming and shaving, tattooing of skin, cuttings of the flesh. (2) We are basically vegetarians, making scant use of certain animal flesh, yet outlawing the use of swine's flesh in any form, shell fishes, scaleless fishes, snails, etc.[10]

Since the cult claims personal divinity through their unique relationship with Haile Selassie I, the believer who claims membership enters into a divine state of "sonship." To assume it, one does not merely join the cult. Membership occurs through a spiritual birth, through self-awakening, not adoption but by right to "sonship." The believer becomes therefore a son of "Jah Rastafari who is god" and, as such, shares in divinity, for it is recorded:

I said ye are gods and all of you sons of the most high.[11]

Beloved, now are we the sons of God, and it doth not yet appear what we shall be: but we know that, when he shall appear, we shall be like him; for we shall see him as he is.[12]

The above suggest that the Rastaman shall be like God— that is both Black and divine at the same time.

On the subject of reincarnation the Rastafarians have a unique teaching akin to Hinduism. They believe that God revealed himself many ages ago in various forms. To the Hebrews, God revealed himself in the person of Moses, who was the *first avatar* or savior, speaking God's word because he was actually God revealed in the shape and form of man. His mission fulfilled, Moses disappeared from the earthly scene and "no man knoweth of his sepulchre unto this day." The *second avatar* was Elijah, who declared the will of God, but the rulers of earth paid him little attention. Elijah did not die as other human beings, but "went up in a chariot of fire." The *third avatar* was Jesus Christ, who said quite emphatically, "Before Abraham was, I am"; and again "I and my father are one."

Now the advent of Ras Tafari is the climax of God's revelation. Ras Tafari will therefore never die. He is eternal and all Rastafarians who believe in him are eternal and shall never see death. "We who are Rastafarians are the disciples who have walked with god from the time when the foundation of creation was laid, through 71 bodies, to behold the 72nd house of power which shall reign forever."[13]

Though they might have lapsed in their relationship with God throughout this long existence, Rastafarians claim this is no longer possible because they now live in the age of theocracy. They therefore do not believe in death but in eternal life. Only the evil of the earth dies. "The wages of sin is death, but the gift of God is eternal life."[14] The brethren attribute the death of a member of the cult to a lack of proper self-preservation, to unfaithfulness to "Jah." Because the dead is no longer one of them, they move away from the scene, justifying their behavior by quoting the Bible:

Leave the dead to bury their dead, but go thou and publish abroad the kingdom of God. . . . There shall none be defiled for the dead among his people: . . . But he shall not defile himself, being a chief man among his people, to profane himself.[15]

Pressing one Rastafarian leader for an explanation on the subject of eternal life, the writer was offered this theory:

Even if a Rastafarian pass away because of old age he really is not dead. The atoms of his body pass back into the totality of things. These same atoms are again utilized into the formation of other newborn babies and life continues as before.[16]

Another leading Rastafarian explained it this way:

Life is like a game of cricket. As long as the player makes the appropriate stroke that merits each ball, he can play on and on for centuries. The only way a good player can be bowled is when he makes an inappropriate stroke. The Rastafarian is the man who has acquired the appropriate spiritual way of dealing with life; he therefore is immortal.[17]

Such an emphasis on eternal life is reflected by the youthfulness of Rastafarian members, many of whom have never seen any of their members die of any natural causes—only by the police. During my early research, the effect of the eventual death of Haile Selassie on the movement was often discussed. To the Rastafarians the question was absurd—God cannot die because he holds the power of death. In Chapter 8 we will review their situation since the death of the Emperor.

The White Person Is Inferior to the Black Person

The idea of Black supremacy comes largely as an echo from the days of Garvey and remains a strong point in both the Black Muslim (United States) and the Jamaican Rastafarian movements. From Garvey's *African Fundamentalism* we read:

If others laugh at you, return the laughter to them; if they mimic you, return the compliment with equal force. They have no more right to dishonor, disrespect and disregard your feeling and manhood than you have in dealing with them. Honor them when they honor you; disrespect and disregard them when they vilely treat you. Their arrogance is but skin deep and an assumption that has no foundation in morals or in law. They have sprung from the same family tree of obscurity as we have; their history is as rude in its primitiveness as ours; their ancestors ran wild and naked, lived in caves and in branches of trees, like monkeys, as ours; they made human sacrifices, ate the flesh of their own dead and the raw meat of the wild beast for centuries even as they accuse us of doing; their cannibalism was more prolonged than ours; when we were embracing the arts and sciences on the banks of the Nile their ancestors were still drinking human blood and eating out of the skulls of their conquered dead; when our civilization had reached the noonday of progress they were still running naked and sleeping in holes and caves with rats, bats and other insects and animals. After we had already fathomed the mystery of the stars and reduced the heavenly constellations to minute and regular calculus they were still backwoodsmen, living in ignorance and blatant darkness.[18]

In the *Supreme Wisdom* of Elijah Muhammad there is a similar emphasis on the superiority of the Black person:

The original man is . . . none other than the Black man, Black man is the first and last: creator of the Universe and primogenitor of all other races—including the white race, for which Black man used a special method of birth control. White man's history is only six thousand years long, but Black man's is coexistensive with the creation of the earth. . . . Everywhere the white race has gone on our planet they have found the original man or sign that he has been there previously.[19]

Eaton Simpson reported (1950) that during his research each night, in typical Rastafarian meetings on the streets of Kingston's west end, this idea was intoned as follows. A speaker will rise and ask, "How did we get here?" *Chorus*: "Slavery." "Who brought us here?" *Chorus*: "The White man. The White man tells us we are inferior, but we know that we are not inferior. We are superior, and he is inferior. The time has come to go back home."[20]

Despite the rhetoric, the Rastafarians, contrary to many reports, are not anti-White. The White race is seen as oppressors, but not all White people are considered evil. Each White person is accepted on merit, until proved guilty of racism. In many cases, Whites often find more acceptance with Rastafarians than do some Blacks. The American hippie cults have had easy entrée to the cult, although they are White. At the moment many Whites have become Rastafarians and are so accepted.

Jamaica Is Hell; Ethiopia is Heaven

The Rastafarians in general represent the lowest segment of Jamaican social classes. Although a sprinkling of new recruits has now emerged from the middle class, this has not significantly changed the character of the group. This level of Jamaican society represents the largest body of the unemployed and underemployed and the greatest number of unemployables; consequently, deprivation within this group has remained unchanged over the years. The flight syndrome discussed earlier is the basis for this millenarian emphasis of the earlier period of the movement. Though this escape ideology still exists among some groups, the younger element has gradually moved away from it.

The Jamaican life condition in the past has generated three observable social responses. The first is *aggression*, exemplified by numerous instances of violence as discussed in Chapter 2. On a middle level it persists in incidents of theft, usually petty, on the streets of Kingston in open daylight, or breaking into well-to-do St. Andrew homes at night. Stealing has been the famous pastime of this segment of society. However, with easier access to firearms, aggression has now taken on a new twist with bloodshed and killing widespread on the island. The economic condition in the city slums has created a seething volcano which erupts each night. Madeline Kerr calls this "intragression," the internalized frustration of a society. The Rastafarians have used this frustration as a means to continue their struggle and gain results.

The second response is *acceptance*—the society may *accept* its hopeless conditions. In Jamaican society this acceptance is symbolized in the Jamaicanism: "Who fe do"; in other words "one does not like it, but nothing can be done about it." The majority of Jamaican peasants seem to settle into this attitude. They can scarcely make ends meet but see no way out of their dilemma. This attitude is rejected by the Rastafarians. Their answer is flight or fight. While in their earlier history, the flight motif was dominant, today they have settled into the latter.

The third reaction is *avoidance*. This attitude, held by the separatist, sees no good in society and no hope of contributing any good even if the effort were made. The Rastas once fitted into this group. Seeing Jamaica as utterly hopeless, in terms of Blacks, they saw no need to hope for a share in Jamaica's future and therefore expected nothing from it. They have often said that the Blacks have given their labor to Jamaica's White rulers for three hundred years, but received nothing in return. Blacks do the work; Whites get the profit. Hence the Rastafarian movement was once united in withdrawing from Jamaica and would have nothing to do with it. As one of their leaders, Samuel Brown expressed it in 1965:

Because of the stand we have taken against white oppression, and the enforcement of their way of life on black people, we have become the target of abuse and murder, perpetuated by the black mercenary policemen, white officered. Contrary to the opinion formed abroad that Jamaica is a black man's land, it is not true where power of rule is concerned, even though we outnumber all races combined. A mulatto bourgeois class holds the balance of power under remote control, while the blacks are held as virtual slaves. The investiture of a black governor-general who is continually reminded to obey orders is the present fake. . . .[21]

Ambivalence still exists in the movement but, as we shall see, there is a gradual rethinking of their position.

Because the Rastafarians claim Africa or Ethiopia as their messianic hope, their homeland, that is where they plan to "sit under their own vine and figtree." According to Brown,

We are the people in Jamaica who are definitely opposed to any form of integration or assimilation with the white oppressor, or any non-African races and ourselves. We are those who do not accept the name Jamaican, knowing we are the Africans in exile. Our view is therefore to return to Africa at any cost. We are also proud to be called Africans or Ethiopians, knowing creation owes to the black man its paternity.[22]

To prepare the brethren for life in Africa, classes in Africanization were developed as early as 1961, especially for the study of Ethiopian history and Amharic, the language of Ethiopia. In Eastern Kingston, the Rastafarian Repatriation Association sponsors films on the culture of Ethiopia and conducts a school at night to upgrade the education of the group for leadership in Africa. But as the possibility of repatriation has gradually receded in the minds of the youth, a new evaluation of the movement's ideology has arisen. To the younger element the liberation of Jamaica is the current interest. A cautious attempt is being made to become involved in transforming Jamaica into a land of Rastafarians.

The Invincible Power of the Emperor

Before leaving Jamaica in 1965, the writer promised the Rastafarians to return in two years to see them; they all expressed uncertainty as to the possibility of this because of their belief in the imminence of their repatriation. Their mode of behavior then was anxiously waiting for the call to go. So convinced were the brethren of this event, that a visit of an African official can set off feverish speculation of immediate repatriation. On July 27, 1966, a news item appeared in the morning newspaper announcing the arrival in Jamaica of the Ethiopian ambassador to Haiti for official talks with the Jamaican prime minister, giving rise to wild speculation that he had come to prepare the way for repatriation. To this end, Ras Roy McDonald of the Ethiopian African National Congress took to the streets of Kingston informing the brethren he happened to meet that they must prepare now for the time for departure had come. Questioned by the writer about the source of his information on this urgent announcement, he replied that the spirit had revealed to him the mission of the ambassador.

This mood of urgency has brought the Rastafarians to the airport time and again fully dressed and ready for immediate departure—all because of a dream. No advice to the contrary can persuade the brethren that Ethiopia is unable to accept mass migration of unskilled or semiskilled peoples.

There is a reality, however, that gives added support to Ethiopia as the Promised Land. That is the Emperor's land grant to all Africans abroad who aided Ethiopia during the Italian-Ethiopian war. Visited by the Jamaican Mission to Ethiopia in 1961, the land is said to be good for settlement. A further support of their hope is the Emperor's message as reported by the Rastafarian brethren of the same mission; he is purported to have said:

Tell the Brethren be not dismayed, I personally will give my assistance in the matter of their repatriation. I want not only men but women and children. I do not want you to suffer any difficulties. It will take some time for careful study and planning.[23]

No other delegates of the mission support this message. It is said to have been a private communication only to members of the Rastafarian faith.

Haile Selassie's visit to Jamaica in 1966 was interpreted as the last step before repatriation. Even today the cultists anxiously await the call recorded in the prophecy of Isaiah: "I will say to the north, give up: and to the south, keep not back; bring my sons from afar, and my daughters from the ends of the earth."[24] Some few brethren have actually migrated to Ethiopia on their own, but recent developments in Ethiopia have dampened the cultists' enthusiasm and the effect of the death of the Emperor has brought new problems to their dreams.

Blacks Shall Rule the World

The Rastafarians believe, based on their interpretation of the prophecy of Daniel 2:31–42, that Blacks are destined to be the ultimate rulers of the world. In this prophecy, the Black person is "the stone hewed out of the mountain without hands." This stone is the rising African nations which have already smitten the great image, interpreted as European nations that once colonized the African continent. The hand of the image, the "fine gold," is Great Britain; the "breast of silver," France; the "belly and thighs of brass," Belgium; and "the legs, part iron and part clay," Germany. All these nations have fallen because of the political blow dealt them by the rise of Blacks in Africa. Here is a typical exegesis of scripture which to the scholar lacks all semblance of historical reality, but to the cultists is full of meaning and truth. Similarly, the Rastafarians believe that Whites are destined to destroy themselves with nuclear weapons after which only Blacks will survive on this planet.

The Rastafarians constantly point to the glorious age of the Black race in Africa before the coming of the European. Habitually they refer to the historical figures of Egypt, Ethiopia, and Greece as Blacks of the past who once occupied intellectual and political positions far superior to any achievements of the Caucasian race. They glory in the riches of Africa, richest of all continents in natural resources, soon to dominate world markets. The tendency to recall the past in support of the future has been observed by C. Eric Lincoln in *The Black Muslims in America*. He writes:

The black nationalist revives history (or corrects it, as he would say) to establish that today's black men are descended from glorious ancestors, from powerful and enlightened rulers and conquerors. This reconstruction of history may reach ridiculous extremes; . . . But a history is essential to the Black nationalist's self respect. Essential, too, is the certainty of a brilliant future, in which the inherent superiority of his race will triumph and he will again rule the world.[25]

Rituals

Certain unique activities have become indispensable parts of Rastafarian cultic behavior—I will call these rituals. These would include called meetings or congregations for inspiration, exhortations, and meditations. They sometimes involve processions and collective ceremonials which are necessary for holding a group together. Rituals often include prayers, recitation of codes, music, sacrifice, fasting, and the observations of certain taboos. Seen separately or as they have merged to encompass Rastafarianism today, these activities merit attention as they now exist.

Meetings

Rastafarians hold various types of gatherings; there are weekly and monthly meetings called for various occasions, the most important of which is known as the "Nyabingi" meeting. Weekly meetings are generally referred to as business meetings where ongoing programs are discussed and problems solved. Typical topics might be community projects or problems involving government activities which affect the group. A chairperson or "leading brother" always serves as the spokesperson of the group. There is often a chaplain, a local treasurer, sergeants at arms, and a recording secretary. The meeting generally begins with prayers and chants, but at weekly meetings this may not be necessary. Despite the hierarchical structure of called meetings, the atmosphere is highly democratic. Every member is given time for full and free debate on all subjects until consensus is reached. Monthly meetings are more of an inspirational type involving music, prayers, and exhortations. While meetings of the first type are generally held at the home of the leading brethren, the second type are usually held at the home of a member.

A typical monthly meeting often begins in the early evening and will last for the entire night with dancing, smoking, and eating. First the group recites Psalm 133: "Behold,

how good and how pleasant it is for brethren to dwell together in unity! " etc., followed by the Rastafarian prayer
(see below) and various scriptures and comments, and ends
with the Rastafarian national anthem. Following this, the
drummers and singers will participate for hours of jollifica-
tion.

The most important meeting of the Rastafarians is the
"Nyabingi," which involves members from all over the island, and is held in various parts of the island periodically.
This is comparable to a movement's convention and may
last from one to three days or even a week.

The term "Nyabingi" comes to us from East Africa and refers to a religio-political cult that resisted colonial domination from the last decade of the nineteenth century to about
1928. There is no agreement as to where the movement began. Robert I. Rotberg in his book *Rebellion in Black Africa*
(London: Oxford University Press, 1971), suggested
Ruanda-Urundi or Uganda. The term might have been the
name or title of a Ruandaise royal princess who was killed
by colonialists because of her resistance. After her death
cults arose which were influenced by her spirit. The members of the cult experienced spirit possession and the
medium of these cults was always a woman. Rotberg believes the word means "She who possesses many things." In
Jamaica the term means "death to the Black and White oppressors."

On July 6, 1975, I was informed that a Nyabingi meeting
was in progress at a district by the name of Nine-Miles (in
the Parish of St. Thomas, nine miles east of Kingston). The
two Rastafarians who gave me the information suggested
that it would be good if I could visit this meeting for a learning experience. My visit turned out to be not only a learning
experience, but also a nightmare I shall never forget. Arriving by car in the community about 5:30 that evening, my
friend, the owner of the car, cautiously left me in the village
and returned to Kingston with much apprehension. Leaving
the main road, my backpack filled with cameras and other
equipment, I ascended into the hills toward the camp lo-

cated two miles from where I started, on what is known as "captured lands"—a bit of land generally not frequented by outsiders unless accompanied by members of the cult. Arriving at the entrance of the camp, I went through what seemed like a Japanese torii. Above the entrance was a sign with a picture of a great lion, with the insignia "I.N.R.I.," which means "I Negus King of Israel." A large crowd was gathered outside the camp looking at what appeared to be an unorganized mass of Rastafarians milling about. This was the period of feasting.

Having dealt with the Rastafarian brethren for years, I was not prepared for the reception I received. It was soon brought home to me that entering a Rastafarian ritual compound was quite different from meeting them in Kingston on neutral grounds. On entering, I immediately felt a mixture of suspicion and hostility. A sudden shout of "Babylon! Babylon!" greeted me, announcing to the group that an intruder had come into the camp. Unknowingly, I had broken several rules. First, I entered the camp with a head covering that was not Rastafarian. Second, I was too well dressed for their occasion; and third, I had equipment of Babylon on holy ground. Sensing my situation, I immediately looked around to locate Ras "H" the gentleman who invited me. Spotting him among the drummers, I moved quickly toward him, calling him by name; he gave a very distant bow and smile, and suggested I take a seat and observe the customs, giving me the chance to look the camp over.

In this camp was a newly built house and a shed under which five drums were being played. Two large bonfires burned in the yard at either side of the camp and inside the shed a Coleman gas lamp burned for added light. About seventy-five people were sitting, standing, or moving about the camp. The majority were "dreadlocks" men and children, but there was also a fairly large gathering of women. The men's dreadlocks were about twenty inches long, while those of their children were approximately ten inches long. Intending to take pictures of the activity and, seeing such beautiful locks, I inquired of one of the "dreads" with whom

I was acquainted, whether this would be acceptable. After his inquiry to a convener of the Nyabingi, he reported that such practices were prohibited at these meetings. I settled down to observe with great disappointment.

All around the camp the air was thick with smoke from the holy herb. Men and women were smoking and making marijuana "spliffs" up to seven inches long. Some smoked chillum pipes and, while gazing into the sunset called out "Fire!" while others simply gazed with a smile. The drums kept a haunting beat while the cultists sang songs such as:

> There is no night in Zion, there is no night there
> Ras Tafari is the light, we need no candle light
> Hallelujah there is no night there.

and

> Dry up your tears and come to meet Ras Tafari.

One tune continued as long as an hour and without a break; another was started and continued on and on throughout the evening until the drummer was exhausted. His place was then taken by another and the singing and drumming continued. Many songs were new creations of the movement, but a great many had been adopted from the native religion and Christian hymns, using Rastafarian tempo and words when necessary.

As the evening progressed, more Rastafarians began to pour into the camp, some on foot, some on Honda motorcycles, and in minibuses. Some came from Kingston and the nearby villages, but there were members from as far as Montego Bay. By 9:00 P.M. the camp held nearly two hundred brethren and the tempo had accelerated. There were dreadlocks of all shapes and sizes, women with multicolored dresses, and men carrying tall poles which had the colors red, black, and green. As the tempo increased so did the smoking of the holy weed. Having decided to spend the entire night at this unusual fete, I sat enjoying these late night activities.

At about 10:00 P.M. that night, the other Rastafarian who

invited me entered the camp. Apparently delighted with my presence, and being deep under the influence of the herb, he suggested I take a picture of him. I informed him that I was forbidden by the host to take pictures; but he insisted with all the authority of a "dread." Being the son of the convener of the Nyabingi, I assumed that his request was sanctioned by the authorities; so without any further questions, I aimed, focused, and clicked. The flash from the camera set off a loud roar of "Babylon! Fire! Burn him!" and with that roar, as many as twenty dreadlocks surrounded me with their tall poles crying, "Death to the spy! Death to the oppressor! Burn the traitor!" My friend tried to intervene, but to no avail. My camera and tape recorder were confiscated and the film burned. Had it not been for my friend whose picture I had taken, the tape recorder too would have been thrown into the fire. All this time the questions were being fired at me, "Are you a CIA? Are you an FBI?" Each time I would try to explain myself and in many cases, some dreads would seem satisfied, but then a new group would gather around me and the explaining would begin anew. The older brethren soon accepted my explanation and, with the help of Ras "T," it seemed that I had successfully gained their confidence. But a set of young Rastafarians would not be satisfied with any explanation. These young men threatened and I felt my life in danger. At this point an older "dread," a man who had once visited the United States, seeing my difficulty, came to my rescue. He led me outside the camp, cranked up his Honda, and told me to get on the rear seat. I was on my way to Kingston. Halfway between Nine-Miles and Kingston, the police picked up our trail and followed close by. The sight of a man with my appearance riding a Honda with a dreadlock was not usual! Thanks to the astuteness of Ras "T," we eluded the police and I headed to my place of residence in safety.

The following day, I returned to the Rastafarian headquarters to investigate what might have created the hostility. It was revealed that the group who threatened me were not true Rastafarians but were young people taking on the appearance of the cultists and most of them were probably wanted by the police; photographs of them could have been incriminating. I was also told that I could have ultimately lost my shoes and my eye glasses to the fire as a penalty for breaking Nyabingi rules.

Incidentally, despite the meaning of the term "Nyabingi" in Jamaica—"death to the Black and White oppressors"—it is more accurately a gathering of the brethren for inspiration, exhortation, feasting, smoking, and social contact.

Prayers

Prayers as a ritual act are done in many ways. Meetings are opened and closed with the prayer which has been associated with them from a very early period:

Princes shall come out of Egypt, Ethiopia shall stretch forth her hand unto God. Oh thou God of Ethiopia, thou God of divine majesty, thy spirit come within our hearts to dwell in the parts of righteousness. That the hungry be fed, the sick nourished, the aged protected, and the infant cared for. Teach us love and loyalty as it is in Zion.

Deliver us from the hands of our enemy that we may prove faithful for the last day, when our enemy has passed, and decayed in the depth of the sea or in the belly of a beast. O give us a place in thy kingdom forever and ever. So we hail our God Selassie I, Jehovah God, Ras Tafari, Almighty God, Ras Tafari, Great and terrible God Ras Tafari. Who sitteth in Zion and reigneth in the hearts of men, and women; hear and bless us and sanctify us, and cause thy loving face to shine upon us thy children that we may be saved. Selah.

Recited with all the emotional tone of a deep worship experience, the prayer has become so popular that even non-Rastafarians have been heard to recite it at meetings. A glance at the prayer will show that it contains all the structure of a classical ritual prayer. There is adoration to the supreme being *Ras Tafari*; then there is supplication for the hungry, the sick, the infant, and for the destruction of the enemy, and finally it closes with adoration. The last paragraph of the prayer is repeated over and over again in meetings where the Bible is read. The Rastafarians are also in the habit of expressing evocatively "Jah! Ras Tafari!" throughout a ceremony with the rhyming phrase "Haile Selassie I," the numeral "I" used as the vowel "I."

Except for the above, no other prayers are known. In the Prince Emanuel group, the Ethiopian National Congress, a new development was observed in my recent visit: prostration on the tabernacle floor in silent prayer. The most religious of the cultists, this group is moving somewhat away from the mainstream of the movement toward a church. For them, Prince Emanuel is now revered as God; but more of this interesting development later.

The nearest thing to a code in the Rastafarian movement other than the prayer is the ten-point moral code written by Sam Brown and strictly adhered to by the movement's members:

1. We strongly object to sharp implements used in the desecration of the figure of Man; e.g., trimming and shaving, tattooing of the skin, and cutting of the flesh.

2. We are basically vegetarians, making scant use of certain animal flesh, outlawing the use of swine's flesh in any form, shell fishes, scaleless fishes, snails, etc.

3. We worship and observe no other God but Rastafari, outlawing all other forms of Pagan worship yet respecting all believers.

4. We love and respect the brotherhood of mankind, yet our first love is to the sons of Ham.

5. We disapprove and abhor utterly hate, jealousy, envy, deceit, guile, treachery, etc.

6. We do not agree to the pleasures of present-day society and its modern evils.

7. We are avowed to create a world of one brotherhood.

8. Our duty is to extend the hand of charity to any brother in distress, firstly for he is of the Rastafari order—secondly, to any human, animals, plants, etc.

9. We do adhere to the ancient laws of Ethiopia.

10. Thou shall give no thought to the aid, titles and possession that the enemy in his fear may seek to bestow on you; resolution to your purpose is the love of Rastafari.[26]

Music and practicing taboos must be left for later chapters. Regarding sacrifice, only the Prince Emanuel group practices this ritual and he has been thoroughly criticized for it. Many feel that such a practice will generate hostility toward the movement from the outside.

The Bible

To the Rastafarians, the Bible is a holy book, but not all its contents are acceptable. To be understood, the Bible must be interpreted as they believe that, due to the various translations of the Bible from the original Amharic language of Ethiopia, many corruptions have occurred. These, they assert, enhance the philosophy of the slavemasters. However, being Rastafarians, they have found the key for detecting the falsehoods of such corruptions. The Bible becomes therefore acceptable to them as a book of symbols and is read in their meetings. In the Prince Emanuel group, the Bible is read in a nonstop fashion for up to three hours—the Laws, the Prophets, and ending with the Gospels, and the Epistles. As a rule, they seldom comment on these scriptures.

Some Rastafarians use the Bible as a source book for their religious practices, especially in defense of the herb. To others, the Bible is a collection of Rastafarian wisdom which predated the scriptures. But the main reason for the use of the Bible among the cultists is the fact that the Emperor advocated it. To substantiate this, Ras Mack produced a quotation of a speech said to have been delivered by the Emperor in 1954, in which he was quoted as saying:

We in Ethiopia have one of the oldest versions of the Bible but however old the version may be, in whatever language it may be written, the words remain the same. It transcends all boundaries of Empire and all conceptions of race, it is Eternal. No doubt you will all remember reading in the Acts of the Apostles of how Phillip baptized the Ethiopian official. He is the first Ethiopian to have followed Christ and from that day onwards, the word of God has continued to grow in the hearts of Ethiopians. And I might say for myself that from my early childhood I was taught to appreciate the Bible and my love for it increased with the passage of time.[27]

In a later section of this long quotation, the Emperor is quoted as saying that he has always encouraged his people to read the Bible and "that they should find the truth for themselves." Disregarding the rest of what might be a contradiction for the cultists, they took this phrase as a directive that Rastafarians would accept no other interpretation of the Bible, but that which they themselves have evolved.

Ganja (Marijuana)

The use of ganja as a religious ritual among the Rastafarians has been the subject of scholarly, popular, and legal debate for some time. The furor has attracted great interest and created much confusion about the nature of ganja and its implication for the social and the religious future of this Jamaican movement. Rastas probably began to use ganja as a religious ritual in the early days of the movement during the wilderness experience in Pinnacle. Since then it has become an inseparable part of the movement's worship and a ritual aid for meditation.

The herb known as marijuana has attracted millions of youth and older people for the past ten years and has become a national phenomenon not only in the United States, but all over the world. Technically, the herb is known as *Cannabis sativa*, a name given to it by Linnaeus in 1753, and was known by the Hindus for centuries as Indian hemp or Bhang. It seemed to have been used in India not only commercially for making rope, but also for religious meditation. The flowering cluster from the tops of female plants is carefully cut; the resin contains special properties capable of producing altered states of consciousness when used for smoking mixtures. The term "marijuana" is a Mexican-Spanish name and has become popular in the United States. In Jamaica, the term "ganja" is the most popular and represents a finer quality of the weed. Ganja, then, is the specially cultivated type of Indian hemp derived from the female plants and is said to be as much as four times stronger than the Mexican variety.

Prior to the emergence of the Rastafarians, ganja was used

by native herbalists as a folk medicine, particularly in teas and as smoking mixtures with tobacco. But as the Rastafarians emerged, ganja took on a new role as a religious sacrament. Its use became a reactionary device to the society and an index of an authentic form of freedom from the establishment. Although the use of ganja was prohibited very early in Jamaica, most of the peasants were unaware of it; the Rastafarians, who were mostly urban dwellers, knew of its illegality. It would therefore be right to assume that as a protest against society, ganja smoking was the first instrument of protest engaged in by the movement to show its freedom from the laws of "Babylon." But, like peyote among the Navaho Indians of North America, ganja has other sides to it; its use produces psycho-spiritual effects and has socio-religious functions especially for people under stress. It produces visions, heightens unity and communal feelings, dispels gloom and fear, and brings tranquility to the mind of the dispossessed. So, ganja gradually became a dominant symbol among the cultists and has remained so to this day.

Among the Rastas, ganja is called by many names, such as *callie* and *Iley* which suggests the essence of the herb. Other names are "the herb," "the grass," "the weed," and so on. Sometimes called "the wisdom weed," it is said that the weed was first grown on the grave of King Solomon, the wisest man on earth. When used in ritual contexts, the name became known as the "holy herb" as various scriptures are given as proofs of its sanctity. The Rastafarians will say that God who created all things made the herb for human use and will cite Genesis 1:12 as their proof text:

And the earth brought forth grass, and herb yielding seed after his kind, and the tree yielding fruit, whose seed was in itself, after his kind: and God saw that it was good.

And

. . . thou shalt eat the herb of the field (Genesis 3:18).
. . . eat every herb of the land (Exodus 10:12).
Better is a dinner of herb where love is, than a stalled ox and hatred therewith (Proverbs 15:17).
He causeth the grass to grow for the cattle, and herb for the service of man. . . . (Psalm 104:14).

These biblical texts are only a few of the many used by the cultists in defense of their rituals.

They are also capable of quoting the history of the herb from antiquity to the present. In a recent interview with a leading Rastafarian, he had this to say of the weed:

Concerning ganja and the amount of publicity it has received of late, it becomes imperative that I should impart some knowledge on it regarding its history and usage among the Rastafarians. We know that in the wars of the Crusades, the Moslems were using a form of Hashish from which they get the name Assassin. This same Hashish was used religiously. In Jamaica, we do not make full use of Hashish in that form; what we use is ganja. The Rastafarian sees ganja as part of his religious observance. He sees ganja as the smoother of mental imbalances and as a meditatory influence. Ganja is really used to bring forth a peaceful and complacent aspect within man. We do not believe in the excessive use of ganja. It cannot be used to excess. In that case it would be bad for man. But in truth, ganja used moderately is not bad. We do not find ganja as a mental depressor, ganja sharpens your wit, and keeps you intellectually balanced. It is not a drug; it is not an aphrodisiac either. We smoke it, we drink it, we even eat it sometimes. We do not find it a poison. I have been smoking ganja since I was eighteen years of age. I am now fifty, and I have never been to a doctor for any ganja related ailments.

Even in Trinidad today, ganja is used by the East Indians in their Temples as a form of worship without any government interference or restrictions. If ganja was not available in Jamaica as a sedative to keep poor people calm, the island would have experienced anarchy already.[28]

A Montego Bay "dread" described his experience of ganja like this: "It gives I a good meditation; it is a door inside, when it is open, you see everything that is good." And yet another: "When I smoke the herb I man is able to see from Jamaica straight to Panama." There is no end to the praise of ganja among the brethren.

Ritual smoking follows the same pattern wherever it is observed. A package of herb is produced, generally wrapped in old newspaper or a brown bag. After carefully mincing it with a knife, it is made into a cigarette known as a "spliff" or packed into a chillum pipe. Just before lighting it, the following prayer is said by all:

Glory be to the Father and to the maker of creation As it was in the beginning is now and ever shall be World without end: Jah Rastafari: Eternal God Selassie I.[29]

Several strong pulls of smoke are taken and deeply inhaled. The smoker then seems to go into a deep trance-like state, exhales, repeating the process two or three times, then the pipe is passed to another person. If it is individual spliffs,[30] the same kind of smoking technique is used. Smoking is done on all safe occasions; but it is required at all called meetings and at Nyabingi services. I saw at least three kinds of pipes: first, a straight hollow piece of wood or iron tube called a "cutchie" which is used by placing a piece of cloth over the mouth end—this is called a "sappie." The second type is the regular chillum made out of cow's horn into which a cutchie is placed. The smoking end is a rubber tube attached to the small end of the horn. The horn is filled with water, while the herb is placed in the cutchie. The third type is made of bamboo and varies in shapes and sizes, but the parts described above are the same. At the Nyabingi service described earlier, various shapes and sizes of chillum were observed; in addition some pipes are so large that they are used only on rare occasions.

There are many taboos among the Rastafarians; some of the strongest are those against consuming rum and all liquors and the smoking of cigarettes, particularly at a Nyabingi service. The brethren insist that drinkers of Jamaican rum have created more serious social problems on the island than all the ganja smokers together. Furthermore, the cultists declare that while rum makes one violent, ganja smoking makes one calm. The Rastafarian poet puts the whole philosophy this way:

What is ganja? We know it's a plant
Created by God to fulfill men's want
The powers that be, say man should not use
They use it in secret, yet show its abuse.

There is no comparison between ganja and rum
The former keeps you "cool" the latter makes you glum
Rum as we know is an agent of death
With the using of ganja you draw new breath.

The taking of rum has eaten out our head
They who continue to take it will wind up dead
Remember, one is created, the other manufactured
On the evils of men we have always lectured.

So cast not your verdict before making a test
True conscience in you will show you the best
For rum as we know will pronounce your doom
All hail to great ganja, the solvent of gloom.[31]

The controversy surrounding the use of ganja or marijuana continues unabated, so it would serve no purpose for this author to indulge in evaluating the pleasures or evils of the herb. This would be beyond his expertise, and besides, even those believed to be experts cannot agree on the matter. One personal observation may, however, be in order. The author has observed that, after ten years of studying the groups most familiar to him, there appear to be no physical, mental, or psychic effects on the Rastafarians from the use of ganja. Most older brethren have been smoking for twenty years and are still as witty, hard working, and creative as other citizens of Jamaica. This observation was recently collaborated by the Official Report of the National Commission on Marijuana and Drug Abuse. On Jamaican's use of the herb they reported:

In the Jamaican study, no significant physical or mental abnormalities could be attributed to marijuana use, according to an evaluation of mental history, complete physical examination, chest X-ray, electro-cardiogram, blood cell, and chemistry tests, lung, liver or kidney function tests, selected hormone evaluation, brain waves, psychiatric evaluation and psychological testing. There was no evidence to indicate that the drug as commonly used was responsible for producing birth defects in offspring of users.[32]

The prolific growth of ganja in Jamaica, its ritual use among the Rastafarians, and the illegal demands for the herb in the world, have created a burden on the Jamaican government in its attempt to control its use. The government has set aside a special squad of police to trace ganja to its places of origin and to destroy the cultivations. On one of my research trips I requested to join the search-and-destroy squad in order to become better acquainted with the care and growth of the plant and the areas in which the plants were cultivated. The following is a field report of this raid.

On the evening of July 19, 1966, police Inspector L. called to say that a raid was scheduled for the following day and that if I could take the rigor of the operation, I should appear at Harmon Barracks, Kingston, that evening at 9:30 P.M. He suggested that I take old clothing, a soft-bottom pair of shoes, a flask of water, and some food to eat. Arriving at the Barracks at 9:15, I met the Inspector, who introduced me to a Mr. B., a reporter from a New York magazine. At 9:45 P.M. we were assembled for briefings in which we were told that the raid was to be carried out in area two of the Jamaica police division which included St. Mary, Portland, and St. Ann. The Herman Barracks police known as the Mobile Squad supervise all island-wide raids with the help of the local divisions. At 10:45, we left Kingston. The unit consisted of one car and two landrovers with a total of ten policemen of all ranks, each heavily armed. Our first stop was to be Moneague in the Parish of St. Ann, where we camped the night in the local police station for a short nap. We arrived there at 1:00 A.M. We were awakened promptly at 4:00 A.M., and in quick military style we left for the town of Claremont where 90 policemen were awaiting us. At 5:30 A.M. the convoy of two trucks, five landrovers, and a car headed for the district of Bensington and climbed the McDougal Mountain where the raid was to be carried out. The altimeter in the landrover began to show 2,500 feet above sea level and when we reached the camp, it was 3,000 feet. The area is made up of sharp, protruding peaks, rising sharply, then dropping off into deep ravines.

On reaching the plateau, we searched for an area where the helicopter with two police spotters could land. At 7:30 A.M. the "chopper" arrived with an Inspector and a Superintendent. After a short briefing, the squad was divided into groups of twenty men and were given the numbers one through five. Mr. B. and I were told to join any one of the groups. I picked group one so that I could immediately get into action. The helicopter took to the air once

more and using air-to-ground radio sets, the pilots began to direct
each group to the fields as they were spotted from the air. At 7:50
A.M. the first field was spotted and group one was directed to
mount the hill to the left. Climbing up the steep mountainside into
what seemed to be an inpenetrable jungle, we came to the summit
where a field of ganja sat in an area 60 × 30 feet. This was a nur-
sery in which the plants were no more than twelve to fifteen inches
high. The police, using their hands, pulled up these small plants estimated at 2,500. These were taken back to the camp were a fire
was already lit, and they were committed to the flames. This fire
was to burn from 8:30 A.M. to 4:30 P.M.; each group would carry the
bundles of herb on shoulders to the flames. As many as 25,000
plants were burned between the time we completed the first field
and the time when group number one was called to do another
task. At 1:00 P.M. my group was ordered to another field. This time
the distance was over two miles away. It took us one and one-half
hours to reach that distance. The field sat in an amphitheatre in
what seemed to have been the crater of a dead volcano. The field
was ten acres of very fine specimens from five to eight feet tall, and
was estimated to contain a half million plants. Fire was kindled on
the spot. There were 20 men, including myself, but the task of
clearing this field was so great that 20 more men were requested. It
took more than three hours to perform the task.

An incident worth mentioning occurred on this operation. While
cutting the herb it was observed that some of the plants were recently cut by people other than the police. Using binoculars to survey the edges of the crater, the police saw men hiding in the distance, overlooking the field. Gunners were called out and a party
set out for a search. 30,000 newly cut plants were recovered and
brought back to the fire.

Because of the caution taken by the hill folks few arrests were
ever made in these raids. But on this occasion, two men were captured and sent to jail. After a hard day's work, we were all tired,
thirsty, and dazed by the smoke of the holy herb. The final raiding
party returned to camp about 5:30 P.M. This last load of herb was
placed on the truck for exhibition and, being cautious not to be
caught in the region after sunset, we left the hills with dozens of
fields of ganja untouched and returned to Claremont where we received refreshments and after a briefing I returned to Kingston with
Superintendent S.

The cultivation of ganja requires a rich, well-cultivated soil. The seeds are sown in nurseries and transplanted when the seedlings are from seven to twelve inches tall. They are then manured with expensive fertilizers and carefully attended for a while. The plant is then cut, stripped of its leaves and its flowers, and dried. This is then placed in a box or bags for sale in large or small quantities.

The gardens are located in the inaccessible mountains, mostly "crown lands," and known only to those who cultivate the fields. The sizes of some of these gardens would suggest that the average Jamaican cultivator is only a middleman, hired by someone who can afford the seeds and the fertilizers and remains in the background, away from the dangers of raids. This is not to say that many local Jamaicans do not engage in cultivating the herb; for many of the hill peasants this is their only way of making a living. The larger portions of cultivated gardens are financed by some big operators and to a lesser degree by the local hillites. The demands are so great that the risks involved are outweighed by the profits to be gained. One field of ganja successfully reaped is enough to make a poor man relatively wealthy. The cultivation of the herb is so widespread that it will be another two years before the police will have a chance to raid this area again. In that time, several poor peasants and some big operators can safely buy homes on the hills overlooking the blue waters of the Caribbean.

Laws suppressing the use of ganja in Jamaica have created a kind of survival system among the cultists. Since the herb is absolutely essential for ritual uses and the cultists cannot afford to buy the "stuff" from outsiders for fear of being exposed, they have become distributors as well as smokers. To guard themselves, they have developed a defensive communication system, and with words and gestures they are able to alert each other of dangers. During my research on several occasions I have detected diacritic signs and have heard phrases used to warn each other until the identity of the visitor can be established. The danger of the police also serves a unifying function in fostering intense intrapersonal relationships among the brethren. Recently, the police seem to have resigned themselves to the cultists' use of the herb. Almost without exception, the police told the author that their least problems of ganja are with the Rastafarians. They now see its use as a ritual of the cult and, as such, are willing to turn their eyes away when it is so used.

Crimes involving the drug are no longer a Rastafarian crime, but that of the average citizen and their foreign connections. One leading Rasta explains this development in the following words:

In the beginning ganja was a poor man's game. He did a little higgler-ing with it, but with the world going desperate for drugs to settle man's frightful situation ganja has become a thing that the rich man suddenly developed an interest in. You have rich men with their big plantations in Jamaica who parcel out these lands to men to whom they pay money to seed the land, plant, and fertilize them until they come to maturity. They are the people with influence, who when they have a large amount of ganja, they take up their telephones, call their clients in the United States or elsewhere, and make arrangements for their planes to land on their properties on which they have built private airstrips. Some even land on remote country roads. A poor man will sell a little ganja, a pound or two of it; but when you see ganja going to the United States, filling ships and planes, you know it's a rich man's game. It is the big people in Jamaica who are carrying the trade of ganja under the masks of de-cency and innocence and it is the poor man who suffers and takes the rap for it.[33]

Of course not all the big people of Jamaica are in the ganja trade, but a careful observation of the trade suggests that the operation is in the hands of the very sophisticated.

Symbols

Ritual Symbolism among the Rastafarians

The study of religious symbolism has become an important part of the history of religion and anthropology, especially for students of social movements such as the Rastafarians.

The study is so involved, its language so technical, that only the simplest level of discussion will be undertaken to underscore the importance of Rastafarian symbols. It was J. J. Bachofen who said that the symbol awakens intimations, while speech only explains. The symbol plucks all the strings of the human spirit at once, while speech is compelled to take up a single thought at a time. The symbol strikes at the most secret depths of the soul, while language skims over the surface like a soft breeze. The symbol aims inward; language aims outward. Only the symbol, which literally means "throwing together," can combine the most disparate elements into a unitary expression. And it was the great sociologist W. Robertson Smith who said that the symbol is the permanent visible object at and through which the worshipper comes into secret contact with the god.

Among the Rastafarians both private and public symbols exist. The private symbols are the most dominant. These involve their hairstyling and their use of foods.

One of the chief marks of a true Rastafarian is the way he wears his hair. Though there are Rastafarians who do not wear long hair, the true symbol of a cultist is his hairy appearance. There has been much speculation concerning the origin of this symbol. Some believe this wild appearance resulted from the mountain experience of the cult—a time when it was impossible to cut their hair. Others believe it was an imitation of Ethiopian tribal warriors that the cultists saw in a newspaper or magazine. But the cultists themselves have defended the symbol as religious and defend their custom with the Bible:

They shall not make baldness upon their head, neither shall they shave off the corner of their beard, nor make any cuttings in their flesh.[34]

They refer to themselves as Nazarites and invoke Samson as their example. According to Sam Brown, the unshaven man is the natural man, who typifies in his appearance the unencumbered life. But there are deeper social meanings to the hair styles of the Rastas even if they are unconscious of it. Hair has always been a problem in Jamaican society in that it is often used as an index of social differences; for example, fine, silky hair has always been considered "good," while wooly or kinky hair is frowned upon. The person with fine, silky hair was considered better and more socially acceptable than the typical Negroid type. Thus the dominant hair styling of the Rastafarians is a symbol of the contradiction in the society—the Rastafarians are unconsciously ridiculing the ambivalence of the society. Long hair worn by men is also considered wild, dangerous, effeminate, and dreadful. Long beards worn by certain classes of the society are a sign of savagery and disorder—a symbol of degeneration. But, most of all, long hair worn by men is a symbol of defiance to the society. The average Jamaican reacts toward the Rastafarians with a mixture of revulsion and fear. The hair-symbol of the Rastas announces that they are outside Jamaican society and do not care to enter under any circumstance other than one of radical change in the society's attitude to the poor. Nearly all conservative Jamaicans dread the locks of the Rastafarians; and the stronger the revulsion, the longer the Rastafarians cause their locks to grow. Today, some Rastas sport locks as long as twenty inches. We have a group of cultists known as "dreadlocks," the sight of which can frighten the newcomer or the weak-hearted. This symbol has served to unify the cultists who refer to one another as "dreads."

The concept of "dread" has taken on new meanings in Jamaican society. To the elite it refers to an unkempt, dangerous, and dirty appearance; to the Rastafarians it signifies power, freedom, and defiance. "Dread" means rebellion or a certain behavior pattern outside of society. In recent years it has become an established word among the youth; for example, if a teacher is severe, that teacher is known as "dread." Subjects such as mathematics and science are "dread." If a man is good at a sport he is "dread." So, the word has been routinized in the society in a value-free way. The top selling record of Rastafarian singer Bob Marley—"Natty Dread"—has made the word even more popular in Jamaica-talk. In this way, the Rastafarians have added new linguistic dimensions to the Jamaican vocabulary. But this is just one of the new words to enter into the speech patterns recently.

As we have seen earlier, one of the public's response to Rastafarians' locks was to cut off their hair. The police began the practice, and were followed by school teachers who were threatened by the children and youths. This reaction by the public brought quick retaliation from the cultists, first by threat of physical retaliation, and then by letters to the editor of the national paper. As physical retaliation increased, both the police and the teachers refrained from this practice. Sam Brown, who has been one of the most eloquent defenders of the movement, stated for the press as a response to one Mr. Scotter:

I will also attempt to set the record straight concerning the hair dressing Mr. Scotter spoke of (and society believes too). The quaint curls of the Rastafarians, known as the locksmen, is not clay-hardened ringlets as generally believed, but the wooly hair of the African, only washed with pure water and left undisturbed by comb, etc., it will curl to the consistency of the locks of its own volition.[35]

Two ideas of Sam Brown's are worthy of further comment. The first is the care of the locks. As disciples of naturalism long before the term "Afro" came into being, the cultists developed special techniques in hair care. The hair and the body of the brethren are washed in water using only locally grown herbs which are quite plentiful. Their rejection of chemically processed goods is almost absolute, so they will not use soap or shampoo. Far from unsanitary, the cultists probably use more water than the average Jamaicans of their class. The second idea is the use of the comb. The dreadlocks, unlike the wearers of "Afros" who carry combs, do not use a comb. The hair simply is left to do as it wills. In this connection contradiction has arisen in the movement. There are hundreds of Rastas who use combs to groom themselves. This is true of some members of the Mystic

Revelation of Rastafari, and also of the great singing group known as Toots and the Maytals. The Rastafarians call these men "combsome." Many well-groomed "crypto-Rastafarians" wear neither locks nor beards; these they call "cleanface" Rastafarians. Then, finally, there are young Rastafarians who have just begun to grow their locks which will take years to fall in the pattern of dreadlocks; these men are referred to as "nubbies."

Food Symbolism

Many anthropologists, including Claude Lévi-Strauss and Mary Douglas, have found food symbolism to be an important index in assessing social groups. These writers contend that foods certain groups prepare and enjoy eating symbolize certain social and religious ideas. This is important, especially among the Rastafarians. The second point of Sam Brown's Rastafarian code states:

We are vegetarians, making scant use of certain animal flesh yet outlawing the use of swine's flesh in any form, shell fishes, scaleless fishes, snails, etc.

The diet of the Rastafarians is very rigid; for example, meat as a whole is considered injurious to the body. When it comes to meats they do eat, pork is not one of them. They refer to pork as "that thing." The author was told, however, that when a Rastafarian is hungry and can find nothing but the gift of a piece of pork, he will change the name to "Arnold, and then partake of it." Here we can observe a typical Jamaican folk rationality, the typical "trickster" mentality. The significance of this is the old Rastafarian theology which states: "There is nothing neither good or bad, but thinking makes it so." Ras "H" explained that one of the reasons for rejecting meat is that it leaves worms in the human body, and that when these worms defecate in the stomach it gives one a sickly feeling.

One of the prime staples of the Rastas is fish, but only of the small variety, not more than twelve inches long. They are fond of small herring known as "sprat" and all fish with scales that meet this strict size rule. All larger fish are predators and represent the establishment—Babylon—where men eat men. But the food of the greatest worth to the cultists is vegetables of almost every kind. Like ganja, the earth brings forth all good things. Food is cooked with no salt, no processed shortening, and few condiments except in its I-tal form. If they need oil, they will make use of the dried coconut in which the richest oil is found. The word "I-tal" is another Rastafarian word that is fast becoming part of Jamaican speech. It means the essence of things, things that are in their natural states. So, the Rastafarian food is now known as I-tal food. There may be great commercial possibility for this word in a short while. Many of the Jamaican foods are now renamed; for example, one of the vegetables known all over the island as Callalu is now called *Illalu* to sound like I-tal. As we have already indicated, the Rastafarians will not drink liquor of any kind, nor milk or coffee, but they will drink herbal tea and anything made from natural herbs and roots. They will not use patent medicines but will use any herbal concoctions used in the folk tradition.

The author was placed under a test in a recent research trip which might be of value to future researchers. Following a lead, I proceeded to the address of a well-known Rastafarian whom I intended to interview. On entering the house, I found his wife just about to spread the table for the midday lunch. As soon as this was done, the Rasta suggested I eat a little food while he attended to a friend who was in a hurry to leave. Two cups of Cirassee tea were prepared and a dish of I-tal food rested on the table. As a Jamaican, I was well acquainted with the tea. It is probably the bitterest herb on the island, but as a boy I could not escape it, because it was considered to be the panacea for all ills. I drank it down appearing to be having a good time, but in much distress. I then proceeded to eat some I-tal food, and to my surprise, found it so tasty that I had to curb myself, being at that time rather hungry. On the return of the cultist, he finding me relishing holy food, was well pleased. But it was my sincerity which was tested, not my hunger, for he later told me that all the information I needed was forthcoming in that, as a stranger, I did not reject his hospitality as others had done.

Another staple of the Rastafarian's diet is fruit and juices of every kind. Although fruits with large seeds like the mangoes are prohibited by some groups, fruits are generally relished. Cane juices and juices from other exotic Jamaican fruits are a daily treat. The Rastafarians are also careful about the preparation of their food, and in some cases exhibit a kosher precaution. Hence they are not in the habit of eating food of unknown sources. They have strict rules even among their women folk. Their wives may not cook for them during their menstrual periods as this is forbidden in their scriptures. The Rastafarians also prefer to eat foods from their own plantations. For this reason, one of the most coveted items among the cultists is land on which they can live and cultivate their own foods. A Montego Bay "dread" put in this way: "We need lands on which we can pitch the tents of Jacob."

The Symbolism of the Lion

One of the most prominent symbols among the Rastafarians is the lion which represents Haile Selassie, the Conquering Lion of Judah. It is seen on the houses of the brethren, on their flags, in their tabernacles, in their homes, and just about any place Rastafarians have any connections. It appears in their artwork such as paintings and sculptures, in their songs, and in their poetry. The lion represents not only the King of Kings, but the dominant maleness of the movement. The Rastafarians simulate the spirit of the lion in the way they wear their locks and in the way they walk. To the public the image of the lion suggests strength, dominance, and aggressiveness. Hence, the presence of a "dread" in any social setting outside of their habitat is a matter of concern to the public.

Rastafarian Colors

The colors unique to the movement are red, black, and green—the original colors of the Garvey movement. Every Rastafarian commune is identifiable by these colors which appear everywhere, even painted on the trunks of trees in the yards. The sticks or staffs carried at Nyabingi services are red, black, and green. The dresses and berets which have become common to most Jamaicans are knitted in these colors with the gold of the Jamaican national flag added as another color. The red signifies the blood of martyrs of Jamaican history, including heroes from the time of the Maroons down to Marcus Garvey. The black represents the color of the Africans whose descendants form 98 percent of all Jamaicans. The green is the green of Jamaican vegetation and of the hope of victory over oppression.

Language as a Symbol

We have already seen how a new type of language symbolism has emerged as a result of the movement. Nothing has been written on the subject and the field is open for the student of linguistics to try out new theories. The Rastafarian speech has been called "soul language," "ghetto language," and "hallucinogenic language." It is all of these and more; it is religious language of a strange type. Few outsiders can make sense of what the average cultist says. In the first place, it is ungrammatical when spoken by the uneducated; secondly, it is Jamaican dialect used on the philosophical level, a burden which it was not created to bear; and finally, the Rastafarian speech is almost devoid of subject-object opposition as well as without verbs. Students of Rastafarianism must be prepared to translate the material into English, or to do research only among the most educated brethren. This is quite possible though, for there are Rastafarians on all levels of Jamaican society. But research done only on a scholarly level would deny the joy of meeting grassroots Rastas.

An example of Rastafarian speech can be gleaned from any of their literature. The following example is from the now-well-known monthly, *The Rastafarian Voice,* published by the Rastafarian Movement Association at 52 Laws Street, Kingston:

The people of Jamaica are near to starvation. Everywhere there is a hue and cry for food. Government claims it is interested in I and I planting the land. Yet still when I and I plant food to feed I fellow African, I and I are harassed and driven off the land. When will this wickedness stop?[36]

Although this quotation is not altogether exemplary of the average Rasta speech, it will serve for our illustration. Notice that the writer refers to his group as "I and I." The words "me" and "you" are almost never used by the cultists. The primary combinations "I and I" are always used, even to noncultists in conversation. The Rastafarians have moved beyond the "I, thee, thou" of the Quakers, and have even gone beyond the classical primary combinations of Martin Buber's I-Thou relationship. Of Buber's combination, Will Herberg wrote:

Primary words do not signify things, but they intimate relations. Primary words do not describe something that might exist independently of them, but being spoken they bring about existence. Primary words are spoken from the being . . . . There is no I taken by itself, but only the I of the primary word I-It . . . . The existence of I and the speaking of I are one and the same thing. When the primary word is spoken the speaker enters the world and takes his stand in it.[37]

The language of the Rastafarians is a soul language in which binary oppositions are overcome in the process of identity with other sufferers in the society. The Rastafarian, when meeting a stranger, does away with the superficial greetings common to polite society and instead tests the "vibration" of the person. If that vibration is positive, it does not matter if one is a member of the movement or not; he or she will be immediately addressed in conversation as "I and I." To the average visitor accustomed to looking at people from the outside, this is very disarming. But the Rastafarians have a way to search the very soul of their friends and visitors. Once they feel the spirit of sympathy and sincerity in the true meaning of these words, the I-Thou and I-It relationships move into the third level of being and become I and I.[38]

It can be seen, then, that long before the philosophy of democratic socialism, which advocates the breaking down of divisions among fellow Jamaicans, was ever heard in the island, the Rastafarians were practicing the philosophy as long as a decade ago.

An Ambivalent Routinization

The period of 1961 to 1971 might be designated as the period of "ambivalent routinization" for the Rastafarians. The word "routinization" is taken from Anthony F.C. Wallace: "Revitalization Movement etc" (1953), suggesting the last stage of the dynamics as a movement attempts to establish itself within society. These years came as a time of high expectation in which the possibility of imminent repatriation and feverish organization took place. As many as twenty groups of Rastafarians were to emerge in the cities of Kingston, Spanish Town, May Pen, and Montego Bay, with satellites in other parts of the island all bearing special names and headed by different leaders. As the hope for imminent repatriation faded, many organizations ceased to exist or merged with others. During these years, a few of these were recorded in the author's notes as: the Ethiopian African Congress and Rastafarian Melchizedek Orthodox Church, led by Prince Edward Emanuel—a movement which has continued to the present; the Rastafarian Movement, African Recruitment Center, 1000 Marcus Garvey Drive, led by Ras Samuel Brown; the Rastafarian Repatriation Association of Jamaica, 26 Adastra Road, operating under the name of "The Mystic Revelation of Rastafari" and led by the three brethren who visited Ethiopia in the government's mission;

the Ras Tafari United Front, Liberty Hall, 76 King Street, Kingston; and various others which seem to have disappeared from the scene or have changed their names.

Factors Leading to Routinization

This chapter seeks to analyze the decade between 1961 and 1971, and to show some of the factors leading to the routinization of the movement in Jamaican society—an event which has contributed greatly to their prestige on the island, and has contributed enormously to aspects of the island's economic, political, and social development.

The University Report on the movement and the subsequent visit of some brethren to Africa made the Rastafarians visible in the island in a very important way; and, as we have seen, contributed to diffuse the excitement for repatriation. But, to the author, three incidents which are now scarcely discussed outside the circle of the brethren might have been the most important factors leading to the routinization of the movement. They are: the candidacy of Ras Samuel Brown for political office; the destruction of Back-O-Wall; and the visit of Haile Selassie to Jamaica. Each of these events have more than historical meaning.

Ras Sam Brown

Ras Brown is one of the most complex personalities within the Rastafarian movement. He combines in his person the attributes of a mystic, poet, orator, saint, painter, and what a government official called "a lovable rascal." In his presence at one given moment, one feels free and relaxed, and in the next moment tense and frightened. Since the early beginnings of the movement he has been one of the most ardent Rastafarians and is today one of its most important poets, if not the best. Born in the parish of Trelawny in 1925, he attended the local elementary school and was so brilliant a student that it is reported he won a scholarship to a prestigious secondary school in Kingston, but failed to accept the offer because of poverty. After working at various trades he became interested in printing. By 1965, when the author met him, he was without a job and was the leader of a group of brethren in Back-O-Wall. He told the author how vividly he remembered the night he heard Marcus Garvey in Edelweise Park, when he was only five years of age—a mere tot brought by his mother who was a member of the Garvey movement.

Three years before my interview with Ras Brown he created a mild sensation in the island when he entered the 1961 election campaign as an independent candidate for Western Kingston under the banner of the Black Man's Party. This was the first time in history that a Rastafarian entered the arena of active politics. Although receiving less than one hundred votes, his famous "Twenty-One Points" platform and his boldness to campaign on it not only gave the average citizen a new insight into the movement's philosophy but, for the first time, drew the attention of the elite to the potentials of the movement. The famous Twenty-One Points are known as the Foundation of the Rastafarian Movement,[1] which for historical reasons will be quoted verbatim from a tattered copy presented to the author during field research. It states that:

1. Members of the Rastafarian Movement are an inseparable part of the Black people of Jamaica.

2. As such we cannot and do not proclaim any higher aims than the legitimate aims and aspirations of the Black people of Jamaica.

3. The Rastafarian Movement consists of the most advanced, determined and uncompromising fighters against discrimination, ostracism and oppression of Black people in Jamaica.

4. The Rastafarian Movement stands for freedom in its fullest sense and for the recovery of the dignity, self-respect and Sovereignty of the Black people of Jamaica.

5. Many deplore and accuse the Black people of raising the colour question in this island. But White supremacy was the official policy of this island for hundreds of years and white supremacists never regarded Black men as good as the dogs in their yards.

6. To white supremacy has been added Brown-man supremacy and the mongrel children of the Black woman came to think and behave contemptuously of Black people.

7. Time has removed some of the grosser aspects of white and brown man supremacy; but discrimination, disrespect and abuse of the Black people are still here in many forms.

8. For instance, in their employment policies, the big guns get generous salaries, house allowance, travelling expenses and bonuses. The poor Black man working in the same industry or enterprise cannot get adequate food, money, and has to accept poor treatment and insults as part of the price of holding the job.

9. In their housing policy, they have houses for the rich, housing for the middle-class and housing for the under-privileged. "Underprivileged" is only another name in Jamaica for poor Black people.

10. God did not say "come let us make underprivileged man, middle-class man, and rich man." He said "come let us make man." The existence of underprivileged man in Jamaica is a product of white and brown man supremacy.

11. The Rastafarian Movement has as its chief aim the complete destruction of all vestiges of white supremacy in Jamaica, thereby putting an end to economic exploitation and the social degradation of the Black people.

12. The Rastafarian Movement stands for Repatriation and power and for the fullest cooperation and intercourse between the Governments and people of Africa and a free and independent people of Jamaica.

13. The Rastafarian Movement, for the furtherance of these ends, must have the backing of its support to, or lead, a political movement of its own.

14. The Rastafarian Movement has the backing of no party. We are subject to persecution and discrimination.

15. The Rastafarian Movement has lent its support to the two big Parties, this support has been in vain because no improvement has taken place in our condition. Neither are we offered or do we see any hope.

16. The Rastafarian Movement therefore has decided to actively join the political struggle and create a political movement with the aim of *taking power* and implement measures for the uplift of the poor and oppressed.

17. Because we have no other aims than the legitimate aims of

all Black people in this island as states in clause 2, this movement
is open to all Black people, irrespective of class, religion or financial
standing.

18. We are not declaring against the political leadership of white
men and brown men because of their colour; but because of the
wickedness that they represent and invite them to repentance.

19. Consequently, if a man be as Black as night, his colour is in
our estimation of no avail if he is an oppressor and destroyer of his
people.

20. All men therefore are free irrespective of colour to join this
political crusade. The only condition is that he must abandon evil.

21. Suffering Black people of Jamaica, let us unite and set up a
righteous Government, under the slogan of *Repatriation* and
Power.

Sam Brown's entry into politics, at that time, was an in-
novation contrary to Rastafarian philosophy and the pronouncements were contrary to Rastafarian beliefs, but
Brown was a realist and, as such, was a man of foresight. His
emphasis lay upon a strong foundation which actually
blueprinted the routinization of the movement which
gradually took place. His ideas predated even the Black
Power Movement in America whose philosophy was similar
to that of Brown's.

A look at the clauses of this document which appeared in
1961 suggests that Ras Sam Brown saw the eventual routinization of the movement within his society. At that period
when most Rastafarians were preparing to repatriate (in
clause 1), he was saying that the movement is an "inseparable part of the Black people in Jamaica." He saw the movement as "not proclaiming any higher aims than the legitimate aims and aspirations" than those "of the Black people
of Jamaica." In clauses 3 and 4, he advanced some ideas that
were to be taken up by the present prime minister of Jamaica
in the fight against discrimination, ostracism, and oppression, toward the recovery of dignity and self-respect and
sovereignty of the Black people of Jamaica. On the subject of
White and Brown supremacy, he again antedated the present
prime minister who, although a member of an elite family of

Rare photograph of a Rastafarian political party symbol.

Jamaica, saw the need to reecho the entrenched problem of racism which has always menaced Jamaican society. In Jamaica, the ruling racial philosophy has always been "If you are Black, keep back! If you are Brown, stick around! If you are White, you are right!" What Ras Brown boldly attacked in 1961 is the same philosophy Michael Manley seeks to destroy at present. The salary differential and working conditions referred to in clauses 8 and 9 are now incorporated by the Manley government. In the last budget speech by Manley, the language attacking the privileges of the upper class and the professionals is identical to that of Sam Brown. In clause 12, Sam Brown linked repatriation with the word "power," which when really interpreted means "liberation and power," and which also anticipated the present stance of the Rastafarians who now see "liberation before repatriation" as their goal. All this would suggest that the Rastafarians were the forerunners of the ideology of democratic socialism, the present political philosophy of the Jamaican government.

After the election, Brown was rejected by the movement as a radical who eventually split the movement. But he continued his political involvement to this day, and remains one of the most advanced thinkers of Rastafarianism.

At the time of my first interview with Ras Brown, the summer of 1965, he was still at his headquarters at 1000 Marcus Garvey Drive. A short review of this personal encounter and references from my field notes will set the stage for the second phase of routinization. The residence of Sam Brown was a small house consisting of two rooms. Just beyond this dwelling was a small yard in which all activities were centered. The signs about the yard impress themselves on the visitor in a symbolic way. Examples are:

Be happy about what is saved rather than gloomy about what has been lost.

The growl of a hungry stomach the rich knows not.

One God, One Aim, One Destiny.

Grudge is sin.

Cowards cannot win.

Informers beware.

All Black men are brothers.

On the day the author visited Ras Brown, he entered the yard through an inner gate within a larger gate. The atmosphere was suspicious until the purpose of the visit was reiterated and finally believed. There were some objections to taping the interview, but this was finally permitted upon the presentation of a few dollars. These preliminaries dispensed with, Ras Brown settled down to a most polished speech which is quoted verbatim:

It has ever been a mystery to the non-Rastafarians to know the standards of this faith. The mystery deepens with the knowledge that there is no textbook or manuscript dating back to antiquity that depicts the cult of the Rastafarians making any impact on the then-present world order. From the day of the first slave landing in Jamaica, possessing the knowledge of forcible displacement from his original habitat Ethiopia, until this day, has caused the slaves to be resentful and at times revengeful to the cause of their enforced exile and ultimate privation. While at the same time, in the majority of cases, such resentment is marked by a mask of abject docility. The resentment of the African to colonialization and domination has expressed itself in many violent slave uprisings in this and other western lands. Quaco, Koffie, Accompong Nanny, Paul Bogle, George William Gordon, and the great Garvey were truly individual exponents of the same Rastafarian thoughts existing in their age. Such thoughts are: (1) basically, unanimity and a common racial heritage; (2) a god as seen through Black men's eyes discarding the questionable or mythical dogma of a European Jesus crucified; (3) the aim from the beginning has been likened to the prodigal son, whom, after many vicissitudes, realized the place for his recovery was his home, hence our demand for an African Repatriation; and (4) one destiny exemplified by the obliteration of tribalism, thereby fostering unity in its entirety.

The Rastafarians are the fulfillers of all these with an additive exclusively his. Indeed, the Rastafarian is he who will never relinquish the fact that he is an African. He also never forgets that Britain was chief signator to the Act of an African return.

It is remarkable what pains the intelligensia will take in an effort to erase from the minds of the blacks of this country that we are Africans, telling us that we are Jamaicans and Negroes. Your Bible that was given us as a means of Christianizing clearly contradicts the . . . plans of both local and universal Christianizers by its declarations: "The leopard cannot change his spot, neither the Ethiopian his skin" and also for the minds genuinely seeking a solution to the problem they have caused, to rid their conscience of hypocrisy, and take a new view of the situation and realize that the only Jamaican is the one originated here. For example, the extinct Arawak and the immediate mulatto. Remember there is no Negro from Negroland, neither Jamaicans from Africa. We have seen planned systems of partial genocide enacted time and again. You cannot kill a problem; it beggars your solution. The seeming fanaticism of the Rastafarians in regards to black and white in all aspects, stems from the knowledge of the past that we were the shackled slaves on the Estates, and even unto this day it remains a fact that the historians of tomorrow will record us the Blacks, notwithstanding category, as the slaves of the present day. It is only a matter of time boosted by extreme pressures of the Europeans and his derivatives, that all black peoples, especially the under-privileged ones, will realize that possessed with the spirit of black emancipation, all the sons of Africa, notwithstanding shades, are one. In Jamaica we see a planned system of propaganda based on isolation of the Rastafarians, not only from society, but even among those blacks who have not yet emerged from the obscurity of themselves. The Rastafarian does not naturally hate any member of mankind, but determinedly detested systems which will not allow the true brotherhood of men to blossom forth in its full richness. We are not bent on the destruction of the figure of God, which is man, but of confederacies bent on wickedness and suppression of the poor.

It is greatly scandalized throughout the world that the Rastafarian is a ready vehicle for communism, a fleshpot who deified ganja. The truth is he deals with all things with a sense of normality, and on "ism," it is purely an African Brand.

The Rastafarian is quite aware of the fact that all past and present government is reluctant to deal with the Rastafarian problem, but instead brands us with the stigma of ganja as a pretext for continued repression. Nevertheless, we of the Rastafarian order know that brutality of punishment is no detriment to the human will. The willingness of the majority of African States to accept their exiled offsprings is enough incentive to continue our struggle to a victorious conclusion, and prove to these twentieth-century

Pharaohs that power of will without discretion or self control leads to destruction.

So in concluding, I take this medium of appealing to the Christian-minded people of Jamaica, to use their unbiased minds and honour the rights of all sections of the people, thereby proving to the world that independence in Jamaica is not only a White Hall dictated mockery.[2]

The first interview with Sam Brown was mainly observational. He took the initiative in supplying much information. At the close of the visit he invited the author to a special strategy meeting on Sunday, July 11, 1965, at which all the brethren of his group were present. (The presence of the author was somewhat disconcerting to some of the group.) Since the same distrust of unbearded men prevailed among these brethren as among all others, Ras Brown introduced the author as a student of African history, asking him to say a few words about his interest in the Rastafarian movement in Jamaica. After a short speech by this author, the tension was visibly relaxed, at the conclusion of which Brown rose and addressed the gathering on the purpose of the meeting. Part of this address, taken in longhand follows:

We are gathered here Brethren to reorganize our groups to save the people of Jamaica. We have to harass the people who have us under their feet. A large river starts with a little stream. This is not a new work; it is the liberation movement of Africans abroad. We will have to fight here with all our means. We did not have the means in 1961 or else we would have toppled the political parties of this country. No rebel army in the world can defeat us. The white man's age is coming to an end; all we have to do is to move. We are starting back but we have to reorganize. Each man among us must take on some responsibility. We are not many but this is a nucleus. We must get back on the street with agitation. We cannot sit down now; we must begin. [Referring to the researcher, he said:] We hope this man writing here will later substantiate our effort with what he will write. This is not the day of Garvey; this is a new day—we cannot stop now. This government will one day beg Africa to take us because England and Canada will not take us, so with no place to send us and with the population explosion there is going to be hunger here. We must start. Algeria has 20,000,000 people but only 3,000 of her men were in the liberation movement at first.

Plenty of our men got discouraged when they did not win. But Jah Rasta helps only those who help themselves. We will fill the roads again.[3]

Toward the end of 1965, social tension, acts of vandalism, and gang warfare became frequent in Shanty-Town. Due to the heavy concentration of cultists in this part of Kingston, this renewed social unrest was attributed to the Rastafarians. This led not only to the arrest of Ras Sam Brown, but also to the destruction of the Back-O-Wall area itself—an act which brought torrents of criticism on the heads of government, but more importantly a dispersion of the various Rastafarian groups to seek greener pastures both at the edge of the city and to other parts of the island.

The Destruction of Back-O-Wall

Although the government had plans to develop the area known as Fourshore Road which included Back-O-Wall[4] as an industrial complex, the social upheavals which grew tense at the end of 1965 appeared to have hastened the need for its destruction. The author was an eyewitness to this historic situation and shall report this incident from notes gathered during the operation.

On the morning of July 12, 1966, at precisely 9 A.M., a regiment of 250 police from all over the city assembled at the Denham Town Police Station, opposite Back-O-Wall. Armed with guns, bayonets, pistols, and clubs, the scene resembled a preparation for battle. Squatters caught without notice saw several bulldozers roaring down the street toward their dilapidated shacks and, with the sharp deployment of the police at key points in the area, the government "clean-up" campaign began. When it finally dawned on the "shantyites" that judgment day had arrived, many made a mad rush to save their few belongings. For the most part, others stood in amazement and watched their homes of many years reduced to rubble by the giant machines. When the first raided camp was demolished, a blazing fire of unknown origin consumed what remained to ashes while the fire company stood by. The sorrows and sufferings of the people were too much to report. In three days, three camps were destroyed and hundreds of people were left abandoned with only the rags on their backs. Hundreds simply moved into the nearby graveyard, setting up temporary shelters; others found some comfort at the Spanish Town Roman Catholic Church and others simply lodged on sidewalks.

Of the three camps destroyed in 1966 the most important were the Rastafarian Movement Recruitment Center of Sam Brown, and the African National Congress of Prince Edward Emanuel. The Rastafarians took the ordeal mildly; they accepted the destruction as only another incident of government's brutality to the poor and needy, further confirming their desire for Ethiopia. During the operation, a Rastafarian woman stood on the sidewalk and sang:

> Since we are squatters in Jamaica
> Send us back to Ethiopia
> We will be citizens there.

As usual the forcible removal of the squatters of Back-O-Wall brought torrents of public reaction, most of it against the government. The national weekly, *Public Opinion*, wrote:

The bulldozers were ordered by government into action and have completed their dastardly destruction, leaving hundreds shelterless and in absolute destitution. Operation "bulldoze and burn" was executed with ruthless efficiency, indicating meticulous advanced planning and anyone who witnessed the devastation of the settlements and the devastation of the poorest of our poor people must wonder whether in the government, we have men or monsters.[5]

A letter to the *Daily Gleaner* entitled "Unfortunate People" asked: "Is this the new independent Jamaica which boasts of decent democracy?" Then, alluding to the squatters in the cemetery, the writer appealed to the citizens of the island to aid the unfortunate youths:

I am asking and appealing to every decent citizen to try and save these young children from sleeping on the tombs of May Pen

Cemetery. I do not see where the living have any right to be mixing up with the spirits of the dead.[6]

The church and the government were later to help many of these people, but Back-O-Wall was no more. The destruction of the area was to become a political struggle, but many of the residents blamed their troubles on Sam Brown and the Rastafarians.

The Visit of the King of Kings

The visit of His Imperial Majesty Haile Selassie to Jamaica took place on April 21, 1966, and continued for four eventful days. It should be noted that the visit of the Emperor had nothing to do with the Rastafarians, but they eventually received great publicity as a result of his visit. Jamaica was included in the Emperor's itinerary when members of the Afro-Caribbean Affairs and other African nationalists organizations were informed that Haile Selassie was to visit Trinidad and Tobago at the invitation of Dr. Eric Williams, then prime minister of that region. A telegram from these Jamaican organizations to their government requesting that the Emperor include Jamaica on his agenda received a favorable reply. When the announcement appeared in the press, the Rastafarian movement was stirred to feverish pitch with the expectation of immediate repatriation. Every cultist in the island began to prepare for what the Greek New Testament called a *"parousia."* On the day of his arrival, Dr. M. B. Douglas, one of the nationalists instrumental in bringing the Emperor and an eyewitness of the airport scene, gave the author this report:

There were no less than 100,000 people at the airport to meet him. The Rastafarians numbered at least 10,000. The morning was rainy and many people were soaking wet. Before the arrival of the plane the Rastafarians said that "as soon as our God comes, the rain will stop." This turned out somewhat like a miracle, because the rain stopped as soon as the plane landed. As soon as the plane had come to a stop, the Rastafarians responded with a roar of joy and surged out on the tarmac, each one pushing to get a touch of the plane.

When the Emperor saw the people, the Rastafarian flags, the cheering and singing,—he wept.

The crowd was so thick around the plane that the Emperor was unable to get out for close to thirty minutes. The police tried in vain to restore order, so I was called by the Haitian Ambassador, I being one of the Nationalist Leaders to speak to the crowd; but not being a Rastafarian I suggested the name of Martimo Planno, who was called over the public address system to the plane. He went up the ramp, shook hands with the Emperor, turned and informed the crowd to clear the way for the descent of the Emperor. This was done and the Emperor came down from the plane, but by this time all the official plans for the welcome ceremony, that is common to ruling monarchs, were completely destroyed. The Emperor got into his car and rode off to King's House. The Rastafarians were not interested in protocol or official welcome, their explanation was: "This is our day! This is our God! It is him we come to see! It is we who welcome him!"[7]

Dr. Douglas said that in his experience no monarch had ever received such a welcome in the history of Jamaica. Several special occasions were planned in honor of the Emperor in which he met with members of the island's African organizations at King's House and at the Sheraton Hotel. At least sixty of the leading brethren of Rastafarians were officially invited. The official invitation cards and the Ethiopian medals in gold which were given the Rastafarian leaders are now sacred items of the movement and many were viewed by the author. The Rastafarians' papers were filled with comments on their evaluation of the meaning of the visit. One read:

For the first time in the history of Jamaica Rastafari Brethren and persons of Back-to-Africa movements were officially invited to King's House: Glory be to the visit of Emperor Haile Selassie I. Although we were born here, the privilege was never granted to us until April 21, 1966. It was a mixed assemblage at King's House. The *Rases* were there, the aristocrats were there, the peasants and outcasts were there. It was a real occasion of the haves and have nots. It took Ras Tafari in person to occasion the reality, "that all men were created equal. . . ." The King of Kings and Lord of Lords did not think himself too highly to leave his High Throne in

Ethiopia to sit on a chair in King's House among the servants of the earth.[8]

Another Rastafarian leader states, "His coming lifted us from the dust and caused us to sit with princes of this country;" while yet another saw his visit as comparable to the triumphal entry of Christ in Jerusalem.

The Emperor's visit gave the Rastafarians a great boost in prestige. Many of the elite who had paid little attention to the movement suddenly saw their Rasta leaders in resplendent robes moving about and receiving greater attention than they in King's House. This was especially true of the Rastafarian brethren who had visited Ethiopia in the 1961 mission. The Emperor, although obviously elated at the outpouring of the praise toward him, had little to say of the daily comments of the press linking his name with the cultists. Dr. Douglas however stated that the Emperor said that, "He never dreamt that he had such a following in this faraway country where people never saw him before."

Two important developments resulted from the Emperor's visit. The first was the special private communication which was said to have been given by the King to some of the leading brethren. This communique was that the brethren should not seek to immigrate to Ethiopia until they had liberated the people of Jamaica. This new ideology, "liberation before migration," has become the routinization technique of the younger members of the movement and has worked wonders in the adjustment of Rastafarians to the realities of Jamaican life. The second development is the celebration of April 21 as a special holy day for the movement. The coming of Haile Selassie to Jamaica, then, proved an important event in the routinization of the movement in the life of the island.

The Process of Routinization

The process of routinization of the movement in Jamaica was aided by many factors and on various levels. First, we look at the role of the government. During the 1960s, the ruling party of Jamaica searched desperately to aid the movement to repatriate to Africa or to Ethiopia.[9] Lacking any practical logistics, this project was quietly dropped. Instead a period of benign neglect appeared to have replaced the government's response. Most official pressures were lifted from Rastafarian activities, which meant less police harassment for small incidents, and some recommendations set out in the University Report were instituted, such as building better facilities for the cultists, providing them with jobs, and incorporating some of their creative activities in the Jamaica National Festivals. On many occasions, the Rastafarians received medals for their outstanding performances and wood work. This new attitude must be accredited to the insight of Edward Seaga, the sociologist and politician who did much to promote the folk culture of Jamaica in yearly festivals. This gradual integration of Rastafarian creativity into the mainstream of Jamaican expressions gave them a feeling of importance to society. On the other hand, the government began to turn its eye the other way to the Rastafarian capture of "crown lands" where communal communities began to develop. On these lands the cultists built their homes where they lived and worked tax free. This new trend aided the growth of the movement immensely. In addition, the government's ministers began to talk favorably about the cultists, to adapt their lifestyle to speech, if not in dress and appearance.

The second factor of routinization must be attributed to the dynamics of the movement itself. Encouraged by the publicity during the emperor's visit, the movement was challenged to prove itself worthy of the positive evaluation given. This immediately set loose a wave of hitherto unknown industry by the brethren. One of their first contributions was music. Almost from the beginning of the Rastafarian movement, a new drumbeat, totally unrelated to any other cult music, came into being. The originator of this beat was the famous Count Ossie, now a legendary figure in the movement. He was a member of the Rastafarian Repatriation Association of Adastra Road in Eastern Kingston from the start of the group. The group is now known as "The Mystic Revelation of Rastafari" and was probably the first to record the music of the brethren in a landmark three-record album called "Grounation." This album was to be the beginning of what has become Jamaican musical industry, for today Rastafarian music is heard in Jamaica, the United States, England, and Africa. No musical event of importance would be complete without the appearance of important Rastafarian artists about whom we shall speak later.[10]

Along with music, Rastafarian art has now become the pride of Jamaica. The etchings of Ras Heartman are sought after by Jamaicans, tourists, and art collectors. Hundreds of sculptors have emerged among the brethren and the tourist sculpture of Jamaica is totally Rastafarian. The author has seen Rastafarian sculptures of fine quality that bring as much as seven hundred Jamaican dollars. Their painters have also received many awards for their work in Jamaican art exhibitions. These few examples show how the Rastafarians have aided in the routinization of the movement within the Jamaican social structure, but it does not say that they have allowed themselves to be co-opted. They are aware of their role as a movement for change and, though their tactics have changed, their strategy remains in their creation and production of songs, music, and sculpture. These have now become the medium through which the message is spoken.

But there is a third and final ingredient to the process of routinization, and that is the acceptance and support by the masses of the Rastafarians, as the avant garde who are carrying the fight for freedom, justice, and a better Jamaica. The overwhelming majority of poorer youths and a large segment of the privileged youth have become either Rastafarians or sympathizers. Ras Brown states that six out of ten underprivileged Jamaicans are now Rastafarians or sympathizers. So influential is the Rastafarian movement that even the government is now turning to them for an answer to the crime wave and violence in the island. A commentary on the times was solicited from Ras Brown during the emergency which these criminal activities created. He sent a written manuscript to the Jamaica Broadcasting Company for use as a national statement of the Rastafarian; it was never used. Ras Brown has consented for it to be incorporated in this book. The content of this tightly-written paper should leave no doubt in the mind of the reader that the Rastafarians are now committed to radical social change in Jamaica. The paper presented here is a slightly edited version:

By this excerpt I will try to give my impressions on the current situation of unrest and violence bedeviling the country, and try to impart advice towards its solution. Brutal severity of punishment is no detriment to the human will. The rapings, maimings, killings of the ghetto must be kept within its confines. The hordes of slaves who are rated the lowest in the society seek a release from their dilemma. The ghettoman, who is introverted, when consciousness of his identity and of his brothers dawned on him, he tends to become extroverted. Natural envy takes hold of his consciousness, he attacks the suburbanites, committing the unpardonable sin. Even the educated slaves who hold the authority of life and death over the inhabitants of the ghetto dare not commit the sin of uncouthness against suburbia. The disturbed ghettoites are not being fused in the melting pot of time. The stringency of enactments will fail to arrest the global movement now taking place. The turbulent ghettoite does not readily see himself distinctly racial, so his struggles are for the opportunities, the rights of man. The angry young man of the ghetto spawned in poverty and filth, coming to maturity, views with alarm and envy the imbalance of affluences and wealth in favor of high society. The inducements of abortion, the stringency of laws and other deterrents will not provide the solutions to the problems. This is definitely a struggle against class bondage; the only solution of which the society is well aware is more equitable distribution of the wealth. As long as society continues to make a mockery of justice by denying the rights of the poor, the turbulence of the ghetto will eventually overspill, leading to ultimate anarchy, the various media of communications coupled with desperation, due to the seemingly impossible position enured the ghettoman to desperate boldness, one who will not be cowed by amoured might or military personnel. If the people are content no one needs live in fear.

Suburbia will not attack itself, so laws for the constraining of violence are laws of the ghetto, wearing a democratic mask. A society of equality and justice does not live by the gun. Without defending a particular system, one would ask, are there ghettos in the U.S.A., Britain, the Soviet Union, or the English-speaking Caribbean? It is futile for the rulers of these ghetto colonies to foster the idea that bias to the ruling society or reliance on the protection of amoured might will be able to arrest the rolling ball of the peoples' revolution. Killing on the whole is reprehensible, yet every life created by divine laws to fulfill a role is important. Yet no national outcry or mourning is experienced at the demise of the ghetto person. If the changing tide of world conflict won't, then economic pressure will, compel all sections of down-pressed people—for example, police, soldiers, and the ghetto people—to look in one direction. As water pressure develops in an insecure dam, its banks eventually give way—so will oppressed peoples' governments. If the rulers really stand for the good of all the people, they must accept the fact that the present system is in error, and bad administration is the parent of crime. Without ownership of lands one cannot amount to much. The overcrowded ghetto needs land settlements, and the status it carries. It is not hidden from the sight of the silent majority that in these colonial territories, whether independent or economically tied, that nine-tenths of the agricultural and arable lands are captured by a small minority class, thereby helping to foster overcrowding ghettos.

The historians with prophetic insight do not marvel at the times. They know that these unrests are the foetal stages of the Black Revolution which is global. It is heart-rending to the leaders of Western democratic systems to know that any land on earth tinged with the poison of colonialism in any guise, will be embattled by the people, the system eventually becoming victims to the hordes of the new order—now being conscious that they who manipulate the system are the barriers to freedom and betterment. It is significant that the majority of riots and demonstrations occurring in the Western Hemisphere are being done by black youths. Youths who now master the construction of projectile arms, who now manufacture most deadly homemade weapons. It seems only a matter of time for the mastery of the complication of the hydrogen bomb to be possible. The winds of change have caused the colonials to unlock their grips on the lands of the East. Yet the Western Hemisphere, democracy's last outpost, stands ready to massacre the slaves other than ceding the rights of man. The democratic countries did pledge on the Charter of Human Rights, without its implementation, lasting peace in these parts is only an illusive wish.[11]

The commentary on the times by Sam Brown is just a sample of the level of philosophical and political astuteness found among the cultists. Their ability to face perceived opponents on various levels keeps the opponent in a state of confusion. On one level the movement is purely religious; on another level the movement appears to be a separatist organization looking toward Ethiopia and immediate repatriation, yet seeking integration within the society. Language like the above with all the rhetoric of a born revolutionary is common. This kind of technique is what theoreticians call "revolutionary judo." This technique aims at emphasizing the gap between the ideal values of the society and the actual behavior which denies them, and by so doing incurs feelings of guilt among opponents. This has the effect of stimulating the establishment to action for social change. Revolutionary judo also allows the cult members to define their perceptions of social reality in ways unfamiliar to the opponent, against which they have no socially defined defense; in other words, the cultists are able to "tell it like it is," while the opponent is more likely to cover up the gaps with hypocrisies. And finally, the word magic of the revolutionary cult movement often creates visions of Armageddon in the mind of the establishment which forces it to commit indiscretions that more often than not turn to the movement's advantage.

As we have seen, the Rastafarian movement in Jamaica has demonstrated all the classical techniques of a real revitalization movement. It emerged from a period of stress brought on by a perceived cultural and social distortion, and moved through a period of heightened tension in search of a reformulation of the mazeway by adopting an ideology, relics of which were well known to the culture; the movement then undertook the task of communicating this ideology, resulting in mass recruitment and a loosely structured organization. By astutely maneuvering against the opposition, the movement attained some acceptance. This acceptance, however, was only a stage in the movement's goals. It further sought to adapt itself to the social and cultural realities of Jamaica by using a variety of strategies which often create confusion in the minds of the opponents. On the strategy of a movement's behavior, Anthony F. C. Wallace writes:

The movement may therefore have to use various strategies of adaptation: doctrinal modification, political and diplomatic maneuver, and force. These strategies are not mutually exclusive nor, once chosen, are they necessarily maintained through the life of the movement. In most instances the original doctrine is continuously modified by the prophet, who responds to various criticisms and affirmations by adding to, emphasizing, playing down, and eliminating selected elements of the original visions.[12]

We have seen that all these strategies have been used by the Rastafarians up to this point. We now turn to the discussion of the movement today and its future on the island.

Dissonance and Consonance

Anyone who listens to Rastafarian music, be it the ritual Nyabingi or the popular reggae, will detect in the lower beats deep structural dissonance which mirrors the social conflicts within the society. But careful attention to the lyrics of such songs as Bob Marley's "No 'oman No Cry" reveals a search for a consonance in his repeated refrain "Everything is going to be all right," sung as by one who is possessed. Dissonances in this context suggest the social and cultural incongruities which the society feel are responsible for its alienation whether real or imagined. These dissonances often create deviant situations of a counterculture which lead either to the death of a society or to its rejuvenation. Cultural dissonance, like musical dissonance, constantly searches for a consonance in which to resolve itself, which in most cases is latent within the culture itself. Often the resolution is revealed to a prophet or a seer, generally from the class of the oppressed; in some cases the consonance emerges from the countercultures. An example of this dissonance-consonance combination may be seen in the Rastafarian evolution—dissonance, and in their cultural contribution to present day Jamaica—consonance-resolution.

For an up-to-date picture of the Rastafarian movement, we

must undertake a short review of their development, high-
lighting some of the predictions made by scholars and journalists who observed them in their struggling days. The first
such scholar was George E. Simpson of Oberlin College,
Oberlin, Ohio. His study was carried out in 1953, in the
West Kingston areas, where he attended open-air meetings
of the cultists. His short paper on the movement was published by the University of the West Indies' *Journal of Social
and Economic Studies* in 1955, under the title "Political
Cultism in West Kingston, Jamaica." The article, though
less than twenty pages and mostly descriptive, contained
some rather important insights into the function of the
movement in that early period. He described it as made up of
"illiterates, or semi-illiterates, confused, poor, and bitter . . .
urban dwellers."[1] They were regarded in those days as lunatics, ganja smokers, and professional criminals. But he also
saw in them budding entrepreneurs, a movement of resistance to political oppression, and a religious alternative to
the other worldly Christian organizations in the slums
which had grown stagnant and irrelevant to the needs of the
oppressed. He observed:

Cult activities provide release from the drabness, drudgery, and
humiliation of everyday living in an economically depressed area.
Members compensate for their lowly status in Jamaican society by
denouncing their oppressors, by insisting upon their superiority
over those now in power, and by rejoicing over their knowledge
that deliverance is at hand. The despised and rejected have responded to their situation by creating a world of their own, and
they exhaust themselves emotionally in their meetings through
singing and verbal violence.[2]

Following Simpson's lead, other sociologists and journalists
began to observe the Rastafarians of West Kingston, mostly
paying attention to the setting out of which the cult
emerged.

Up to the late 1960s, Rastafarians were to be found mostly
in areas of the city which used to be called "dungle"—a
word which signified "dung" and "jungle." These were the

worst areas of the city, even lower than ghettos. A true picture of these areas is to be found in Sam Brown's poem
"Slum Condition," written to describe the situations of life
for the Rastas in the 1960s. However, two good descriptions
of that era were written by the brilliant sociologist, Orlando
Patterson, and the Oxford scholar, Katrin Norris. Patterson,
in his book *The Children of Sysiphus*, described the Rastafarian district as follows:

. . . on the left were shacks; dreadful, nasty little structures—a
cluster of card-boards, barrel sides, old cod-fish boxes, flattened tar
drums and timber scraps. A few of the more luxurious, consisted of
carcasses of old cars.[3]

A less poetic description of the same place is given by Katrin
Norris in her book, *Jamaica: The Search for Identity:*

Only a few hundred yards beyond the harbour and the central
shopping areas [of Kingston], in a most conspicuous position along
what should be a waterside boulevard, is a horrifying sight. This is
one of the squatting settlements of the Rastafarians. . . . They live
in the utmost squalor in huts of boards, metal scraps, motor car
parts, tires, cardboard, and anything they can lay their hands on.[4]

The areas described by Patterson and Norris no longer appear in Kingston. In 1966, the government recaptured them
from the Rastafarians by sending in a fleet of bulldozers
under police guard and ploughed them under. Many Rastas
from these areas found other lands to capture or moved away
to the country where they have built new villages of a more
permanent quality. Today, the Rastafarian communities are
no longer so depressing, although conditions are in no way
ideal among the new camps. The writer paid a recent visit to
the Adastra Road community, which in 1965 was nothing
but several shacks such as those described above. He was
greatly surprised at the improvements. Many Rastafarians
who once lived in broken-down shacks were now living on
the same grounds in middle-class dwellings made of concrete blocks with running water and other amenities. Their
community hall, which was only a "bush-arbor," is now a

permanent hall of substantial concrete where classes in sculpturing and music are held for community youths. It is from this community that the now famous Mystic Revelation of Rastafari has emerged. Their famous drummer, Count Ossie, the father of Rastafarian drumming, was until his death a member of this community. They have cut many records and are now known all over Jamaica and the outside world.

One-quarter mile from the Mystic Revelation group is the Rastafarian settlement known as Lennock Lodge, once described by the "Saint," under the caption "Rastas are Cave Men," in the *Star* of April 9, 1962. In that article he described the area as follows:

At the foot of the Long Mountain range of Wareka Hill commencing . . . at the end of Sligo Avenue, numerous members of the Rastafari cult eke out a miserable existence on the rugged hill slope owned by the forestry department. Among sharp pointed rocks and cactus they erect unsightly shacks cut out of cardboard, old wooden boxes, tree branches and other materials, with which the land is littered. The less fortunate ones, such as the newcomers to the settlement, live in shallow caves like animals.[5]

Today, this camp, described by the "Saint," is a massive settlement of Rastafarians who have built permanent dwellings on the hillside. As many as fifteen acres of the most enviable housing lands overlooking the bay area and the airport have been captured by the Rastas. Houses of all sizes and shapes with their red, black, and green colors perch precariously on the hillside. The life style remains much like that described by the "Saint:"

The cultist live on the land without any water. To get water they either go further down the Mountain areas, where there are standpipes, or to the public park. . . . To make a living I understand that these hill people cultivate small gardens in back of their shacks, burn charcoal, or supply homes with fence posts. To get their supply of wood, or coal, or fence posts, the Brethren travel up the steep mountain range, barefooted and partly nude. Trees are felled, trimmed and cut up in small bits for the kiln, and conveyed on the head down the hill side.[6]

Contrary to the popular belief of most elite Jamaicans that the hillites are lazy and all criminals, the new Lennocks settlement with its colorful building proves without doubt that these Rastafarians are creative people, hard working, and above all proud. If the "Saint" were to follow up his research on hillites, I am sure he would have to write a piece with the caption "From Cavemen to Concrete Dwellers."

Such development was unforeseen in 1962. The Rastafarians have confounded the skeptics on every hand. For out of these "cavemen" have come some of the best drummers, singers, dancers, and carvers of present-day Jamaica. There are many more such "phoenix-like" communities among the Jamaican Rastafarians which we shall discuss later. But this is not the end of the story. A few of the more exceptional of these cavemen have by now acquired middle-class homes in the suburbs. All this indicates that a new approach to the Rastafarians in Jamaica needs to be undertaken.

Contemporary Observations

Having studied the Rastafarians since the 1960s, and having watched the dramatic development of the movement in such areas as art, music, and language, I wanted to observe and to study more carefully those changes that had taken place since my last research. So, in the summer of 1975, I set out to do an extensive re-study of the movement. What I found was convincing enough for a revision of my previous work published in 1968.

The central tenets of the Rastafarians have not changed to any great extent. Haile Selassie of Ethiopia (even though he was dethroned during my research, and died within a few days of my return from the field), is still god. The returned messiah in the flesh, he is now even more powerful in the spirit—a belief central to the movement. This is the belief that separates a Rastaman from all others. There are thousands of people whose hair and general appearances look like Rastas, but hairdos and outward appearance do not a Rastafarian make. It is the belief that Haile Selassie is god and the love and worship arising from that belief which makes one a Rastafarian.

On the subject of repatriation a slight shift has taken place at the edges of the movement. I would estimate that close to 50 percent of the movement's membership still holds to the doctrine of repatriation; that is, the miraculous return to Ethiopia by the supernatural power of the king. This belief is the view of the older members of the group. The younger and more militant members have added a new twist to repatriation. Their argument revolves around a new myth, said to have originated during the visit of Haile Selassie to Jamaica in 1966, when he was supposed to have said that the Rastafarians should "liberate themselves in Jamaica" before they repatriate. The phrase now current among them is "liberation before repatriation." This group seems more ready to enter into a sociopolitical struggle with the government. They are politically alert and involve themselves in all political enterprises aimed at liberating Black people both in Jamaica and abroad. They celebrate African independence such as the recent independence of Mozambique. They readily involve themselves with organizations like OAU and other movements in Jamaica whose aim is to lift the awareness of the Jamaican masses. Somewhat disdainful of the repatriationists, they see them as somewhat backward. Although they view Ethiopia as their eventual home, they feel that only by taking a political hold in Jamaica and becoming a part of the decision-making process can they ease the way to repatriation.

Structurally, the movement remains basically the same—it is ascephalous. No leader has arisen to unite the separate branches of the movement and there is no desire to do so. The Rastafarians are deathly afraid of leaders because they feel that a leader would destroy the movement. There are still "leading brethren," but these are men around whom various groups are organized. Their power is mostly organizational, they do not speak for the members as leaders, but simply serve as an inspiration for their specific groups. Despite this amorphous collectivity, the movement has nodes of connection island-wide. Ras Sam Brown pointed to this nature of the movement when he said:

The Rastafarians movement is not a movement with a central focus. All Rastafarian movements in this country have an affinity with each other. In every Parish of the island, you will not just find a one here and a one there. You can find sizable colonies of Rastafarians all over, along with thousands of sympathizers too. In every colony of Rastafarians you have brethren who see to the guidance of the youth who must be taught the philosophy of the movement. What affects Rastafarians at Morant Point, becomes the concern of those Rastafarians at Negril Point. We do not look at it as just a personal and isolated case. We look at it as something that the whole structure of the movement must set right.[7]

It is clear from the observation of Sam Brown that although each colony is separate, the movement can escalate when there is a need to do so. Segments of each movement from the far end of the island can be found in the other, especially on special ritual occasions which we have already discussed. At present, the movement is very mobile. The use of minibuses and motorcycles has made the movements' involvements easier than in the 1960s.

Unlike the 1960s, when the movement was an alien "bird of passage" cult, the Rastafarians today are a very visible entity on the island. They have carved an identity of their own and are sure of themselves. They have "won their spurs" so to speak and see themselves as contributors to the cultural and economic fibre of the island. Rastafarian musical groups such as the Lights of Saaba, the Mystic Revelation, and Toots and the Maytals, and performers such as Bob Marley are internationally known artists. Their performances have top billings in both Jamaica and the United States. Their recordings, banned from the Jamaican radio stations for years, have replaced the soul music of the United States, which was once the only Black music thought acceptable in Jamaica. Not only have they gained a personal identity, but the island which once saw them as the "boogiemen of the slums" now acknowledge them as "brothermen." From the slums of Kingston to the palatial drawing rooms of the St. Andrew Hills, the Rastafarians are the current subject of conversation. Their quaint mode of speech is the current language fad of both the people in the street and the professors at the senior common room at the University of the West Indies.

The Rastafarians, who are living examples of Jamaican social and cultural deprivation, are now the prophets preaching to the elite about the conditions of squalor. Their songs carry the message to the living rooms of the rich; they are the social catalysts of the island; and no one can escape this message. The reality of the Rastas cannot be ignored by the politicians: their voice is the voice of the people and the success or failure of Jamaican leaders henceforth must grapple with the power of these modern day "John the Baptists" whose voices call out from the electronic wilderness. The Rastafarians must be seen above all else as the champions of social change on the island. Despite their messianic-millenarian doctrine, they are the first Jamaicans since the time of Marcus Garvey to venerate Black culture. Few islands in the West Indies have been so schizophrenic regarding their true culture. With regard to dress, language, taste, and Black pride, Jamaicans have been last on the scale of identity. Few middle-class Jamaicans would consider themselves dressed up unless they are suffocated in Scottish tweed and mohair clothing made for cold climates and not for weather that is close to ninety degrees most of the year. The Manley government in recent years has introduced a national dress for men known as *Cariba* or *Kareba*, but this national dress has been scorned by the elite. The mere fact that it is "Jamaican" is enough to reject it outright.

Despite the work of Louise Bennett Coverley and her excellent effort toward making Jamaican dialect respectable, and despite the fact that most Jamaicans know their dialect—English being a second language—few middle-class or aspiring middle-class Jamaicans dare to use what is properly theirs in public. Their grammar may be atrocious, but they will insist on the "proper accent," meaning the accent of the BBC news reporter. This they feel is the way one speaks. In other words, to copy England is good; to speak Jamaican is bad. With respect to taste Jamaicans are the world's greatest consumers of foreign goods. Average Jamaicans would go out of their way to obtain foreign things, despite the wide range of tasty Jamaican foods. The visitor to Jamaica looks in vain for a Jamaican restaurant only to find a Chinese restaurant on nearly every street in Kingston and will have no trouble finding an Indian or even a Korean one. There are Chinese clubs; German clubs; American, French, Spanish, and English clubs; but no Jamaican ones. One can find such societies as the Rotary, the Lions, the Junior Chamber of Commerce, the Elks, and other imported organizations, but not a Mongoose, an Anacy, or a Gutu club, because these would be Jamaican, and that is bad. It is fashionable to adhere to any religion if it has foreign connections, but a native religion is out of the question. All this social and cultural schizophrenia accentuates the significance of the Rastafarian movement as an instrument of social change in Jamaica.

A contributor to the *Daily Gleaner* of June 29, 1969, pointed out this fact very forcefully:

It is significant that the Rastafari founded perhaps the only real piece of culture Jamaica has experienced, and it fed on a hope that did not lie inside the island society. The Jamaicans who reacted against European aesthetics and grew their hair to resemble the jungles of their lost heritage rather than the straightened smooth gloss of England's green fields, instinctively sought for a symbol of black pride which they could not find then or now in Jamaica. When they coated themselves with honest earth, it was a symbolic, if unrealistic, rejection of the pusillanimous middleman way of life existing parasitically upon the creations of others.[8]

The writer who seems to be a Jamaican and middle-class himself, zeroed in on the point I have been trying to make in this summary, admitting:

In muted terms, I am convinced there was a lesson in the Rastafari evolution for all classes of dispossessed in Jamaica. Yet we leapt upon them furiously, afraid to listen to what they had to say. Later, when compromised with a Machiavellian mission to Ethiopia, Rastafari symbols appeared from everywhere, swamping any official hope that the embarrassing movement might subsequently disappear. The Rastafari represent the extreme of an almost paranoiac search for an identity on the part of Jamaicans. How can this be so if we are one people? [9]

The writer, whose article is entitled "The Rastafarian Evolution: A Lesson for all Dispossessed," seems suddenly awakened to the stagnation of his society and sees the Rastafarians as an instrument of social transformation which has slowly reawakened the society to its heritage, its reality, and a pride in being Jamaican. His observation is not an isolated one. But it will take some time before all Jamaicans will agree with those who have seen the mission of the cultists.

Two Contemporary Case Studies

My recent research on the Rastafarians was prompted by the large publicity they had begun to receive in such papers as the *New York Times* and the *New York Post*. Much of the publicity was negative, involving gang warfare and drugs. On the other hand, Rastafarian music and paintings had also begun to receive popularity in the United States. I was interested in studying the development of the movement in Jamaica from 1966 to the present to see the strength of their organization in Jamaica, the sources of their creativity, and their impact on the wider world. Three months of research were undertaken in Kingston and nearby St. Thomas, Montego Bay, and short trips to other parts of the island. To get a comparative picture two groups were carefully observed: The Rastafarian Movement Association headquartered in Kingston, and the Ethiopian National Congress of St. Thomas. These two groups represent the wide diversity now existing in the movement from the standpoint of goals, beliefs, and practices. Much of what follows will be given in the words of the cultists themselves, with a minimum of editorial work when necessary.

The Rastafarian Movement Association

The Rastafarian Movement Association consists of an office in Kingston which also serves as a shop in which Rastafarian arts, crafts, and literature are sold. Two rooms only, the front and rear serve as both office and workshop for artists. Its administration includes a president, a vice president, and a secretary who is always present to give information to visitors and to show the items for sale. The RMA serves as coordinator for important meetings such as the celebration of the independence of a new African state (for example the Mozambique independence of July, 1975), and by sending out flyers to various other groups for a meeting at the Marcus Garvey shrine; it also supervises a youth program in the city, where underprivileged youths are supplied entertainment and food. An important function is the printing of the monthly paper known as the *Rasta Voice*, which carries an editorial on current interests of the movement, community news, news about Africa, a short history of the Rastafarian movement and the Garvey movement, the history of Ethiopia, pictures, and poems. The RMA also undertakes aid to Rastafarians who come in conflict with the law, by providing legal advice and securing a lawyer when possible.

During my visits to the RMA, the headquarters literally teemed with activities. Members from various groups arrived from time to time to get advice on various matters, there were researchers from universities, women and children from the city, or just casual visitors curious to find out what is happening in a building where so many dreadlocks are assembled. The history and function of the RMA were given to me by a leading spokesperson in the following words:

The organization came into being in order to bring about a centralization of all the movements. Prior to now, there were many little groups but no recognized organization. In 1969 we felt the need for an organization and a constitution, so we met at Waltham Park Road and talked with Brethren from all over; they all agreed that these things should be done. About three weeks after these meetings we drew up a constitution and brought about this organization. With the contributions of the Brethren we acquired this place and we have been here since. Here, we try to rally the Brethren together for reasoning and to build a framework of the culture, but this place has even become too small for our operation.

The organization of the RMA does not see its duty as responding only to Rastafarian brethren but also to the needs of a larger community of African people. Our membership consists of Rastafarians and sympathizers who want to see the Rastafarian brethren move forward.

We realize that the struggle for freedom and liberation cannot be the work of the Rastafarian brethren alone. Most of the people you see out there are Rastafarians but because of the conditions prevailing in the Island, most of them are not sure just where they belong. So it is the duty of I and I to rescue them from this dilemma. What the RMA is doing now is to involve the broadest amount of people so that we can evolve an organization to help the black people of Jamaica. That is what we are working for. Over the years if you notice, our government has turned its eye and ears away from the conditions of the Black people whom it represents. Take the celebration of the Independence of Mozambique that you attended the day at Marcus Garvey's Shrine; this should not have been a Rastafarian meeting alone, but the Rastafarians are the only people in Jamaica who speak of Africa. Our government officials speak of Blacks and Africans only when they are outside of Jamaica. So we have the duty to educate our people about their race and their origins here. Not only Rastas, but all the Black people.[10]

The above should offer the reader an insight into the present outlook of some segments of the Rastafarian movement. This RMA official is a man socially and politically alert. A dreadlock, five-foot-ten-inches tall, he possessed a charming but commanding personality. He once worked for the government, during which time he organized his fellow workers into a bargaining unit; so his leadership capabilities were demonstrated long before he became the president of RMA. He was originally a Roman Catholic and had his early education through that church but, at age sixteen, he left the church because, "I decided that I would not worship images anymore." In 1960, while discussing religion with a friend, he was introduced to Haile Selassie. At first he could not be-

lieve that a man could be God; but after reading and studying his Bible he became convinced that his friend was right.
He did not convert until 1965 when, after a trip to the
United States where he experienced some humiliating racial
problems, "the White man did it for me." Returning to
Jamaica, he took up the faith resolved to be Black. At that
time he knew His Majesty only by his pictures, but when
the King visited Jamaica in 1966, "then I realized that he
was the Divine Majesty. Since then I have been doing my
bit."

Sensing the rather liberal interpretation of Rastafarianism
among the RMA officials, my conversation then turned to
the present situation on repatriation. His answer gave me an
insight into the new orientation of a sizable segment of the
movement. He explained:

We realize that Rastafarians over the years have been clamoring for
repatriation and that is the spiritual goal of all Rastafarians. But
now we have come to the understanding that I and I cannot get repatriation under the present condition because we are not liberated. We are now saying therefore that we must gain true liberation
as a people in order to gain true repatriation. Repatriation involves
government-to-government contact; we are not a part of government so we cannot exert ourselves on this matter. When we are
truly liberated in power, then we shall be free to go as we please.[11]

In answer to my question: "Do you envisage a time when
the Jamaican government will be in the hands of Rastafarians?" he said: "We believe that freedom can only come to a
people when the people become a part of the decision-
making process of the government. So I and I have come to
the conclusion that we must become a part of the
decision-making body of the government." This is indeed a
new trend, for since the campaign of 1961, when Sam Brown
entered politics as a member of the movement, politics as
such was not the interest of the cultists. But the present
interest might have been provoked by the astuteness of the
present government, the popularity of which drew the attention of all classes of Jamaicans; even the Rastafarians became political as the following will show.

Speaking of the present government, our speaker had both a positive and a negative assessment:

In the last election Prime Minister X went to Ethiopia and met with the King of Kings and had a conversation with him. He came back to Jamaica and showed the people a Rod, which he said was given to him by the King, Haile Selassie the First, to bring freedom to the Black People of Jamaica. He carried that Rod all around during the campaign. The Rastafarians heard this; the Dreadlocks heard this; and this rod caused him to win a landslide victory for the Party. Well, I and I welcome that, because the former government did nothing for the cause of Africa, Rastas, or no one. As you know, we Rastas do not vote, because you cannot take out a rat and put in a cat, but the Prime Minister came to power talking like a Rastafarian. He started some progressive moves on behalf of the African peoples of this country. But after a while he forgot the Rod; he forgot to talk about Africa; he forgot to talk about the Rastafarians. What we now know, is that if the Prime Minister even wanted to do something good for the African peoples of this country, his lieutenants will not allow him to do it.

After he came back from Ethiopia he called himself Joshua, the one who was to take us to the Promised Land, but the only freedom we have seen up to now is the word "Socialism."

To be honest, he had done better than the other party, for the other Party was so anti-Black that not even Elijah Mohammed could enter Jamaica as a Black man. Today, it is a little better; there is freedom of speech for I and I. As you see, we even got the Marcus Garvey Park to use. Here and there we have seen a little change on the part of the government but not enough to bring the Black masses out of the slums they are in right now.[12]

Much of this leads one to believe that we are dealing with the religio-political segment of the Rastafarian movement. At least eight or nine groups are in association with the RMA. Their aim is to bring mother Africa into Jamaica. They are intelligent, politically sophisticated, socially aware, and, although organizationally weak, they have the making of a strong syndicate. One service rendered by the RMA is to help artists find exposure for their work. It was through some of these artists whose works were on exhibit at the prestigious Gallery of the Institute of Jamaica that I was introduced to the RMA. We shall return to the artistic phase of the movement later.

The Ethiopian National Congress

During my interview with the president of the RMA, the name of the Ethiopian National Congress under Prince Edward Emanuel was brought into the conversation. Speaking of this group, the RMA official paid high respect to its superb organization, its spiritual orientation, and its hesitancy to join the political and economic wing of the organization. Having studied this group in my earlier research and knowing of the destruction of their camp in 1966, it was exciting to learn that they were still in existence and had now become stronger. I decided to travel to St. Thomas to observe them and see what changes had taken place. Locating an X98 bus to Bull Bay, St. Thomas, I settled down for the hour's ride heading east from the city. Fearing I might miss the camp, I inquired of the bus conductor if she had any knowledge of its whereabouts. She assured me that she was well acquainted with the group, which she described as "one of the most congenial groups of Rastas she had ever met."

She then proceeded to give me valuable information about their behavior. "I always find it a pleasure to pick them up at the bus stop where they congregate. They are so well-groomed and pleasant. If any of them boarded the bus and their fares were overlooked, they would come right back to me and pay. They are not like the rest of those rowdies who call themselves Rastafarians." Then eyeing me carefully she asked: "Are you one of the clean-faced Rastas?" I told her that I was not, but she had contributed greatly to my research with her unsolicited testimony of the group. She concluded: "The camp is on your left, far in the hills, sit back and keep cool, for you will be having a long walk." Not long after our conversation, she rang the driver to stop and, pointing to what looked like a citadel on the hill, directed me to Mount Zion.

Armed with a traveling backpack filled with cameras and

tape recorders, I began the slow walk upward. The camp sits on the edge of the mountain two thousand feet above sea level, about two miles in from the main road, with a view of the sea almost indescribable. It occupies seven or eight acres of "captured lands," on which sit a large tabernacle, a small school for Rastafarian youths, a shed for broom making, another for the making of sandals, the living quarters of the prince, and about eight houses for the followers and many others in various stages of completion. The camp is surrounded by a wire fence with entrance through a large gate guarded by a sergeant at arms. To enter the compound, all secular goods and instruments must be left at the gate under the protection of the guard, but in my case, these rules were waived.

Prince Edward's group represents the religious wing of the Rastafarian movement, and in nature and function they are almost monastic had it not been for a few women found among them. The members wear an unusual outfit consisting of a turban, a modified form of the Ethiopian religion, with flowing robes mixed with the colors red, black, and green, and the Rastafarian sandals to round this off. At the head of the hierarchy is the Prince himself, who now claims to be a priest after the order of Melchizedek, and to whom worship is given as one of the triumvirate of the movement over which he rules. The three are Haile Selassie, Marcus Garvey, and the Prince. Very close to him is the lady, who may or may not be his wife, known as the empress who controls the women. Below her are priests, apostles, and prophets. The camp is run like a commune and a court. Members bow in his presence with the verbal greeting "My Lord," while placing the right hand over the heart. The same manner of greeting is given to the invited guests in the camp. Hands are not shaken as is done on the outside. While it is forbidden to smoke cigarettes in the camp, the holy herb is used under ritual conditions. This group follows the dietary and hygienic practices like all the rest.

The activities of the camp are work and worship. Special days are set aside for memorial services honoring the

A door keeper in a hill camp.

Two Rasta officials
who visited Ethiopia.

Emperor and Marcus Garvey. There are special days for fasting and prayers, and the regular Sunday service is attended by
members and followers from the outside. Very strange practices may be seen in this group such as are unknown to the
RMA. For example: sacrifice is a ritual practice, the washing
of the saint's feet, and prayer by prostration. The daily services resemble that of the Pukumina, but with Rastafarian
chants, drumming, and dancing. Services are continuous
from 7:00 A.M. until late at night. During the week members
go out of the camp to sell such wares as brooms, sandals,
ceramics, and knitted crafts.

Prince Edward's group is moving toward a regular church;
and as such is moving away from the militancy found
among the dreadlocks. Although known to cooperate with
the mainstream of Rastafarianism, the Prince showed some
resentment when classed with all Rastafarians. It should be
remembered that he represents one of the oldest of the
groups, having been in operation since the earliest days of
the movement. As a leader, he is strict in morals, and is
probably the only leader who stands out as the sole head of a
group. The reverence shown to him approaches that of a
paramount chief, or a bishop. But he is much less articulate
than the average militant Rastafarian leading spokesperson,
and his age does not allow him to take the strenuous tasks
that he once undertook. All members of the camp may take
unto themselves a woman who must obey the rules set by
the Prince. The rules seem so strict, that on my several
visits only two women were counted as dwellers of the
camp. One small incident on my last visit may throw light
on the strictness of the Prince's rule over Zion.

At the end of my last visit to the Prince, one of his priests
accompanied me to my bus. On reaching the gate of the
compound I saw a princess dressed in the headdress of a
Rasta woman—a beautiful green headdress with the insignia
of the group on the front. She stood outside the gate fully
dressed but made no attempt to enter. This aroused my
curiosity and further down the hill I inquired of the priest
about her identity. Turning to Ras Rupert I asked if she was

a princess of the movement. "Yes," was the reply, "she was a queen, but because of her behavior she was placed under prohibition from entering the camp for an indefinite period." "For what?" I asked. "She was a queen of one of the brothers, but her behavior did not come up to standard. You see when one comes to Zion, one must first put off the outside ways, or else it can create disruption." Further prodding revealed that this queen had the habit of falling in love with several apostles and prophets which created tension in the house of Prince Edward.

The presence of the queen outside the gates dramatically showed the strict discipline of the camp of Prince Edward. One dare not enter that gate without "a clean hand and a pure heart." Her gaze toward the tabernacle on the top of the hill reminded me of the scripture which reads: "I will lift up mine eyes unto the hills; from whence cometh my help." The queen looked lost. On reaching the main road, I said goodbye to Ras Rupert and took one more look at Mount Zion, and promised myself that one of these days, I would return to spend a week with the Prince.

The Rastafarian Impact on Jamaican Culture

For over three hundred years scholars have been documenting the impact of the Africans on New World civilization. This includes music, dance, sculpture, religion, literature, sports, and almost any field that one might investigate. Looking at the United States, the contribution of the Africans is so outstanding in all fields that it is now highly praised rather than denied. The art, literature, and creativity of the Haitian people have long been astounding to the outside world despite the poverty of the island. Countries such as Cuba and Brazil would be barren without the contribution of the African descendants. The Blacks have been freedom fighters, art inspirers, and the creators of folk literature and the very life of these New World cultures. In Jamaica, although we have had our freedom fights and a strong African folk dynamics, very little art and sculpture has emerged out of the grassroot population until the emergence of the Rastafarians. It is true that Jamaican artists have been acclaimed in several countries for their sculpture and ceramics, but most of these artists came from a very minute segment of the elite White and East Indian communities. Very rarely did a Black man emerge from the African roots. The first internationally known sculptor to break into the Jamaican scene was the famous Pukumina leader known by the name of Kapo. His works have had worldwide publicity, all of them produced under religious inspiration.

Only among the Rastafarians did the long suppressed African creativity find wing. Today, all over the island, Rastafarian paintings, sculpture, and ceramics can be bought. From the common folk art sold to the tourists to expensive Rastafarian heads which may sell for as much as five hundred dollars; from the primitive paintings of Ras Dizzy to the superb etchings of Ras Daniel Heartman; from the rough sculpture of Ras Canute who works under the coconut tree in front of the Casa Montego in Montego Bay to the refined pieces in Joe James Gallery in front of the Holiday Inn at Rose Hall, St. James—Rastafarian and Rastafarian inspired art can be found everywhere.

We shall look briefly on the art and poetry of the Rastafarians, allowing the cultists themselves to say what brought about this new expression. Almost all the Rastafarian artists I interviewed convinced me that their work is not merely "art for art's sake," but the medium through which they project their social and spiritual message. When one looks at the works of Ras Daniel Heartman, one cannot fail to see the spiritual message of the Rastafarian movement in such a piece as "Chanting Brethren," in which a dreadlock sings the Ethiopian chant, mouth opened, locks drooping on all sides, beard lying on the chest; or his "Daniel in the Lion's Den" in which a most handsome dreadlock is surrounded by five lions, most vividly executed; and his "Dread Trinity" showing a head of a dreadlock with three noses, three mouths, and three eyes—a modern Picasso.

One of the several Rastafarian artists whose works were

exhibited at the Gallery of the Institute of Jamaica gave me an extended interview from which a general idea of the cult artists' role may be extrapolated. Ras "T" is a bright, young painter-poet. He is educated above the average cult member, and has traveled both in Bahama and the United States. He has read widely in art and literature. In answer to my question: "What kind of art do you do, and what do you seek to express in your work?" he stated:

In terms of style, one of the things that comes into that is materials. As for me anything can express my feelings. I used old boards, glass, cardboards and anything that is around me. I use them to express my feelings. As a Rastafarian in the ghetto, I cannot buy expensive stuffs, that is not possible. So, because of economics, materials will at all times dominate or dictate the idea.

Art to me is the integrator of all mankind. As a Rastafarian , I am a humanist and in art I try to integrate all mankind. Art has the power of liberating man from certain drudgeries and their way of life. A man who was born in the ghetto can't afford to be a Sunday painter, his whole life is involved in getting across his ideas; Rastafarianism, politics, Black culture and all that. Even our meeting here now is an artistic involvement. Some people do art with love here, politics there and so forth; now, to me art is one cosmic consciousness. The way you love, live, and even the way you hate: even your negative expressions connote a certain art-form. So I really do not separate my art from my other sphere of life. Art does not belong in a museum nor is it an investment. Some people buy Picasso because it will sell six months after for a certain price. You are not concerned with Picasso's troubles . . . it is not the spiritual experience in which they are interested. Such people have a cocktail-party-mentality or something like that.

My main theme in art is not only the portrayal of oppression the daily experience of the ghetto-man, but there is also joy. I do not only portray oppression, I try to point a way out. Art is vision, every object you portray can be a symbol of something. . . . From the grain of sand to the great big mountain, there is meaning to be conveyed by them. This is what art is all about. It is vision, it must lead somewhere. It must lead to the enrichment of life.

The religious aspects of one's art is not really bounded by one particular theme. Whatever you do can be religious. One cannot say that this piece of my art is Rastafarian and this is not; all expression can be religious depending on your mood of meditation at the time of its inception. Rastafarian is not a physical image; it is a spiritual concept. So you do not have to draw a facsimile of a Rasta woman or child; the content of your life expresses itself in various ways, even in abstract forms. For example, in one of my paintings you will see forms of people, some visible, others invisible, but they are all there. People are part of the Rastaman's life. As a Rastaman, when I begin a painting especially with human forms, I cannot just draw one person. In the ghetto there is always a crowd. People keep crowding in your consciousness; you have to involve them, because they ask to be involved. As you walk the street, you do not have to see people, you can feel the weight of the people in the ghetto. They are there crowding your consciousness.

The Rasta theme is now a convention. Years ago no one would stoop so low to paint a Rastaman. Today it is the thing. For many it has become a commercial gimmick.[13]

Space will not allow me to continue the Rastafarian philosophy of art from the mouth of Ras "T". The small sample above is just one page from my taped transcript, which would delight the hearts of art critics. What I am trying to show is that, among the Rastafarians, various levels of sophistication live completely hidden from the elite society of Jamaica. The little that has been written about the cultists has been mostly peoples' impressions of them. This is why I want to provide samples of their own thinking.

One of the concerns of Rastafarians today is the commercialization of the cult creativity. As Ras"T" expressed it, "the Rasta theme is now a convention." The wider society has now accepted the creativity of the Rastafarian visions; their sculpture, paintings, and etchings are now seen as highly valuable collector items and some of the prestigious travel magazines in the United States encourage visitors to Jamaica to buy the carving of the Ras Tafari sects. But as Ras "T" puts it: "Rastafarianism is not a matter of hairstyle, it is a spiritual force, it is a rebellion, it is the need to ask questions about a better way of life. It is this message he would like the world to hear; and probably through these carvings and paintings they will. Ras "T" is also disturbed about the art critics of Jamaica, who see art as a mere academic exercise and habitually refer to Rastafarian art as folk art. He sees this as an "infra-dig," representing the same colonial mentality as of old, praising everything done by foreigners, while at the same time degrading indigenous creativity. Commenting on this mentality, Ras "T" concluded with this observation:

Artists are pioneers of the spirit. We younger Rastas must preserve the heritage of yesterday. The Rastaman who was the object of all the derogatory statements and oppression in the past, has now come into his own. We are the ones who must add richness to the Black culture. . . . When I look upon the so-called European civilization which has been forced upon us, and when I look upon the Benin Kingdom of Nigeria, the culture of Dahomey, and see the rich work of art: metals, gold, tapestry; all these things that Black people have contributed to civilization, it is the Europeans who destroy culture. We are shown in our day the works of Beethoven, Mozart, and Van Gogh, but we are never shown the works of Black Africa, Brazil, and other places. So we the Rastas are the pioneers of the Jamaican society; and we are the ones who must open the eyes of the middle-class to our heritage.[14]

These are the words of the Rastas. A people politically, socially, and historically aware of their reason for being.

Ras "T" is not only an artist of the brush, but also one of the budding poets of the movement. Before I left him, he read one of his poems as a contribution to this book. He called this poem, "A Hymn to the Concept of Ras Tafari." The poem is in the style of Edward Brathwaite of the University of the West Indies. Although the poem is long, it is not often that one is privileged to get such a gem in field research. I shall therefore present it in its uncut version.

Rasta is love	Rasta is ends
Rasta is hope	Rasta is water
Rasta is vision	Rasta is geometry
Rasta is good.	Rasta is round.
Rasta is beauty	Rasta is here
Rasta is a river	Rasta is heaven
Rasta is spirit	Rasta is Universe
Rasta is.	Rasta is beginning.

Rasta is I	Rasta is bread
Rasta is light	Rasta is magic
Rasta is joy	Rasta is a child
Rasta is night.	Rasta is blood.
Rasta is coming	Rasta is curve
Rasta is divine	Rasta is humor
Rasta is inside	Rasta is water
Rasta is cuss.	Rasta is Africa.

Rasta is.[15]

Painting and sculpture are not the only talents of the awakening consciousness of the Rastafarians. Their poetry as we have seen is equally well-developed or developing. Diderot once said that poetry wishes for something enormous, barbaric, and wild. Such a thing is present in Jamaica today. The climate for poetry according to Diderot occurs in times of crisis:

It will be after times of disasters and of great misfortunes, when harried peoples begin to breathe. Then imaginations, shaken by terrible spectacles, will depict things unknown by those who did not witness them. Genius is timeless: but the men who carry it within themselves remain benumbed unless extraordinary events heat up the mass and make them appear. Then feelings pile up in the breast, torment it; and those who have a voice, anxious to speak, release it and relieve their minds.[16]

One of these poets whose works we have already quoted is Sam Brown. His images of the slums in "Slum Conditions" are vivid; in it one can hear the sounds and smell the odors. His many hundreds of poems are yet to be printed, but the world will soon be hearing from him. In an interview with this genius, this is how he depicted poetry:

To me poetry is the inner voice of God speaking. When I write poetry it is the appeal of God through my heart. Poetry to me is attunement with the divine. In poetry, I intend to carry a message to the people; not only to the oppressed, but to all people. It is another way of giving verbal expression as a warning against the evils of man as God shows me. I see poetry as a language which all emancipated minds can understand; it is a universal language. I write a

A Rasta sculptor with his work.

Rasta poet reading his work
to the author.

realistic form of poetry. I speak of the condition of the people: In-equity of justice, religious masks, and things like that. I write to re-veal the oppression of man to man by man.[17]

The poetry of the Rastafarians is the message of a people shaken by horrible spectacles of fire, hunger, nakedness, and fear. Benumbed by these extraordinary events which are to this day common experiences, they release their minds in word magic. Prophets of a new day of Jamaican creativity, no more looking outside for redemption, they now focus on the transformation of the society they know best. How success-ful has their impact been on the elite? Though few will admit it in public, the admiration of the Rastafarian's con-tribution is now seen as the cultural renaissance of an island that for centuries had looked to Europe and America for its inspiration. The Black proprietor of one of the most progres-sive art shops in the island, and one who specializes in Ras-tafarian sculpture, can be considered an example of this ad-miration when he states:

For me, I look at the Rastafarians from many different views. One, as an artist myself, the features which they carry are features of dedication, one which makes them peculiarly different from all other Jamaicans around them. This is a religious thing; a desire to create an independency as a nation of people; I should say rather, Black people. In the faces of most of these people there is a feeling of endurance, the feeling of suffering, the feelings of tremendous hope. Now all these things are melted together in a face which de-picts high spirituality. In this type of face, one really cannot make a line which is not saying something. Each lock of hair that falls off the head is significant because he knows it is there. These are the things that make the man what he is. In their creative works they have shown this mainly in iron, pottery, art, and music.

I am not a Rastafarian myself, but I understand the feelings of the Rastafarians. But as an artist, when I try to create those lines in the face of a Rastaman, it is as much a mental traveling to me as it is to the Brethren.

Beginning with the year 1929, which is about the period when their religious and social activities began, they have influenced politics and art, both here and abroad. They have given us to realize that a nation cannot exist with only transplanted elements but that there should be a feeling of "base-source" of existence—some writers called it "a grassroot." Therefore, I must say that the Rastafarians, whether others wish to believe it or not, have created a social pattern which most of us have accepted though we may try to show otherwise. In Jamaica today, Rastaism includes all people, not only the Black man. There are Chinese Rastas, Indian Rastas, and white Rastas which has nothing to do with Hippyism. You see, Rastaism is a thing of the soul.[18]

This kind of testimony can be multiplied a hundred-fold, but this will suffice as a sample of the Rastafarian impact in the creative area of Jamaican culture. We now turn to their impact in the field of music.

Rastafarian Music

Even the nineteenth-century philosopher of racism, Count Joseph De Gobineau, in his *Essays on the Inequality of the Human Races* (1915), acknowledged that "the source of the arts is foreign to the civilizing instincts. It is hidden in the blood of the blacks." And further, "For the Negro, the dance, along with music, is the object of the most irresistible passion."[19] This is, like all racist statements, an exaggeration, yet there is some truth to his observation at least. Music is the "soul" of Blacks. Through music they express their joys, pains, and sufferings. It is mostly through the medium of music that they project a spell or incantation on the objects of oppression. The powerful often kills, even though in the wrong. The powerless sings. This is true of the blues of the American Blacks and has become true of the Jamaica Rastafarians. Rastafarian music emerged in the early days of the movement when Count Ossie introduced his ritual drumming. Rastafarian music reflects the cultists' perception of the society. The downbeat of the drummer symbolizes the death of the oppressive society but it is answered by the *akette* drummers with a ligher upbeat, a resurrection of the society through the power of Ras Tafari. This is not the music of adoration but the music of invocation; it is a call to Africa. This ritual music has withstood all the new creations of the non-Rastafarians, from the Jamaica Ska to the Rocksteady and has remained basically religious.

But, beginning in the late sixties, a new beat—closely patterning the ritualistic music—emerged in the island; since then it has captured the very souls of Jamaicans from slums to suburbs. This beat is known as *reggae*. Professor Rex M. Nettleford, O. M., said of this music:

The sheer hypnotic ritual of the earlier Rastafarian-inspired beat no longer satisfied the need of protest. However, in the late sixties the reggae songs (musically akin to the traditional mento than the contemporary revivalist) went back to the Rastafarian themes while maintaining the *rudie* social comment on poverty and general distress.[20]

The term "rudie" in Professor Nettleford's statement represents a gang-related group of young people who existed at the edge of the Rastafarian movement in the sixties. Many came from middle-class families but were turned off by the society. Most were what in America would be called drop outs. Many of them finally entered the Rastafarian movement. It is out of this group that the new music was to emerge with a strong Rastafarian flavor. If the story is correct, it was one of these "rudies" whom we know as "Toots Hibbert" who wrote "Do the Reggae" about 1968, that brought the name into existence. Today, this famous reggae group known as "Toots and the Maytals" has become internationally famous. Their appearance in New York, Philadelphia, and San Francisco is described by one writer as "a mind-busting experience." But the most popular Rastafarian group to American audiences is the musical high priest of them all, Bob Marley and the Wailers. Bob Marley performs with the typical hairstyle of the dreadlock, giving him and his movement instant publicity. Reggae was first introduced to Americans by Johnny Nash, with the song "Stir It Up" written by Bob Marley, but since then, reggae in its original form has taken over Jamaica and is fast becoming an acceptable beat in England and America, although its future is yet to be established.

The author was privileged to hear a concert by Bob Marley and the Wailers in Philadelphia in April, 1976—an unforgettable experience. The concert took place in one of the mainline suburban theaters, in a middle-class community, consequently not well publicized in the Black community. The audience consisted of mostly White middle-class college youths and professors from departments of anthropology, sociology, and music of nearby colleges and universities. The Blacks, who composed a sixth of the crowd, appeared to be Jamaican with a sprinkling of Afro-Americans.

On reaching the theater a large crowd was rushing to the first show. By 8:30 P.M. it was standing room only in the three-thousand-seat theater. Enthusiasm mounted as the pre-show preparations concluded. The lights blinked and the MC approached the audience who, by this time, was on cloud nine. Marijuana smoke floated everywhere. In a clear voice the MC announced: "Ladies and Gentlemen, straight from Trench Town, Jamaica, I present to you Bob Marley and the Wailers." A spasm of frenzied joy greeted Bob Marley as he jumped, spun, and shook his dreadlocks in front of the audience. With raised hands, in true Rastafarian style, he psyched the audience with his familiar yell, "Yeah!" The audience responded, "Yeah!" Then, reverently, he positioned himself in front of the drum and with bowed head and drooping locks, invoked the god of Rastafarianism, "Jah." This ritual invocation by Bob Marley was a solemn Nyabingi chant depicting a traditional Rastafarian meeting. The music in this ritual performance was slow and included such lyrics as:

> I'll wipe my weary eyes,
> I'll wipe my weary eyes,
> Dry up you' tears to meet Ras Tafari,
> Dry up you' tears and come.

The tempo built with the Jamaican favorite: "I'll Fly Away," and concluded with the chant "One Lord, and One God, in Mount Zion." With this invocation, dramatic displays of flags were projected over the entertainers: first the Ethiopian flag, and a second flag with the Lion of Judah, followed by a picture of Haile Selassie. The chants ceased and Bob Marley moved in a ritual dance toward his guitar; the audience seemed uncertain about the meaning of the performance. They knew the music was not reggae, yet, they were totally hypnotized. A pause, and suddenly guitar in hand, Bob Marley faced the audience and the reggae beats floated out in driving polyrhythms, as the third flag appeared with a view of Marcus Garvey. It was clear that the audience had come to hear these rhythmic beats and for the next hour and a half they remained completely under the spell of the Trench Town "sorrow songs" and the bouncing beats. The first songs were new releases, but soon Marley was in the American favorites such as: "Forget Your Troubles and Dance," "I Shot the Sheriff," "No 'oman No Cry," "Lively Up Yourself," and "Belly Full, But We Hungry." After a session that seemed only minutes long, Bob Marley bowed and disappeared, the audience standing and roaring for more. The clapping continued for seven minutes; The Wailers reappeared with Bob Marley to render two encores: "Rasta Vibrations" and "Stand Up For Your Rights." The audience stood with hands raised while many did the reggae in the aisle. On leaving the theater, an equally large crowd waited patiently for the second show in lines two and one-half blocks long, five rows deep.

To me the evening's experience was a delight and a revelation! A revelation which many Jamaicans may never appreciate. Never since the time of Marcus Garvey has any Jamaican personality so excited an American audience with a revolutionary message as this Rastafarian band. The exciting fact is that out of Trench Town, a district seldom visited by Jamaican elites, has come a new voice with a unique message in songs, inspiring the hearts of American youths, Black and White, and a new musical sound, full of mystery and dissonance, disturbingly Jamaican. History may yet prove my statement correct that, the spiritual ethos of Rastafarianism which produced reggae may be the most exciting thing to come out of Jamaica for many years to come.

Reggae music is often characterized as a "slow-driving throbbing rhythm that just won't quit." Others describe it as "heart-music, natural, free, with no inhibition." Bob Marley calls it "earth-feeling music." Although reggae is a new beat, pleasing to the ear, hypnotic, and relaxing, it is only one part of the reggae phenomenon. To fully appreciate the force of reggae one must listen to the songs of which it is a part. Most of these songs are caustic social comments, they speak of "the hungry man who is an angry man"; they speak of the crying women, of sorrows, troubles, weakness, and sickness; they also speak of police brutality, jails, and freedom. Jamaican heroes such as Marcus Garvey, Sam Sharpe, and the old Maroon heroes are also honored in them, and last but not least, they sing praises to Ras Tafari and of ganja, the "holy herb." The music of Rastafarians is not only an artistic creation in the Jamaican society, but an expression of deep-seated social rage. Rastafarian music should soon be the subject of those capable of writing about it; this author is not so endowed. We shall now turn to other subjects which will round out the picture of the Rastafarians today.

The Rastafarian and the Wider World

We have seen how the Rastafarian movement has become well known to people all over the world. Some literature is written on them, their arts and crafts have been taken to several parts of the world by tourists as exotica (and in recent time even a race horse in New Jersey has become known in the daily double as Ras Tafari). Two of their singings groups have now made their debut in America, England, and other parts of the Caribbean. In the Island of Dominica, there is a group called the "Dreads" copying the hairstyle and food habits of the Rastafarians, many of them are reported to believe in the divinity of Haile Selassie. But the most paradoxical element in the story of the Rastafarians is that the movement has extended itself from Jamaica and is now to be found in England and the United States. As early as March 24, 1966, a column in the *Daily Gleaner*, bearing the name of "The Advocate," reported that a group of Rastafarians had formed a new political party in England, with headquarters on a West London street, as a political expression of the Rastafarian movement in Jamaica. The name of this party was the "People's Democratic Movement." Since 1966, very little has been heard from this group or the other Rastafarians in England for that matter. But we have inside reports that a large segment of the movement now resides in the British Isles.

If little can be said of the Rastafarians in England, much can be said of the cultists in America, especially in New York City. According to police estimates, as many as fifteen thousand Rastafarians are in New York City, primarily in Brooklyn and the Bronx; this number is rather debatable. They also estimated that fights between the two Rastafarian groups from these boroughs have taken the lives of from twelve to twenty cultists and other Jamaicans since 1974. The Rastafarian reputation in New York is not praiseworthy. Large headlines have appeared in the New York papers like the following: "Three Cultists Seized on Gun Raps," "Rastafarian Link Seen in Shootout," "Two Dead in Cult War." All these appeared in the *New York Post* in the years 1974–75. The major causes of the "war" have been tied to the selling of ganja. The name of Jamaica has received such bad publicity as a result of this gang activity that Jamaica's consul general found it necessary to give an explanation of the movement on the Columbia Broadcasting Station, in which he defended the good name of Jamaica and that of the "true Rastafarians."[21]

But who are these New York Rastafarians? The police reported that many of these dreadlocks were illegal immigrants; others are believed to be political exiles from the island. They also reported that many of them after committing criminal acts in New York fled to Toronto or Montreal, Canada. Through field research the author was informed that many of the so-called dreadlocks in New York and other cities in America are children of Jamaican parentage some of whom are native-born Americans; the rest migrated to the United States from the island. Many of these youths know very little about the doctrines of Rastafarianism but, having been rejected in American society, without jobs and roots, have adapted the hairstyle of the cultists and are generally under the leaderhsip of someone who might have been marginally Rastafarian before coming to the States. All the trappings of the movement are simulated by them; they conduct Nyabingi in homes, follow the hygienic laws of the cult, and smoke the herb when it is available. It also appeared that leading ganja exporters in Jamaica have been supplying the cultists with the weed—through middlemen—finding it a lucrative market. It is therefore quite possible that the control of the market may have been the cause for the gang warfare. Although every effort was made during my New York research to get a proper picture of the situation, few people were bold enough to talk. New York Rastas will probably soon settle down to more creative tasks. What we have seen up to now is a part of the growth processes.

To get a broader picture of the New York Rastafarians, I explored the matter among the Jamaican cultists. I shall refrain from using the names of my informants and shall use only spurious initials. One of the New York Rastafarians, Ras "X," had this to say:

As for the youths in America whom they say are Rastafarians lots of the youth may be genuine believers but the majority are people who claim to be Rastafarians and are not. These are the people who give Rastafarians a bad name. There are many who were sent to the United States in "mothball" by party officials to hide away until the time when election should come. They will then be sent for to do work for the politicians and then disappear again to the States. They are instructed to use the mannerisms and hairstyles of the Rastafarians that they may blend more readily in the community on their return. But if they were true Rastafarians they could not be used that way. Lots of these youths in the United States firing guns are political refugees, sent to the States by party bigwigs. The man who is a true Rastafarian does not condone violence, robbery, murder, rape, stealings, and things like that. The situation in the United States needs clarification from people who know the movement. And I believe the sooner this is done the better it will be to set the mind of the world at ease.

The Rastaman keen at his base knows as a fact that he came from Africa and wants to return there eventually. So a true Rastaman would not want to sojourn in the United States. We see only Africa as our home.[22]

And from Ras "Y:"

Jamaicans are always migrating. Many of the youths born in Jamaica are now in the United States. Some children born to Rastafarian parents are also in the United States. Some of these children after entering the United States decided to identify themselves with their homeland and the only thing really Jamaican they could remember was Rastafarianism. These youths may also have been strengthened by Garveyism which is still strong in New York; Rastafarians in Jamaica have never really opened any dialogue with the American and Canadian groups, but we know of their existence.[23]

Evidence leads us to inconclusive conclusions. The American and Canadian Rastafarians are Jamaicans, who, before leaving Jamaica, might or might not have been members of the cult. But, in that the cult has no official lists of membership, some might have been true Rastafarians, who if we are to believe the pronouncements of the leading brethren do not go in for criminality. Some might be children of Rastafarian parentage who, after reaching a foreign land, decided to identify with the religion of their parents. Others are pseudo-Rastafarians, who might be in America as middlemen and political refugees. This author has met with only a few Rastafarians in the United States and those few seem to be real brethren who, like their Jamaican counterparts, are sincere adherents to the movement. In every religion there are many counterfeits; the good will have to live with the not so good. The pseudo-Rastafarians have created many anxious moments for the Jamaican community in New York but this is also true in Jamaica.

The Ethiopian Orthodox Church

Elements of the teachings of the Ethiopian Orthodox church seemed to have been in Jamaica soon after the emergence of the Rastafarians in 1930. In 1965, the author was introduced to a small group of brethren on the Spanish Town Road at that point known as "Four Miles" where a small church bearing the name "Ethiopian Coptic Church" was in operation. It now appears that a group of the Rastafarians had desired the establishment of the church in Jamaica quite early in their development. This desire was highlighted in one of the ten recommendations of the University Report to the Government in the following words: "The Ethiopian Orthodox Coptic church should be invited to establish a branch in West Kingston." Quite possibly because of this recommendation, the Ethiopian Orthodox church appeared in Jamaica in 1969. Since then, the church has gained a foothold among the members of the Rastafarian cult, and is now moving toward becoming an incorporated body in the church structure of Jamaica. The new religious development is of great interest to students of Rastafarianism for many reasons. First, the Ethiopian Orthodox church, though a minor branch of Christianity, is one of the most ancient and historic. It falls not in the rank of Protestant denominations but with the Catholic, Eastern Orthodox, and older churches including the Coptic and Syriac churches. Second, the introduction of the Ethiopian Orthodox church to the Rastafarians, and the possible conversion of this cult to one of the most ancient branches of the Christian church, could be a development church historians would find most important.

A short analysis of this development is necessary in a book on the Rastafarians and will probably be only the first such discussion of a new development that will be written about for many years. First, a short history of the Ethiopian Orthodox church, its teachings, literature, liturgy, and hierarchy; then the response to the church as the Rastafarians themselves have seen its appearance in Jamaica.

The history of the Ethiopian Orthodox church[24] is shrouded in legends based on Ethiopian oral traditions. In most books on church history this branch of Christianity is often referred to as the Ethiopian Coptic church but, to the modern-day Ethiopian, this is incorrect. The word "Coptic" is the Greek and Arabic word for Egypt and although the Ethiopian church was governed by the Egyptian Coptic church as late as 1950, the two churches are organically and doctrinally different bodies. The name Abyssinian church would be more correct, but the name Ethiopian Orthodox church is now the acceptable name.

Legend traces the founding of the church back co the Apostles, especially to Matthew and Bartholomew who were supposed to have been missionaries to Axum. Some attribute the founding of the church to the Ethiopian Eunuch of Acts of the Apostles, Chapter 9. Others attribute it to Jews who heard the new teaching of Peter on the Day of Pentecost, when Ethiopian Jews visiting Jerusalem became converts to Christianity and returned as missionaries to Ethiopia. But the historically approved date of Christianity in Ethiopia is set at A.D. 330, the date when two Syriac Christians (Aedesius and Frumentius) escaped from a shipwreck off the coast of the Red Sea and were brought to the emperor's court. Their acceptance at court also introduced Christianity to the ruling dynasty. The missionary work of these two men was so successful that Frumentius was later ordained by Athanasius, the Patriarch of Alexandria, as the first bishop of Ethiopia. He took the name Abuna Salama (our father of peace), and from that time Christianity was to become the dominant religion of Ethiopia.

Prior to Christianity, Ethiopia, like other parts of Africa, had its own traditional religions which still remain a strong expression of many of its people. A strong Isis cult remained common to both Egypt and Ethiopia. There seemed also to have been a strong Jewish cultic tradition based on pre-Talmudic Judaism in which governor-high-priests like the Melchizedek of Genesis 14 ruled over the people. These were called *Mukaribs*. After these priests there appeared kings

known as Malkanas, who later took the name *negashi*—
which meant treasurers and collectors; later this name became *Negus Negast*, which is translated today as King of
Kings. This title is said to have appeared in the second century A.D. All these earlier religious expressions were poured
into the Christian mold, making Ethiopian Christianity a
unique mixture of old and new, continuing from the fourth
century A.D. to the present.

Ethiopian Christianity represents that branch of the
church that parted company with Western Christianity and
the Eastern Orthodox church over the interpretation of the
nature of Jesus Christ. The Eastern and Western church hold
that Jesus was both human and divine. That is, he had two
natures. The Coptic church and the Ethiopian church believe Jesus had only a divine nature. The division came
about at the Fourth General Council of Christendom, held
in Chalcedon in A.D. 451. The theology of this branch of the
church has been called Monophysitism, or the believers in
one nature. This argument is so involved that it is best to
leave the subject at this point. All I intend to show is how
ancient this branch of the church is. After the break of the
Ethiopian Orthodox church with the Western, in the fifth
century, it experienced a period of decline caused by the rise
of Islam in the seventh century A.D. The Ethiopian Orthodox
church was not to be heard from again until the thirteenth
century.

In the thirteenth century the name "Prester John," legendary priest-king of Ethiopia, reached Europe. This king (who
was supposed to be White, governing a Black nation) was
considered an important contact in Africa in Christianity's
war against Islam which at that time was considered menac-
ing to the faith. This legend among other things sparked
what is known as "the Age of Discovery." Inspired by the
tale, Portuguese explorers and missionaries entered Ethiopia
in the early decades of the fifteenth century and a new phase
of Ethiopian Christianity began. But European Christianity
was ill suited to Ethiopia; after about a hundred years of controversy over the person of Christ, European Christianity

was thrown out and the Ethiopian Orthodox church again asserted its domination. From 1632, to the present, the church has had ups and downs but has remained uniquely Ethiopian. Until the year 1950, the head of the church, the Abuna, was an appointee of the Egyptian Coptic church but, since then, the head of the church has been Ethiopian. In 1955, the Ethiopian Orthodox church joined the World Council of Churches and turned its emphasis to world mission.

As mentioned, the Ethiopian Orthodox church accepts only the creeds of the first three General Councils of Christiandom—the Nicene Creed of 325, that of Constantinople of 381, and that of Ephesus of 431. Unlike the Western Orthodox church, the Ethiopian Orthodox church does not believe in original sin or purgatory. It accepts the Seven Sacraments called the "mysteries"—Baptism, Confirmation, the Eucharist, Penance, Holy Unction, Holy Matrimony, and Ordination. Of these seven, the two most elaborately performed are Baptism and the Eucharist. The Eucharist is accompanied with singing, drums, bells, rattles, cymbals, and dancing. The dance of the priests in the communion is said to be unique in the Christian church.

The Bible of the Ethiopian Orthodox church has created quite a stir in recent years. It contains eighty-one books: the thirty books of the Hebrew Bible and the twenty-nine canonical books of the Christian New Testament; and numerous noncanonical books which are found in their complete form only in the Ethiopian Bible, such as the Book of Enoch and the Book of Jubilee. These are preserved in Ge'ez, the holy language of Ethiopia, said to be a Semitic tongue very closely related to Hebrew. Among the literature of the Ethiopian Orthodox church is the *Kebre Negast* (Glory of the Kings), which traced the ruling dynasty of Ethiopia to the marriage between King Solomon and the Queen of Sheba. The tradition states that from this marriage was born Menelik son of Solomon (Ben-Melek), who was king of Ethiopia after 900 B.C., and that the erstwhile Haile Selassie represented an unbroken line of rulers from that time until now. It is this tradition that allows the king to take on all the great titles, King of Kings, Conquering Lion of Judah, and so on. Other important literature of Ethiopia governs almost every custom of the country, from legal decisions to Sabbath worship, dietary laws, and the training of monks. It is commonly believed that no other nation on earth has so firm a foundation in Holy Scriptures as does Ethiopia.

The liturgy of the Ethiopian Orthodox church is exemplified by its beautiful pageantry of songs, music, dancing, and symbolism, enlivened with resplendent robes, vestments, and other ritual accessories. One unique accessory is the praying stick called Makutaria, used to support the priests in the long liturgy and for the special ceremonial dance. As we have seen, many of the rituals resemble those of the Hebrew religion. One of the temple's accessories is said to be the Ark of the Covenant in which tradition holds that the original Ten Commandments handed to Moses are kept. Ethiopian tradition says that this was taken to Ethiopia by Menelik the son of Solomon, along with Levites who adapted some of the Hebrew liturgy in the church. The great churches of Ethiopia even contain a section known as the Holy of Holies in which the Ark is kept.

At the head of the Ethiopian Orthodox church is the Abuna, sometimes known as the Patriarch. His official residence is Addis Ababa; he anoints all bishops and members of the clergy and anoints and crowns the king. The clergy include archbishops, bishops, priests, archdeacons, and deacons. There are also monks, abbotts, and various other church functionaries too involved for our purpose. Above all there is the King of Kings, who must give his approval to all high offices.

Although this church has branches in New York and in Trinidad, its meaning to the Black world has not been clearly assessed. Its appearance in Jamaica is of great interest to the Black world. Few New World Blacks have had any knowledge of the church, so it is with great interest that many scholars await the outcome of this new mission among Blacks in the West.

The Rastafarians and the Ethiopian Orthodox Church

Our intention is not to write a history of the Ethiopian Orthodox church in Jamaica, but merely to give some impressions of the impact of this new church activity among the
Rastafarians. Less than ten years ago the mission was established; consequently, it has just begun to settle in on its
work. Since its appearance in 1968, it has not found a permanent place for a church although plans are on the way to
build a temple. At the moment its program is being carried
out in rented facilities in West Kingston.

The appearance of the church in Jamaica was welcomed
by the Rastafarians, by other African nationalist groups, and
by the government authorities who invited them.
Thousands of Rastafarians flocked to the initial ceremonies
of the church and many sought membership from the start.
But it was not long before most Rastafarians recognized that
the Ethiopian Orthodox church was not what they perceived
it to be. Many of the more religious groups sought affiliation
and with some minor changes in their religious views were
accepted. But the majority of the locksmen and others of the
militant variety have not found the church to their liking.
First of all, the church was more Christian than they had expected it to be. Second, the leadership were not locksmen
and the central tenets of the church has nothing to say about
the divinity of Haile Selassie. These and other matters have
greatly disturbed the true Rastafarians who, although deeply
interested in the African church established with the blessings of the King of Kings, find it to be a very puzzling affair.

In the following quotations, samples of this deep ambivalence among the brethren appear. The names of the speakers
will be withheld for prudent reasons. One of the leading Rastafarian brethren had this to say about the church:

The Church has been here for a short period of time and I am in
favour of it but I am not yet a member. I am not opposed to the
Church but I do not approach things of this sort until I am sure it is
the thing for me. I help and encourage other Black people to join an
African Church, but the administration of the Church does not suit

the ideals of I. Nevertheless I told the brethren that the Church is important and that we must go into it in order to get hold of the administration of it. There is a whole lot of Rasta brethren now in the Church and it was because of the great amount of the brethren who desired membership why the Church came here. Some of them have been baptized, but as you know the E.O.C. baptize in water, and the Baptism that I and I desire is that of blood not water.[25]

From another leading brother:

From the beginning the tenets of the Rastafarians were based on religion. Religion was a dominant part of it. In these days the movement has taken on a threefold aspect. That is economico- politico- and religious. But as to the inception of the Ethiopian Or- thodox Church in this country, that is another thing. I do not think it will greatly enhance the movement.

The coming of the E.O.C. to Jamaica in my view does not really aid the achievements of our goal in an easier manner. We do not see our fight as one that is enhanced by religious means. The Church in itself as far as I see, will be of help to those yet benighted of an Afri- can opinion, but it is of negligible worth to the struggle we have now—that is, the rights of man in Jamaica. In some respect I see the Church as something to soothe the minds of men; something that blunts the militant will of the people. So, I am not a church per- son.[26]

And yet another:

The Rastafarian movement in Jamaica is a very heterogenous group and as such it is hard to centralize the organization; that is why the E.O.C. came to Jamaica. But I am not going to conform with this kind of religion. Peoples' minds must be free. The E.O.C. is stag- nated and I do not believe that a real Rasta will cope with the church. The movement has a better chance of conforming with something identifiably its own. Many have joined it because it is an African Church, but I do not believe that in the long run it will be successful.[27]

These were taken from my research in the city of King- ston. To get a broader picture I traveled to Montego Bay to see what that group of brethren thought about the church. My first interview was with one Ras "B," who operated a mul-

ticolored stall where Rastafarian wares are sold at a brisk
bargain. After some talk, we turned to the church. Ras "B"
sees little meaning in the church. He sees it dividing the
brethren. He observed that many "dreadlocks and Comb-
somes" have joined the church, more of the latter than the
former. He believed that many brethren joined the church
because of a lack of knowledge. He continued:

Anyone coming from Ethiopia to form a Church in Jamaica is a
convincing person among the brethren. So when the Ethiopian Orthodox Church entered Jamaica in 1968, it immediately drew
members of the Rastafarian movement and other Black Nationalist
organizations. The visit of the Abuna of Ethiopia made a great impression on the Rastas, and since then the Church has had a mild
success. There are now about 6000 members all over the island. A
temple is to be built in Kingston, the land is acquired and a building
fund is underway.[28]

Having interviewed members of the Rastafarian movement who are non-members of the Ethiopian Orthodox
church, I next sought out some of the members who had for
some time been members of the Ethiopian Orthodox church
to get their reaction. One specifically recommended was reluctant to speak and would do so only off the record, but I
later wrote down notes on the interview. The other, a
woman, gave her impressions quite freely and at some length.
The man, Ras, has mixed feelings about the new church. He
explained:

I joined the Ethiopian Orthodox because its "fi wi church." [In English, this would be translated, "I joined the Church because it is a
black Church."] We had a bishop but we drove him out, this man
cut his hair and his wife straightened hers. This was too much and
we "blow him about." This was too much for us Rastas. We Rastas
now control the Church, and as soon as we get a man in the administration we will make it our Church. Up to now things are not to
our liking but "we a gwan bad." When the priest talk nonsense
contrary to our doctrine we raise *rass* in the Church and stop him.
The man is not a Rasta, so we can't have him as our preacher. One
day the Brethren asked if he believed in Jah Rastafari, and he could
not give a definite answer. We can't have that.[29]

The above conversation recorded in dialect is rich in Jamaicanisms, and I decided to retain it in the original especially for Jamaican readers.

My last informant is a well known Rastafarian woman known for her Rastafarian handicrafts. In her opinion the church is a good thing for the Rasta movement. This female opinion is important because, for years, the women of the movement have remained in the background of this male organization.[30] She enjoyed the Sunday services of the church, its Amharic language classes on the weekdays, and the social get-together of the women. Most members were Rastafarians trying to understand the church. Some were dreadlocks finding it hard to do away with their hair. Some have complied with the church; others have not. Although a member of the E.O.C., she still attends Nyabingi services and smokes a little of the herb now and then, but not as before. She, like other Rasta women, believes in the superiority of man and abhors birth control. It is her opinion that the church in time will win most of the moderate Rastafarians but that many of the dreadlocks will avoid the strict rule of the E.O.C.

Reactions to the church are mixed. Hundreds of the Rastas have joined the E.O.C. because it is uniquely Ethiopian. Many expected to join the church have avoided it because of its Christian features. Those who have become members are looking to the day when the church will be in the hands of Rastafarian leadership, an event which is quite possible when one remembers the fissionary tendency of Jamaican church life. On the other hand, many leading Rastafarians may become members of the church in order to learn some of its rituals with the intention of adapting them in their segment of the movement. This is already beginning. The praying stick has already been adapted by most Rastafarians and is now used in their Nyabingi services. The Ethiopian National Congress has adapted the ritual robes of the E.O.C., and many rituals such as bowing low to the ground to the prince have been introduced in their services. What seems certain is that a strong syncretism of Rastafarianism and Ethiopianism is about to take place.

7

Where Go the Rastafarians?

We have shown that the Rastafarian movement is the most recent expression of that large class of Jamaican society which historically resists domination in a society where power at the apex is enjoyed by the few well-born, perpetuated and maintained by this small elite at the expense and sufferings of the masses. We have also seen that resistance by the powerless mass of African descent most often took on a messianic-millenarian overtone, deeply religious in nature, with victory rooted in the hope that the power of the supernatural would overcome might with moral right. The religious roots always form outside of the institutional churches in the island whether it be the Black Baptists with their African syncretism or the mythic identification with ancient Ethiopia.

Our study of the Rastafarians took us through their emerging stage, which we alluded to as the stage of revitalization; people under stress deliberately organizing themselves in a movement to construct a more satisfying alternative to oppressive conditions. Generally, this first stage of the movement may take on the spirit of flight referred to as millenarianism; or it may offer aggressive resistance to the society under charismatic leadership in which case the movement is called messianic. The Rastafarians exhibit examples of both. This dual nature of the Rastafarian movement is seen in our analysis entitled "ambivalent routinization." We further saw that socioreligious movements such as the Rastafarians develop momentum as they begin to routinize within the society. Aspects of this are discussed under rituals, symbols, and other cultural dynamics, all of which often prove fruitful as social catalysts for the emergence of new identity and cultural creativity.

Under normal circumstances, the writing of a book such as this would end in a summary or conclusion, but just as this research came to an end, a new chapter of the Rastafarian movement was opened with the death of Haile Selassie, the God-figure of the movement. At this point this new chapter, "Where Go the Rastafarians?" arose in my mind. In light of this new development we must now look at the effect of the death of Haile Selassie on the movement, paying particular attention to the words of the leaders themselves, and seeking to place the movement in perspective by comparing it with similar events in other movements. We shall close the chapter with some predictions based on the movement's strength and the *real-politik* of the Jamaican society at present.

The Death of the Deity

When news of the political upheavals in Ethiopia was made known to the outside world, very few people imagined that it would eventually lead to the dethronement of Haile Selassie, one of the most revered monarchs in history. But developments were so swift and the implications so grave that the outside world could do nothing but gaze with astonishment. Very few Western nations knew of the internal politics of this fabled land. The spiritual aura surrounding the King of Kings gave the impression that everything was well in "the land of the gods," but this was not so. The wind of change had now caught up with Ethiopia and the end of Haile Selassie's reign. Throughout these developments, the Rastafarians remained undisturbed. To them the king stood above politics and whatever was being written in the Western press was nothing but dangerous propaganda. It was my privilege to interview a few of the leading brethren on their opinion of the incidents leading to his dethronement just three weeks before the death of Haile Selassie. This is how Ras "B" saw it:

Rastafarians have seen the overthrow of many kings and heads of states since I was born. Many who have been overthrown have either been assassinated, exiled, or things like that. In the case of Haile Selassie, we have seen no such thing. What we do believe are the things told us by people coming out of the land, and we have been assured that his removal is only an internal constitutional change within the Ethiopian government. What the Zionist presses throughout the world have told us concerning the King still leaves the Rastafarians unshaken in our beliefs in the King's divinity and the imminent return. The Rastas are not in the habit of believing the press. Nothing that takes place in Ethiopia politically affects our beliefs. Our beliefs in the divinity and invincibility of the King are ones that are unshakable.[1]

Here is the attitude of a true believer. He is not confused with so-called facts, his belief is his truth. The King is invincible and anything that suggests the contrary must be disbelieved. Faith so expressed needs no proof. The following statement by Ras "D" is even more enlightening about the faith of the brethren in their King. To my question: "What is your assessment of the present situation in Ethiopia?" he replied:

What I and I have read in the so-called Press does not satisfy us. I and I realize that a situation exists in Ethiopia. The soldiers and students were asking for certain things and His Majesty had agreed that these things should be given. The armed forces got militant and carried out some reforms. But we say that these reforms were carried out with the consent of His Majesty and we have concluded that what is taking place is the cleaning up of Zion. Zion must be clean. Certain of the hierarchy surrounding His Majesty have been dishonest and the armed forces have gotten rid of them. I and I in Jamaica do not see that it is our concern to go into the internal politics of Ethiopia. Right now his Majesty is free. He is free to travel

Rastafarians returning from a visit to Ethiopia, 1963.

and to perform his duty. If he leaves the throne he is still King of Kings and Lord of Lords for us. As soon as his mandates are carried out, the soldiers will re-instate him.[2]

My next question was: "Would his death cause any problems in the movement?" or "Would it be similar to that of the leader of the Black Muslims?" Ras "D" replied:

Well, Elijah Mohammad was only a Messenger of God. Haile Selassie is the Almighty God. If death should come into the picture, we would have to return to the Bible to clarify that. Death does not figure among the Rastafarians. God is a God of the living, not of the dead. So we do not think about death. Even so, take Christ, when the Messiah first revealed himself in the person of Christ, he said at his departure that he would come again. He did not die, he gave himself. Should this happen again, the second return would be like the first. We do not know now, but the time will come when this will be revealed. It is only a Rastafarian who can understand this. One must seek first the kingdom of His Majesty before one can understand these things.[3]

A careful reading of this quotation will show that the Rastafarians have a rather explicit theological foundation for the movement. The speaker was quick to distinguish between the role of Elijah Mohammad and that of Haile Selassie. Elijah Mohammad was a Messenger of God; Haile Selassie was the Almighty God. And influenced by the Christian doctrine of Christ being God revealed, he associates Haile Selassie with the messiahship of Jesus as contained in the Gospel of St. Mark. Haile Selassie, then, is the returned messiah whose nature is revealed only to true Rastafarians. Death does not figure in Rastafarian theology, so the death of the King would only be a transformation from the temporal body.

The idea of a revelation was brought out in the answer of Ras "T" when he said:

As to the so-called dethronement, I and I who believe firmly, Ras Tafari is still our divine Imperial Majesty. His so-called removal is only a temporary thing, he is still our spiritual head and God and King of Earth. To some who are not grounded, it is a great shaking up; but it has not caused any deflection. If anything, it has caused deep reflection and even a deeper replenishing of our faith. We see this as a part of the prophecy of the Bible which speaks of great tribulation in heaven. The Bible says that there will be a time when the King will be persecuted for many things and will be called names and things like that. His experience in Ethiopia is just one experience of the problems that Rastafarians will pass through. This, however, is merely temporal. The spiritual side is enriched as a result of this. It has been a healing process. Since the King came here in 1966, we Rastafarians have been looking for a revelation.[4]

The most dramatic revelation has been the death of the King in August of 1975. His death caused many to seek out the Rastafarians for some words of wisdom about their future. But to the surprise of many, the Rastafarians, true to their doctrine about death, did not show any emotional response. To them, the King had not died, he had only moved away from the temporal scene in order to carry out his work as God and King in the spiritual realm. As spirit, he will be much more accessible to his followers both in Ethiopia and in Jamaica. One needs only to call his name and enter into his spiritual vibrations to feel his power.

Students of religious movements should find this nothing new. Of the many deaths of religious founders one comes vividly to mind—the well known leader Father Divine whose missions in the United States, Germany, and Australia have been written on, and whose enterprises were believed by many to have been dependent solely upon the charisma of the founder. Many thought his movement would suddenly fall apart at his death, but this has not come to pass. In every one of his multimillion-dollar enterprises his presence is acknowledged. The present author, who has visited the Father Divine headquarters yearly since 1953, can find no evidence for the imminent demise of this movement. In their services and banquets, the empty chair of Father Divine represents his living presence among his followers. He is addressed as if alive and members testify to their continued communication with him.

The death of founders does not severely affect religious movements; it often deepens the faith of the followers as the last quotation implies. In the case of Rastafarians, Haile Selassie is not seen as a founder; he has only a religious connection with the movement. He is only a God-figure to the members who see him as a mythical ancestor of the Black race and this only because Haile Selassie occupied the throne of Ethiopia, which really is at the heart of the movement. Ethiopianism, then, meant more than Haile Selassie. The King, his throne, and the land, have a combined ontological concept in Rastafarianism; the King played but one part. The concept of the King played only a unifying function in the development of the movement, a collective self-discovery device for that segment of the society from which the movement evolved. The real force of the movement is the concept of Ethiopianism, Haile Selassie being only a part of the Godhead.

The Herb Is the Thing

If it is agreed that the God-figure Haile Selassie may not be the most dominant force in the movement's ideology, what then is the real center? The real center of the movement's religiosity is the revelatory dimensions brought about by the impact of the "holy herb." Under this influence the person of Haile Selassie is transformed into that supernatural reality or a cosmic significance befitting a racial redeemer. To the Rastafarians the average Jamaican is so brainwashed by colonialism that his entire system is programmed in the wrong way. He is thus unable to perceive of himself as a Black man; his response to the world is conditioned by unseen forces due to European acculturation. To rid his mind of these psychic forces his head must be "loosened up," something done only through the use of the herb. The herb enables one to see one's true self. A true revelation of Black consciousness brings about the proper love for the Black race; it rids the mind of social and psychological "hang ups" by altering one's state of consciousness, revealing the true nature of the world to the inner consciousness. This done, one's true identity can be experienced, including the revelation that Haile Selassie is God and that Ethiopia is the home of the Blacks.

According to the Rastafarians, the structure of Jamaican society is inhuman and cannot provide the psychic nutrients demanded by the Blacks who originated in the satisfying cultures of Africa. They see Jamaica as death oriented; redeeming values for human life are absent; success in the society is defined largely in terms of having money and a certain standard of living. To them the work roles which yield this money and standard of living are spiritually demeaning and unsatisfying; so, rather than strive for this kind of upward mobility, they have opted for the simple life. This poverty, however, is voluntary, free from the pressures and dictates of a dying culture. By withdrawing from the acquisitive society into a counterculture, they believe that they will be able to redefine themselves and restructure their values with new norms and goals.

The herb is the key to new understanding of the self, the universe, and God. It is the vehicle to cosmic consciousness; it introduces one to levels of reality not ordinarily perceived by the non-Rastafarians, and it develops a certain sense of fusion with all living beings. According to a leading Rastafarian:

Man basically is God but this insight can come to man only with the use of the herb. When you use the herb, you experience yourself as God. With the use of the herb you can exist in this dismal state of reality that now exists in Jamaica. You cannot change man, but you can change yourself by the use of the herb. When you are God you deal or relate to people like a God. In this way you let your light shine, and when each of us lets his light shine we are creating a God-like culture and this is the cosmic unity that we try to achieve in the Rastafarian community.[5]

The Rastafarian movement is presently alive and well. The movement has not been visibly affected by the death of their deity. If anything, his death strengthened the group, for the real source of the movement's vitality is not in a belief but in an experience brought about by a liberating ideology. The hallucinogenic state caused by the herb reinforces this.

The sacramental use of the herb has the similar effect of the spirit-filled consciousness of Christianity; it is the vehicle to the spiritual world, the revealer of hidden things, and the comforter in times of distress. Through this energizer of life great feats are accomplished. The totality of the Rastafarian experience, as they themselves report it, seems sufficient to establish the movement's existence as a religious alternative for its followers. The future of the movement can only be predicted with caution.

Assessing the Future

Predictions about the shape of a socioreligious movement like the Rastafarians are risky matters, but other movements of this kind provide some guidelines. Caution must revolve around the fact that no two cultures are alike. Thus observable models developed in the United States may be inapplicable to Jamaica. And too, movements' behaviors are erratic to such an extent that most of their declared objectives may change almost overnight, thus making one's predictions useless. A case in point is the radical change in the Black Muslims' attitude toward Whites. One of their strongest rules was that no Whites could visit their temples, all Whites being devils. Recently this doctrine was changed without warning.[6] We are, however, sure that most movements of this type undergo change when reasons for their emergence no longer exist. Thus, the strength of revitalization movements is directly proportional to the stress experienced in the society. When the stress no longer exists, the movement may either fade away or it may organize itself into a benign organization merely celebrating those values it once represented. Many church organizations of our day fall into this category.

Jamaican society is now undergoing dramatic social changes, many indirectly brought about by the challenge of the Rastafarians to the plastic lifestyle that once existed. The resistance to these changes is adamant. Should the forces for change be successful and a "steady state" come

into being where all its citizens are seen as equally meaningful to the future of the island, then the repressed energies
that go into movements of resistance will be set loose in
creative channels for the good of the whole; only then will
movements such as the Rastafarians have outlived their use-
fulness. But, as this "steady state" seems to be a utopian
dream not likely to appear anywhere on earth, we envisage
that four basic developments will eventually take place in
the Rastafarian movement. First, a unique Rastafarian
church is likely to emerge as one of the sects of the island;
second, an equally large body of what Professor Rex M.
Nettleford calls "functional Rastafarians"[7] will continue on
the island, secularizing the movement further from its
strongly religious orientation; third, a large body of Rastafarians will opt for the Ethiopian Orthodox church as a syncretistic religious body; and fourth, the movement could become the vanguard of resistance should the socioeconomic
situation in Jamaica be reversed.

The Rastafarian Church

We have already seen the church which now exists in St.
Thomas under the leadership of Prince Emanuel Edward.
This group may provide an example of what a uniquely Rastafarian church may be. Separatist in nature, communal in
its associations, nonmilitant, repatriationist, it devotes itself almost totally to religious activities. Its high priest
functions only sacerdotally and is perceived as God. The
members are readily identifiable from other Rastafarians in
dress, mannerisms, and occupations. Over against Rastafarians who are amorphously structured, this group is responsible to a strong religious leader who demands discipline and
accountability to the membership. They maintain a tabernacle specifically for worship in which some of the rituals of
the Ethiopian Orthodox church are adopted, with blood sacrifice and all. Despite this syncretism, the main tenets of the
Rastafarians are observed: drumming, dancing, and the
smoking of the herb are all part of the church; however,

their hairstyle is covered at all times by a turban, rather than displaying their "locks." The church has within it a hierarchy of men called priests, apostles, and prophets, suggesting the possibility that this organization will soon see the need to establish branches in other parts of the island.

The Functional Rastafarians

A careful observation of the Rastafarian movement suggests that this category will always remain the largest in number. Included in this group will be the large body of "dreadlocks" who represent the most radical element of the movement. Many will be the uneducated, the unemployed, and the unemployable, but proud sons of the soil. Represented are the self-employed farmers, craftsmen, fishermen, and those who just like the unencumbered life. Also prominent will be those converts to the drug culture, with no real religious conviction, but who are mere followers of a segment of people who see liberty as their goal. A large segment of these will be escapees from the law using the anonymity of the Rastafarian as a disguise.

Also incorporated in this large group are the dynamic youths who will still find themselves unwanted in the Jamaican society. At present many youths in the Rastafarian movement represent that growing body of young people who cannot get an education even though they desire it largely due to an insufficient number of schools on the island. Recent figures estimate this group at eighty thousand. These youths have no recourse but to gravitate to functional Rastafarianism. Among the functional Rastafarians we shall include the clean-face Jamaicans, those who share the whole value system of the movement but are integrated into the "straight" world to provide for their families. Most are men and women in their thirties; some highly trained university and secondary school individuals whose social acceptance allows them to articulate the Rastafarian ideology with the possibility of being heard and believed. Secret Rastafarians capable of social mobility will remain the apologists for the movement, insuring the force of its ideology for many years to come.

Sculptors, painters, poets, and musicians will also serve as functional Rastas who will carry on the theme of African identity which should continue to be a major emphasis in Jamaica from now on. I can even imagine a development in which a school of Rastafarian art might evolve similar to the ethnic art forms of Africa and Haiti. An African example would be Sneufu, Baule, or Dogon art. All these patterns are well known to art experts and are identifiable on sight. The functional Rastafarian artists will realize that their art form is a new creation with a specific societal role to play. One can easily foresee Rastafarian art moving from its now primitive period to the classical, through modern and stylistic developments. Some creative personalities will emerge such as restauranteurs specializing in I-tal foods similar to the kosher foods of other religions. At present there are Rasta medicine men in Montego Bay who sell medicine in which the herb is a major ingredient, which is presumed to be good for certain ailments—a point which the author will not debate. This could well be a trend toward meaningful uses of the herb when laws against it are lifted. All this suggests that the contribution of the Rastafarian movement in Jamaica is still in its infancy.

A New Syncretism

Presently a large number of the Rastafarians are members of the Ethiopian Orthodox church, and many new recruits are in a state of great ambivalence. Looking into the near future it would not be difficult to predict that, if the membership of the church becomes predominantly Rastafarians, they will eventually reject the Christian element of this denomination and institute the Rastafarian doctrine alongside those rituals of the church believed to be basically African. Already some Orthodox rituals are adapted in most Rastafarian communities. Such syncretism is not new to Jamaican religious movements.

This process of ritual adaptation began in Jamaica as early as the late eighteenth century when the Black Baptist church entered Jamaica and grafted itself onto Kumina. Later, it evolved into present-day Pukumina and the Native Baptist church of which Bedford was one of its best known leaders. All Revival churches in Jamaica are syncretisms of African and Christian rituals. In present-day Africa this kind of syncretism has yielded six thousand new movements since the last research was done.[8] Most missionary churches in Africa are now seeking ways to make the church more relevant to an African religious expression. One of the setbacks in Jamaican institutionalized religion has been their rejection of the drum, which represents all things African. Most denominations represented in Jamaica are also in Africa, but while the African branches of the church are moving toward an incorporation of the African ethos, the Jamaican churches remain plastically colonial. It would be a great mistake, then, for the Ethiopian Orthodox church to copy the attitudes of these churches for the outcome would be unfortunate.

Counterculture movement such as the Rastafarians do not easily submit to any organization whose attitudes remind them of aspects against which they have developed psychic resistance. Any cues of the oppressive society are like waving the proverbial red cloth in front of a bull. Traditional missionizing psychology needs special refinements in dealing with a movement that has developed for itself alternative modes of religious expression more suitable to their status in life. This has already been achieved by the Rastafarians; whatever else they accept should be aimed at enriching their experiences, broadening their visions, and building upon foundations already laid. This then will be a syncretism, not a conversion. Anything less than this approach will be a fission. What the Rastafarians need at the moment is an organization that can provide for them a

framework in which they can feel at home; should this vision be grasped by the new denomination, it could be an instant success.

The Rastafarian phenomenon is merely an infant. Many
more books will be written on them in the future. From
humble, despised beginnings they have emerged with a new
and vital message to the Jamaican society. They have proved
themselves to be a vital socioreligious movement for necessary change, which has been heeded by the larger society.
Although the implementation of some of their social visions
has yet to be accomplished, Jamaica is moving toward a
more equitable society. For the first time in the island's history there is a conscious attempt to grapple with the problems of the dispossessed mass in such things as land reform,
education, housing, medical care, and equitable justice.

Jamaica is presently a leader of the Third World ideology
advocating that those who have had the privilege of amass-
ing great wealth at the expense of the poor must now see
that a portion of this wealth is utilized in lifting the economic levels of the "have nots"—the alternative of which
will certainly bring on a social Armageddon. It is useless to
state that this kind of philosophy is unpopular to the
privileged class. Most of the present struggles in Jamaica revolve around this radical sociopolitical philosophy which
was declared by the present government. There is no question in the author's mind that the present trend to a more
equitable society is an ambiguous adventure, filled with
many risks and pitfalls, but then all social change will
initially involve disagreeable situations. But with steady,
resolute, and imaginative leadership, backed up with the
enlightened self-interest of those who have for generations
enjoyed the "fruits of the land," there could emerge in
Jamaica a society never before attained.

Social movements such as the Rastafarians are signs of
deep social commotion, a stirring among people, an unrest, a
collective attempt to reach a visualized goal, and a change in
social institutions; neglected, they can become volcanic. An

attempt to remedy these conditions is the responsibility of imaginative leadership which can be overlooked only at the peril of the wider society.

A Movement of Resistance

In Chapter 2 we observed that one of the causes of revolutionary movement resistance is the frustration of high expectations. This frustration may come about in several ways; first among these may be the ambiguous language of desperate politicians—the multi-vocality of whose language, though reassuring to the traditionally privileged, may dangerously threaten the high expectations of the oppressed. If a society such as Jamaica is to move toward equitable democracy, it must speak a single language, a language of love and hope, a language that gives assurance to the weak and hopeless. Any leader perceived to cater to the privileged class, ignoring the poor as a whole, may expect to see a deterioration of movements such as the Rastafarians into pockets of resistance. The ambitious politician, whose sole aim is power, may be blind to his image reflected in the eyes of the poor. Jamaican society today cannot afford the luxury of political ambivalence; the high expectation vested in national independence is fast dying out. Many of the sociopolitical and economic conditions before independence persist. The symbols of wealth and affluence are still in the hands of those who had them before independence, and color and class preferences remain glaringly obvious. Present trends toward equity of opportunities need the support of the enlightened elite if a catastrophe is to be avoided. The Rastafarian movement with its unorganized militancy could be fertile ground for guerrilla resistance, solidifying deep-seated emotional resentment.

A second ingredient for the frustration of high expectation may come from outside pressures. Covert intelligence activities often carried out by the developed nations seek to maintain the status quo of developing nations. This misreading of the internal Zeitgeist of developing nations often plunges a small country into social and economic turmoil. The shortsightedness of the developed nations, insensitive to the hopes and aspirations of Third World peoples, cause them to back the party or politicians who support foreign exploitation at the expense of the future. Such leaders are strawmen whose future is generally short-lived. The Rastafarians are highly aware of this possibility of foreign infiltration. My experience at the Nyabingi service referred to in Chapter 4 proves without a doubt that the movement is well aware of the dangers of outside pressures such as those against Cuba, Mozambique, and Angola. Any such pressures in Jamaica can expect resistance of a high intensity by the Rastafarians, meaning serious setbacks for social and economic advancement.

Any party or politician choosing to be the instrument of foreign pressures may for a short while receive the accolade of foreign multinational corporations and other agents of the status quo, but the social and economic problems that brought about the emergence of the Rastafarian movement will remain. Nothing short of political despotism could offset the terrorism of a civil war. Examples of this kind of frustration may now be seen in Ireland, Lebanon, Argentina, and Africa. Outside pressure and chaos are often brought to the Third World by withdrawing viable industries from operating in a country when levels of profits decline. Behavior of this type has only punitive intent and results only in upheaval. In present-day Jamaica, a potentially frustrating situation is growing—it bodes further ills.

The message and visions of movements like the Rastafarians often point the way to new patterns of society. Though often unheeded, new movements generally have clear visions of where society should be going. The constant cry of Rastafarians is for land on which to live and work; as one of their leaders put it "lands on which to pitch the tents of Jacob." Any social scholar will agree that new movements possess a dynamic which, if given the right channeling, can create possibilities beyond expectations. This can be documented among the members of the Black Muslims of

America whose motto—"do for self"—has changed the psychology of Black communities in America. They have attempted to develop grassroots industries in the cities and rural areas, staffed by their members, giving incentives to Blacks to exert themselves for their own good. Today, the movement operates a multimillion-dollar industry. Other examples are numerous the world over where socioeconomic development has been generated by new religious movements without outside help. If there is one thing that the Rastafarians have taught Jamaica, it is that one must accept what one has and seek to make the best of it. No one can do for Jamaicans except Jamaicans. The messianic-millenarian syndrome is deeply rooted in the Jamaican psyche. Throughout the island's history, there has ever been a looking to the outside for the redeemer and for the "cargo," which would bring about miracles and plenty. This philosophy can bring only disenchantment. Messianism and millenarianism are useful only to a society as instruments of revitalization toward self-fulfillment.

The Rastafarians have passed through the rhetorical stage of their movement; they have shown what a revitalization movement can do; their examples must be capitalized on for the good of all. They have rejected stagnation in a country where the zest for life and creativity had grown placid; their examples should now be promoted by making them models for the masses. The good book tells us that "where there is no vision the people perish." This is especially true of building a nation. The future growth of the Rastafarians into a well-respected cult may in the long run mean more to Jamaican history as a people than all the multinational corporations in the world. Their farms would mean much to the hungry; their art would bring much revenue to the economy; their music would lift the drabness that now exists in all parts of the island.

Worth mentioning is the fact that the Rastafarian movement is more capable of dealing with the neurotics, the maladjusted, the unbalanced, and the psychotic personalities than any government institution. Anyone who has done research among them cannot be but amazed at the Rastafarians' sensitivities to these types. The excitement they bring to life, their uninhibited way of expressing themselves, their capacity to absorb deviant behavior, and their love for their kind make them one of the most therapeutic communities to be found in Jamaica. The same thing can be said of the Black Muslims of America where a large number of their followers were either prisoners or societal misfits. Once they became members of the Muslim faith, a rapid recovery took place. This is not to equate the Muslim movement with the Rastafarians, for these two movements are rather different in teaching and techniques. But, movement dynamics of this type should be channeled and not blocked. Vision is needed to champion causes of this kind; they call for enlightened leadership.

Not only should there be a conscious effort to place the Rastafarians on land on which to build permanent communes, but there should be an effort to preserve the Rastafarian heritage. There should be a Rastafarian museum to preserve their artifacts, their sculpture, paintings, music, and other items for future generations of Rastafarians, other Jamaicans, and foreigners who will all get a feel for one of the most creative periods of our history. Portraits of Ras Heartman and others should now be preserved. Portraits of the great Rastafarian musicians should be made and exhibited before they pass off the scene. One of the important things about a nation is its pride in its creative people—not only the lawyers and politicians, but the radicals, the saints, and the infidels. The history of American cowboys and gangsters is preserved in museums all over the United States and fed to generations as folk heroes through movies and television. This is the folk tradition of the nation. It is encouraging to note here that examples of the above vision are already taking place under the creativity of Professor Rex M. Nettleford, who recently choreographed Rastafarian dance and music in the Jamaican National Dance Theater.

A constant statement made by the Rastafarians is, "This is fi wi country," or "This is our country." This statement reveals a lot to the Jamaican researcher. Most of the author's colleagues who have migrated from Jamaica left the island because they were unable to feel at home. Many of the elite Jamaicans now living in the island would rather be somewhere else. It is somewhat surprising that the Rastafarians who emerged with the strong desire to repatriate to Africa now echo the contradictory statement, "this is fi wi country." This contradiction is felt by all Jamaicans who are abroad. The love for Jamaica can never be erased but, despite the deep longing for our country, there is that ever-present contradiction that deters us from wholly casting our lot to reside there. The land we love has never been ours, because we have never been accepted fully as citizens. Like split personalities we have sought a home outside our home, seeking but never finding. The Rastafarians are showing us the way. The way is reflected in their sculpture and expressed in their songs. For the first time, Black faces are being appreciated and not lampooned in cartoons by foreigners, projected in all their sorrows, aspirations, and dignity. For the first time Jamaican people, aspirations, and protests are being expressed in songs—not songs of caricature but experiences of sorrows.

Where go the Rastafarians? No one can tell for sure, but one thing can be said: they have brought us a long way toward understanding ourselves and our possibilities. Great social developments are not always made in the halls of parliament or in the citadels of learning. These institutions merely react to the dreams of the creative mass. Some of the most creative trends in nations' development are born in the dreams of the visionaries, the radicals, the seers, and the charismatic prophets. This is the cunning of history. It may yet be true that the heretics of today will be the saints of tomorrow.

Appendix

A Selection of Rastafarian Poetry

Poetry is one way in which the Rastafarians have been able to convey their messages to the wider world. The earliest poets used themes dominated by the Back-to-Africa ethos. In these poems, their hero, Marcus Garvey received a prominent place. Following this, reggae songs appeared. This musical phase, although retaining elements of the messianic-millenarian theme, began to focus more on the conditions experienced by the Rastafarians in Jamaica. Along with this new sorrow-songs type, a poetry also developed around African liberation themes. In the following selections we shall deal only with those of the first and third types. Much of the Rastafarian songs are now on records, the printing of which would demand clearance from record companies. These printed here were gathered in field research and are not yet under copyright laws. Many of these would have been lost to us in a very short while. Some date back to 1968, while others are only of very recent date.

A Rhyme for the Times

The following poem appeared in the *Daily Gleaner* of August 4, 1960, in a column written by Thomas Wright under the caption "Candidly Yours" and summed up the feelings of the public to the findings and recommendations of the research team of the University College of the West Indies, on the possible repatriation of the Rastafarians to Ethiopia at government's expense.

Three cheers for the U.C.W.I.
For asking Mr. Manley why
He does not send the Ras Tafari
On an African Safari

While we are out to save the nation
By such pat repatriation
Why not get our Marxists pushed off
To the land of Mr. Krushchev?

Why not send us all back home?
Send all Catholics to Rome
Ship our Scots back to their heather
English back to rainy weather

Send our breadfruit back to Fiji
Welshmen back to Llanfair P.G.
Why twist the tail of Judah's lion
When all our Jews could go to Zion?

Mangoes, Indians should not stay
Send them all back to Bombay
Finns to Finland, Swedes to Sweden
Grantley Adams back to Eden!

Send the Irish to Tralee
Germans back to Germany
Economists home to L.S.E.
For spiritual homeward bound are we.

Send every single person back
To Syria, China, Cayman Brac
And should we population lack
Go out and find some Arawak

So, free of speech and free from fright
Peace comes at last to Mona Heights
When Lewis, Augier and Smith
Have not a soul to argue with!

The Lion of Judah Hath Prevailed

Worship idols, worship Buddah
Worship Romans fail
But we claim the Lion of Judah
Because he hath prevailed

You read not of his speeches
You hear not of his tales
But true inspiration teaches
Judah's Lion hath prevailed

A smoking flax shall he not quench
But bring forth judgment unto truth
He lay himself on David's bench
And call upon the youth

Through the schemes of evil nations
His words we seldom hail
But who can conquer revelation
When the Lion hath prevailed?

His love for man is widely spread
Can we forever fail?
To know for us his blood was shed
But now he has prevailed

But lack we may of more to know
Still we are satisfied
Because we now have seen the glow
Of Haile Selassie I

We care not who denounce him
We care not who agree
But now we have accepted him
The vine of David's tree

How could the seven seals be broken
To depart us from travail
Now that Zion's King has spoken
We know he has prevailed.

—*Author unknown*

Repatriation an Unfinished Business

Repatriation not migration
Set the people free
It is known to every nation
Each vine to his fig tree

Repatriation not migration
A difference you will see
One stands for all the people's freedom
The other not for me.

Repatriation not migration
Then shall captives free
From savage and oppressive rule
To justice and equality

Repatriation not migration
It is for us to see
Three hundred years of hard oppression
Was read in history

Repatriation not migration
Our homes we long to see
Now comes the end of tribulations
As told in prophecy

Repatriation not migration
United we must stand
To claim our promised portion
With true determination

Repatriation not migration
All aliens now must flee
We know the truth of revelation
What is to be must be.

REPATRIATION: YES!
MIGRATION: NO!

—*Author unknown*

1961 Turn Upside Down Remains 1961

1961 turn upside down remains 1961
This proves Marcus Garvey was not wrong
Of the black man's redemption he spoke
From underneath colonial yoke.

1961 turn upside down remains 1961
Let us strike oppression down
No more shall we be pushed around
Underneath colonial crown.

1961 turn upside down remains 1961
United we must stand
And pray for God to guide us on
To that Promised Land

AFRICA FOR AFRICANS—THOSE AT HOME AND
    THOSE ABROAD.
AFRICA: YES! JAMAICA: NO!

*   *   *   *

Never let the new flag fall
For we love it the best of all
We are out on the march for Africa
The flag we raise is the Red, Gold and Green.
Join our ranks to fight the foe
Raise a standard for the race!
Selassie is a leader bold
Never let the new flag fall.

OUR HANDS AND HEARTS MUST BE CLEAN
TO RALLY WITH THE RED, GOLD AND GREEN.

Reformation Truth

There's a mighty reformation
Sweeping o'er the land
God is gathering His people
By his mighty Hand
For the cloudy days descended

And morning sun now shines
Yes! The reformation truth must stand.

Chorus:

It's the Ethiopian story
The mighty Church now takes its stand
Spreading righteousness forever
In its truth we all must stand.

Zion walls again are building
As in the days of old
All the clashing of opinion
And its strife will cease
For we all will be united
As the saints are joined in one
And the will of God in all be done.

Surely Negus has come back
To take his people home
He shall rule in righteousness
As His word go forth
We shall stand in one opinion
To defend this Holy Church
For the reformation truth must stand.

*   *   *

Emperor Haile Selassie I
Who sits on David's throne
He's King of Kings and Lord of Lords
He comes to Claim his own

Chorus:

Thou mighty King of Kings, Thou Tree of Life
Thou Father of the free
Thou Elohim Jehovah Jah
We stand secure in thee.

Stand up with might ye *Rasses* all
In righteousness arrayed
Put on your Robe and face the foe
With courage and with right.

Archangel Gabriel gave the sound
Ethiopia must be free
Arabia Desert Ranger said
They all shall bow their knee

As Babylon lift up his eyes
To spoil the Saints of God
Selassie stand up on his feet
To give them their reward.

*   *   *

Rule Ethiopia

Rule on! O gallant Ethiopia, rule!
Millions of foes around thee press;
But, ere the ruthless fiends find their tools
Will reach that wished-for-spot, that blissful, hallowed rest!

Rule on! for thou alone must lift
The weight from off the shoulders of thy sons, who drift—
The rafters that thy daughters clung to, in their plight
Must be abandoned for the sacred ark of Right!

Rule on in triumph, tho' the foe
Oppress us, as we onward go
Singing the song, "Ethiopia Rules the Waves."
We've vowed that Ethiopia no more shall be slaves.

And whilst thou rulest, let they children, far and wide
Thro' the medium of our MARCUS be gathered to thy side;
For the tri-colors that shall win us back the land we love so well
Must be the RED, the BLACK, the GREEN, our loyal hearts to swell.

Three ringing cheers for Garvey—God bless Jamaica's son:
Hurrah for Ethiopia, whose joys are but begun!
Ten thousand joybells peal aloud the song NEW NEGROES sing
Ring out the old, ring in the New, and ring, ring, ring.

—Iris Lucille Patterson

Dem Call Dem

The following poem written by Ras Gill Tucker is in Jamaican dialect and is a satire on the Jamaican political system of what the author calls "the hide-and-seek political games played on the Jamaican masses by the politicians." The various metaphors used in the poem represent various politicians, and they are so called by the masses, "Dem Call Dem" may be translated, "They Call Them." This poem is edited for the non-Jamaican reader.

Dem call dem political bull frog
Dem call dem shadow and brine
Dem call dem teethless lovers
Dem call dem white skin in black mask
Dem call dem lion in monkey clothes
Dem call dem footstep without foot
Dem call dem promise and empty promise
Dem call demselves what others no call dem
Dem call dem paper tigers
Dem call dem bonehead dunces in the Queens court
Dem call dem soft-face idlers hiding behind big desks
Dem call demselves the peoples' saviours
Dem ride upon dem back and ride upon dem head
Dem call demselves God-fooling and God-fearing
Yet-dem die without vision
Dem die without us—
Dem 'trive 'pon we children hunger
Dem get drunk 'pon we homeless and our fondest hope
Dem call demselves democratics dying in lies
Dem gwane living and dying in a wi nakedness
Dem white God wi' bless dem for dem works
And dem empty words and empty promise spread before wi empty
    table
    Dem call dem.

Abortion

O terrible sin abortion! It is the worst of all
Eight letters spell the deadly sin, so is downfall

The wickedness of murderess destroy the yet unborn
They never gave the seed a chance to see creation's Morn.

There are many who defend such acts based on economy
Heartless creatures—if they had been aborted—they'd be
    non-entities
It is said man should multiply, he should replenish earth
Yet in the eyes of wicked men, the unborn is of no worth.

It is given to man to use all things, yet life is God's control
If God had aborted First Man, there wouldn't be a living soul
Some shades of people take hormones, they try to live forever
Yet for the other shades of men, destruction is their endeavor

The earth create with broad expanse that men should be prolific
But the crude acts of the seeming wise, prove men's minds are sick
When the enemies are at thy gates, thine offsprings are arrows in
    thy bows
With thy large united house, the enemies are laid low

Some people love their people, they control food not birth
From the born to the yet unborn each has a place on earth
So it is for all to shun such acts that man may live his days
Dread repercussion shall be their lot for persistence in evil ways.

—By permission Sam Brown

Notes

Preface

1. Bob Marley, "Them Belly Full (But We Hungry)," *Natty Dread* (Nassau, Bahamas: Island Records, Inc., 1974).

2. Leonard E. Barrett, *Soul-Force: African Heritage in Afro-American Religion* (New York: Doubleday Co., 1974). For an up-to-date review of research done on the Rastafarians and articles written by Rastafarians, see J. V. Owens, "Literature on the Rastafari: 1955–1974. A Review," *Savacou*, ed. Edward Brathwaite (Kingston: Caribbean Artists Movement, 1975).

Chapter 1

1. This belief is held only by the older brethren. The younger group is now focusing on liberation within Jamaica.

2. The movement does not have membership statistics, as is true of all such movements.

3. See interview with Sam Brown noted below.

4. These figures are modifications of the *Annual Abstract of Statistics*, no. 24, table 8 (Kingston: Department of Statistics, 1965).

5. Ibid., p. 49.

6. Frederick G. Cassidy, *Jamaica Talk: Three Hundred Years of the English Language in Jamaica* (London: Macmillan Co., Ltd., 1961).

7. Ibid.

8. Ibid.

9. Madeline Kerr, *Personality and Conflict in Jamaica* (London: Collins Publishers, 1963), pp. 74–84.

10. These figures represent the development in Jamaica up to 1960, and were taken from *Facts on Jamaica*, no. 1 (Kingston: Government Printing Co., 1960), p. 2. The number of children now in all schools would be three times these figures.

11. This figure is taken from my research notes as given to me in interviews with the assistant registrar in 1975.

12. *Facts on Jamaica*, 1965. These figures are still basically accurate.

13. Notes taken from interviews in the Department of Economics, University of the West Indies.

14. This figure is only an estimate based on the author's interviews with leading economists.

15. Transcribed from a taped interview in the summer of 1975. Used here by permission of Ras Brown.

16. Martha Beckwith, *Black Roadways: A Study of Jamaican Folklife* (Chapel Hill: University of South Carolina, 1929).

17. See text of prime minister's speech in "Local Government Reports," *Jamaican Weekly Gleaner*, North American Edition, September 16, 1975, pp. 6, 7, 12, 29.

18. Ibid.

19. Barrett, *Soul-Force*, pp. 68–71.

20. Ibid., pp. 19–20.

21. George Eaton Simpson, "Religious Cults of the Caribbean: Trinidad, Jamaica, and Haiti," *Institute of Caribbean Studies*, no. 7 (Rio Piedras: University of Puerto Rico, 1970), pp. 11–112.

22. Migene Gonzalez-Wippler, *Santeria: African Magic in Latin America* (New York: Doubleday Co., 1975). One of the most recent books on Cuban native religions.

23. Herbert G. DeLisser, *Twentieth Century Jamaica* (Kingston: n.p., 1913), p. 73.

24. Barrett, *Soul-Force*, pp. 61–72.

25. J. H. Buchner, *The Moravians in Jamaica* (London: Oxford University Press, 1885), p. 121.

26. R. C. Dallas, *The History of the Maroons* (London: Oxford University Press, 1803). This is a rare book on the beliefs of the early Jamaican rebel slaves called the Maroons. Dallas is the only one to mention this belief. See p. 93.

27. Thomas Coke, *A History of the West Indies, Containing Natural, Civil, and Ecclesiastical History of the Island with an Account of the Missions . . . etc.*, 3 vols. (London: Clarendon Press, 1810). This work is by far the most elaborate history of the nonconformist mission in British West Indies. Highly biased toward Methodism and English rule. See the chapters on Jamaica in all three volumes.

28. "Religion in Jamaica," *Jamaica Information Service,* Fact Sheet no. 7 (Kingston: n.p., n.d.), p. 1.

29. Ibid.

30. Coke, *History of the West Indies,* pp. 15–16.

31. William J. Gardner, *A History of Jamaica . . . etc.* (London: Clarendon Press, 1873), p. 464.

32. P. D. Curtin, *Two Jamaicas: The Role of Ideas in a Tropical Colony* (Cambridge: Harvard University Press, 1955), p. 68.

Chapter 2

1. Examples of Jamaican slavery can be gleaned from books written by eyewitnesses. Among these are J. M. Phillippo, *Jamaica: Its Past and Present State* (London, 1843), by a Baptist minister who went out to Jamaica in 1823 and worked in the island for twenty-five years; and Henry Bleby, *Death Struggles of Slavery, . . . In a British Colony During the Two Years Immediately Preceeding Negro Emancipation* (London: Dewar's Limited Edition, Florida, 1973), by a Methodist minister from England who worked in the island for seventeen years. Both were eyewitnesses to the Samuel Sharpe Rebellion. The author has relied heavily on Bleby's account of the rebellion. Two books of more serious scholarship are Lowell Joseph Ragatz, *The Fall of the Planter Class in the British Caribbean, 1763–1833: A Study in Social and Economic History* (New York: Octagon Books, Inc., 1963); and Edward Brathwaite, *The Development of Creole Society in Jamaica, 1770–1820* (London: Oxford University Press, 1971).

2. Kenneth M. Stampp, *The Peculiar Institution: Slavery in Ante-Bellum South* (New York: Vintage Books, 1956), p. 146. Quotes Frederick Douglass, *My Bondage,* pp. 250–51.

3. For a study of Maroon communities in the New World, see *Maroon Societies,* ed. Richard Price (New York: Doubleday Co., Anchor Books, 1973). Also Roger Bastide, *African Civilizations in*

the New World (New York: Harper Torchbooks, 1971). For a study on Jamaican Maroons, see R. D. Dallas, *The History of the Maroons,* vol. 1 (London: Clarendon Press, 1803). A recent edition of *The History of the Maroons* has been published by Frank Cass & Co., Ltd., London, 1968. Edward lived in Jamaica for some time during the nineteenth century and had access to much of his materials. But the men who were true eyewitnesses to Maroon life were Bryan Edwards and Edward Long. See Edward's materials in *The History, Civil and Commercial of the British Colonies in the West Indies,* 2 vols. (London: J. Stockdale, Co., 1793), and 3 vols., 1801. In addition, see Edward Long's *History of Jamaica* (London: n.p., 1774).

4. Dallas, *History of the Maroons.*

5. Long, *History of Jamaica,* p. 340.

6. Ibid.

7. Dallas, *History of the Maroons,* p. 33 (Frank Cass edition).

8. Ibid., pp. 66–77. Dallas reported that "Under their chief quao [sic] they [the Windward Maroons] had desolated the Parish of St. George's and committed every excess in the course of their depredation."

9. Ibid., p. 120.

10. Ibid., p. 41.

11. J. Stewart, *A View of the Past and Present State of the Island of Jamaica* (Edinburgh: Oliver and Boyd, 1823), pp. 316–18.

12. The articles of the peace treaty between the British and the Maroons are taken from Dallas, *History of Maroons,* pp. 58–65. There were two treaties; one with the Trelawny Maroons which I here produce, and the other with the Windward Maroons. Except for three minor differences, they were identical in content.

13. For a short survey of this incident, see Carey Johnson, *The Fighting Maroons of Jamaica* (Jamaica: William Collins and Sangster, 1969), ch. 12. A more extensive treatment can be found in Thomas Coke, *Ecclesiastical History,* vol. II.

14. Ragatz, *Fall of the Planter Class,* p. vii.

15. Among the leading defenders of slavery in Jamaica were Edward Long and Bryan Edwards. Of the two, Long was the most virulent denouncer of the African character. To him the Negro was a beast. See also, Winthrop Jordan, *White over Black* (Baltimore: Penguin Books, Inc., 1969); on the chain of being, p. 228; Negro life, p. 249; Negro poetry, p. 285; Negroes' place in nature, pp. 491–93. His ideas influenced American White attitudes greatly.

16. I will be using the shortened term Sam, a name used more often in Jamaica.

17. Bleby, *Death Struggles.*

18. Ibid., p. 126.

19. Ibid., p. 127.

20. Ibid.

21. Ibid.

22. Ibid.

23. Ibid., p. 128. My emphasis.

24. Robert C. Tucker, "The Theory of Charismatic Leadership," *Daedalus: Journal of the American Academy of Arts and Sciences* (Summer, 1968), p. 747.

25. David Aberle. For a further discussion of this theory, see William A. Lessa and Evon Z. Vogt, *Reader in Comparative Religion: An Anthropological Approach,* 3rd ed. (New York: Harper and Row, 1972), pp. 527–31.

26. Bleby, *Death Struggles,* p. 6.

27. The Reverend William Knibbs was a Baptist minister and missionary of the London Baptist Association. He was a contemporary of Bleby and was later to become one of the greatest champions of abolition in Jamaica.

28. Bleby, *Death Struggles,* p. 8.

29. Ibid.

30. Some Jamaican scholars see Sam Sharpe as the forerunner of such men as Gandhi and Martin Luther King, Jr. Such men are always ahead of their times. Such a theory was improbable during slavery.

31. Bleby, *Death Struggles,* p. 7.

32. Ibid., p. 8.

33. For a further discussion of the origin and development of the Jamaican militia, see Edward Brathwaite, *The Development of Creole Society in Jamaica from 1770–1820* (London: Oxford University Press, 1971), *Death Struggles,* ch. 3.

34. Bleby, *Death Struggles,* p. 11.

35. Ibid., p. 29.

36. Ibid., p. 33.

37. Ibid.

38. Ibid., p. 130.

39. Ibid.

40. The Native Baptist church, sometimes called the Black Baptists, was founded by George Liele (sometimes referred to as George

Sharpe), in 1784. He was an American slave who fled to Jamaica with Colonel Kirkland, a loyalist, during the American war of independence. Though a slave, he was a noted Baptist preacher in the United States and is often acclaimed as being the founder of the first Baptist church among Blacks in Georgia. On reaching Jamaica, he received permission to preach and founded the first Baptist organization on the island. He was later joined by other American slaves who, along with him, developed a thriving Baptist organization throughout the island. When the London Baptist Mission later appeared in the island, a large number of the slaves remained with the Black Baptists, since their leadership was Black.

One of the few studies done on the Black Baptists is Mary Reckord's unpublished Ph.D. thesis, University of London, 1964. The following excerpt is quoted from Edward Brathwaite, *Creole Society in Jamaica*, p. 162.

The slaves expressed their political interests in the religious groups which developed outside the mission churches. [These] groups represented a form of sectarianism which mingled the slaves' African religious beliefs, the Negro Baptist tradition established by George Liele and his followers and mission Christianity. [These] groups reflected primarily the slaves' interest which satisfied more completely than mission services their emotional needs. [Moreover], freed from the supervision of the missionaries and their emphasis on conformity and obedience, the slaves were also able to express their political interests and use religion to sanction their hopes.

41. Geoffrey Dutton, *The Hero as Murderer: The Life of Edward John Eyre, Australian, Explorer and Governor of Jamaica, 1815–1901* (London: Collins, 1967), p. 223.

42. Ibid., p. 219.

43. For a study of George Gordon and Paul Bogle, see Dutton, ch. 15; also Hamilton Hume, *The Life of Edward John Eyre, Late Governor of Jamaica* (London, 1867). Both of these books attempt to show Governor Eyre as a victim of circumstances. Hume's book is a real defense of Eyre's good character; while Dutton's book is somewhat in the same vein, he is a little more objective. Bernard Semmel, *Jamaican Blood and Victorian Conscience: The Governor Eyre Controversy* (Boston: Houghton Mifflin Co., 1963), presents a more balanced view.

44. Dutton, *Hero as Murderer*, p. 222.

45. A vestry consisted of twelve elected men, mostly magistrates, which came into being by a Royal Act in 1664. The parochial rector and the Custos Rotalorum jointly chaired this body. Its

function was to carry out local administration such as running the local workhouses, gaols, the protection of slaves, and the general welfare of the community.

46. Hume, *Life of Eyre*, pp. 124–26. My emphasis.

47. Great emphasis is placed on this letter by all the historians of this controversy. See Hume, ch. 5, and Dutton, ch. 14.

48. Hume, *Life of Eyre*, p. 132.

49. Ibid., pp. 134–35.

50. Ibid., p. 137.

51. Dutton, *Hero as Murderer*, p. 253.

52. The loyalty of the Maroons to England was always a paradox to those who study their history. Considering them stooges to the British, most Englishmen who supervised them spoke in a derogatory way about their worth. During the Morant Bay Rebellion their White commander, A. G. Fyfe, said of them: "The Maroons are the children of the mist (referring to the dense mountain fog seen after a rain). The sound of their wild war horns as they rush without warning and without apparent discipline to the plains, strikes terror into the hearts of every one that hears it. Their charm consists in their very seclusion: bring them into everyday contact with the people, and that charm, which in effect quadruples their number, would be dispelled" (quoted from Dutton, *Hero as Murderer*, p. 263).

53. Dutton, *Hero as Murderer*, p. 285.

54. Ibid.

55. Ronald V. Sires, "The Experience of Jamaica with Modified Crown Colony Government," *Social and Economic Studies*, vol. 4, no. 2 (Institute of Social and Economic Research, University of the West Indies, 1955), pp. 150–59.

56. Ibid., p. 156.

57. Garvey studies are so voluminous that it is unnecessary to list all the research. This short sketch is based on *The Philosophy and Opinions of Marcus Garvey*, compiled by Amy Jacques Garvey and published by Frank Cass & Co., Ltd., London, 1967. The author has also had two extended interviews with Garvey's wife, Amy Jacques, in 1963 and 1969.

58. St. Mark 6:4.

59. A. J. Garvey, *Philosophy and Opinions*, Part 2, pp. 37–38.

60. Ras Samuel E. Brown, "The Truth about the Rastafarians," *The Liberator*, vol. 3, no. 9 (Jamaica: n.p., 1963).

Chapter 3

1. For a classical study of this outmoded scholarship see C. G. Seligam, *Races of Africa*, 4th ed. (London: Oxford University Press, 1968). For an up-to-date discussion on race, see Paul Bohannan and Philip Curtin, *Africa and the Africans*, rev. ed. (New York: The Natural History Press, 1971), ch. 3.

2. Cheikh Anta Diop, *The African Origin of Civilization: Myth or Reality*, ed. and trans. Mercer Cook (New York: Lawrence Hill & Co., 1974).

3. Ibid., p. 5.

4. Ibid., p. 27.

5. Ibid., p. 28.

6. Ibid., pp. 281–82.

7. For a good discussion of the evolution of the Black church see Carter G. Woodson, *The History of the Negro Church*, 2nd ed. (Washington, D.C.: The Association Press, 1945).

8. The opinions of Edward Wilmot Blyden are contained in his several books. One of the most important is *Christianity, Islam and the Negro Race* (1887), and the recent work by Hollis Lynch, *Edward Wilmot Blyden: Pan Negro Patriot: 1832–1912* (London: Oxford University Press, 1967).

9. A. J. Garvey, *Philosophy and Opinions*, 2nd ed. (London: Frank Cass & Co., Ltd., 1967), p. 34.

10. Ibid., p. 57.

11. Ibid., pp. 60–61.

12. Ibid., Part 2, p. 19.

13. Ibid., p. 120.

14. Ibid., p. 140.

15. Edward Ullendorff, *The Ethiopians: An Introduction to Country and People*, 3rd ed. (London: Oxford University Press, 1973), p. 92.

16. *The Jamaican Daily Gleaner*, January 5, and March 17, 1934.

17. *Gleaner*, July 15 through August, 1941. These issues devoted extensive reporting to the movement's activities. The material presented here on the Pinnacle enterprise is taken from this period.

18. M. G. Smith, Roy Augier, and Rex M. Nettleford, "The Report on Rastafari Movement in Kingston, Jamaica," *Social and Economic Studies* (1960), pp. 12–13.

19. *The Star*, March 6, 1958, p. 1.

20. *Star*, March 24, 1958, p. 1.

21. *Gleaner*, March 10, 1958, p. 6.

22. Ibid.

23. From research notes of 1965. Courtesy of Ras Brown.

24. *Gleaner*, October 6, 1959, p. 1.

25. *Gleaner*, October 7, 1960, p. 1.

26. *Gleaner*, April 7, 1960, p. 1.

27. Smith, Augier, and Nettleford, *Social and Economic Studies*, p. 38.

28. "Report of Mission to Africa" (Kingston: Government Printing Office, 1969).

Chapter 4

1. Smith, Augier, and Nettleford, *Social and Economic Studies*, p. 38.

2. Alexander Vavoules and A. Wayne Colver, *Science and Society: Selected Essays* (San Francisco: Holden-Day, Inc., 1960), p. 12.

3. Notes from field research.

4. Samuel E. Brown, "Treatise on the Rastafarian Movement," unpublished manuscript—notes collected in field research, Summer, 1966, and subsequently published in *The Journal of Caribbean Studies*, vol. 6, no. 1 (1966), p. 1.

5. Ibid.

6. The concept "peace and love" is unique in the movement. This is their formal greeting. It is used in all ritual greetings of brethren and strangers alike. The shaking of hands is generally dispensed with among Rastafarians, but this greeting is standard. It serves as an invocation and a benediction. The Rastafarians could easily be called the Peace and Love Movement.

7. Taken from field notes, summer, 1966.

8. A. F. C. Wallace, "Revitalization Movement," *American Anthropologist*, vol. 58 (1956), pp. 264–281.

9. Orlando Patterson, *The Children of Sisyphus* (Boston: Houghton Mifflin Co., 1965), p. 23.

10. Copied from unpublished manuscript by Samuel E. Brown, summer, 1966.

11. St. John 10:34 reads: "Jesus answered them, is it not written in your law, I said, Ye are gods?" This Rastafarian version is expanded.

12. I John 3:2.

13. Samuel E. Brown, "Treatise."

14. Romans 6:23.

15. St. Matthew 3:22; Leviticus 21:1 and 4.

16. Notes from interview with Ras Moses, Rastafarian Repatriation Association—now Mystic Revelation of Rastafari, 1966.

17. Ibid.

18. "African Fundamentalism" was presumed to have been written by Marcus Garvey and supplied to the author by E. Monroe Scarlet of the Afro-West Indian League of Jones Town, Jamaica, 1966.

19. Quoted by C. Eric Lincoln in *The Black Muslims in America* (Boston: Beacon Press, 1963), p. 33.

20. Simpson, "Religious Cults," p. 135.

21. Brown, "Treatise."

22. Ibid.

23. Verbatim statement from Ras Douglas Mack R.R.A., summer, 1966.

24. Isaiah 43:6.

25. Lincoln, *Black Muslims*, p. 44.

26. Brown, "Treatise."

27. Transcribed notes from the notebook of Ras Douglas Mack, July, 1966.

28. Taped interview with Ras Sam Brown, summer, 1975.

29. To appreciate this benediction one must hear it spoken—the "i" in Rastafari rhymes with the "I" in Selassie I.

30. A spliff is the Jamaican name for the American "joint."

31. Taken from taped interview as read by the author Sam Brown.

32. *Marihuana: A Signal of Misunderstanding, The Official Report of the National Commission on Marihuana and Drug Abuse* (New York: The New American Library, Inc., 1972).

33. Taped interview with Ras Samuel E. Brown, summer, 1975.

34. Leviticus 21:5.

35. Taken from clippings in Sam Brown's notes, summer, 1966.

36. *The Rastafarian Voice*, July, 1975.

37. Will Herberg, ed., *The Writings of Martin Buber* (New York: The World Publishing Co., 1961).

38. There are numerous unwritten words and expressions among the Rastafarians which are difficult to translate; one will

hear such words as "heights" which means "one who is great or high on the herb"; another is "irie" which means "knowledge-able, mysterious, or deep wisdom."

Chapter 5

1. Unpublished one-page manuscript collected in field research, summer, 1965.

2. Transcribed verbatim from taped session at 1000 Marcus Garvey Drive, summer, 1965.

3. Ibid.

4. This report is from the author's eyewitness field notes, July 12, 1966.

5. *The Public Opinion* (The National Weekly), vol. 30, no. 22 (July 15, 1966), p. 1, under the editorial heading "Man or Monsters?"

6. Letters to the *Daily Gleaner*, July 17, 1966.

7. Taken from taped conversation with Dr. M. B. Douglas, July, 1966.

8. Quoted from Rastafarian weekly, *Ethiopia Calls*, vol. 16, no. 6, p. 4.

9. The party in power during 1960 was the People's National Party, under the leadership of the Honorable Norman Manley, Q.C., who was deeply sympathetic to the movement's aspiration.

10. The untimely death of Count Ossie (Oswald Williams) reached the author when this book was in the advanced stages of publication and therefore mention of his death is not cited in the text. Count Ossie's death, which occurred on October 18, 1976, is a loss not only to the Rastafarian movement to which he was dedicated from its beginning, but to the cultural community of Jamaica as a whole. The author remembers quite vividly his first meeting with Count Ossie in 1965, during which recordings of his drummings were made. Count Ossie was a man of deep spirituality and humility. His music and his dedication to African culture will certainly go down in history.

11. This article was given to the author by Samuel E. Brown in 1965 and is used here with his permission.

12. Anthony F. C. Wallace, "Revitalization Movements," eds. William A. Lessa and Evon Z. Vogt, *Reader in Comparative Religion: An Anthropological Approach*, 3rd ed. (New York: Harper and Row, 1972), p. 509.

Chapter 6

1. George E. Simpson, "Political Cultism in West Kingston, Jamaica," *Institute of Social and Economic Research*, vol. 4, no. 2 (Kingston: University of the West Indies, 1955), pp. 145–47.

2. Ibid., p. 147.

3. Patterson, *Children of Sisyphus*, p. 23.

4. Katrin Norris, *Jamaica: The Search for an Identity* (London: Oxford University Press, 1962), p. 36.

5. *The Star*, April 9, 1962, p. 1.

6. Norris, *Jamaica*, p. 36.

7. Taped interview with Ras Sam Brown, summer, 1975.

8. *The Jamaican Daily Gleaner*, June 29, 1969, p. 13.

9. Ibid.

10. Taped interview with Rastafarian Movement Association officials, summer, 1975.

11. Taped interview, 1975.

12. Ibid.

13. Taped interview with a Rastafarian Movement Association artist, summer, 1975.

14. Ibid.

15. Transcribed from field notes of summer, 1975. Used by permission of the poet.

16. Quoted in J. P. Makouta Mboukou, *Black African Literature* (Washington, D.C.: Black Orpheus Press, 1973), pp. 28–29.

17. Taped interview with Ras Sam Brown, summer, 1975.

18. Taped interview with art shop proprietor, summer, 1975.

19. J. A. De Cobineau, *Essai sur l'inegalité des races humaines*, bk. 1, ch. 7 (Paris, 1953), quoted in Cheikh Anta Diop, *The African Origin of Civilization: Myth or Reality* (New York: Lawrence Hill and Company, 1974), p. 280.

20. Rex M. Nettleford, *Mirror, Mirror: Identity, Race and Protest in Jamaica*, 1st ed. (Kingston: William Collins and Sangster, 1970), pp. 98–99.

21. *The Jamaica Daily Gleaner*, August 20, 1971, p. 2.

22. Taped interview, summer, 1975.

23. Ibid.

24. The materials presented here were gleaned from several sources: Ephraim Isaacs, *The Ethiopian Church* (Boston: Henry N. Sawyer Co., 1968); Harry M. Hyatt, *The Church of Abyssinia* (London: Luzac & Co., 1928); Edward Ullendorff, *Ethiopians*; and

Leonard Morsley, *Haile Selassie: The Conquering Lion* (London: Weidenfeld and Nicolson, 1964).

25. Taped interview, summer, 1975.

26. Ibid.

27. Ibid.

28. Ibid.

29. Field notes of summer, 1975.

30. Leonard E. Barrett, "Aspects of Jamaican Family Organization," *The Rastafarians: A Study in Messianic Cultism in Jamaica*, Institute of Caribbean Studies (Rio Piedras: University of Puerto Rico Press, 1963).

Chapter 7

1. Interview with Ras Samuel Brown, summer, 1975.

2. Interview with a member of the Rastafarian Movement Association, 53 Law Street, summer, 1975.

3. Ibid.

4. Ibid.

5. Interview with Ras Sam Clayton, Mystic Revelation of Rastafari, summer, 1975.

6. *Newsweek* reported that at the Savior's Day celebration of the Nation of Islam (commonly known as the Black Muslims of America) there were several White visitors and some White members. The first White member to join the movement was Sister Dorothy 13X, who is married to a Muslim. *Newsweek*, vol. 86, no. 11 (March 15, 1976).

7. Nettleford, *Mirror, Mirror*, p. 94. Professor Nettleford coined the concept in the following quotation: "A group of such young people are found among the University undergraduates and may be termed *functional Rastafarians*, who have served to secularize the movement away from its strongly religious orientation and blur the lines yet further between those who want deliverance in Ethiopia and those who desire it in Jamaica."

8. David Barrett, *Schism & Renewal in Africa: An Analysis of Six Thousand Contemporary Religious Movements* (London: Oxford University Press, 1968).

Bibliography

Aberle, David, "A Note on Relative Deprivation Theory as Applied to Millenarian and Other Cult Movements," in *Reader in Comparative Religion: An Anthropological Approach*, edited by William A. Lessa and Evon Z. Vogt (New York: Harper & Row, 1972).

Anta Diop, Cheikh, *The African Origin of Civilization: Myth or Reality*, edited by Mercer Cook (New York: Lawrence Hill & Co., 1974).

Annual Abstract of Statistics, no. 24. Kingston: Department of Statistics, 1965.

Barrett, Leonard E., *Soul-Force: African Heritage in Afro-American Religion* (New York: Doubleday, 1974).

Bastide, Roger, *African Civilizations in the New World* (New York: Harper Torchbooks, 1971).

Bleby, Henry, *Death Struggles of Slavery, . . . In a British Colony During the Two Years Immediately Preceeding Negro Emancipation* (London: Dewar's Limited Ed., 1973).

Blyden, Edward Wilmot. *Christianity, Islam and the Negro Race* (London: Oxford Press, 1887).

Brathwaite, Edward, *The Development of Creole Society in Jamaica, 1770–1820* (London: Oxford Press, 1971).

Brown, Samuel E., "Treatise on the Rastafarian Movement" unpublished manuscript in *The Journal of Caribbean Studies*, vol. 6, no. 1 (Kingston: University of the West Indies, 1966).

Brown, Ras Samuel E., "The Truth About the Rastafarians," *The Liberator*, vol. 3, no. 9 (Kingston, 1963).

Buchner, J. H., *The Moravians in Jamaica* (London: Oxford University Press, 1885).

Cassidy, Federick G., *Jamaica Talk: Three Hundred Years of the English Language in Jamaica* (London: Macmillan Co., Ltd., 1961).

Coke, Thomas, *A History of the West Indies, Containing Natural, Civil, and Ecclesiastical History of the Island with an Account of the Missions . . . etc.*, 3 vols. (London: Clarendon Press, 1810).

Curtin, Philip, *Africa and the Africans*, rev. ed. (New York: Natural History Press, 1971).

Curtin, P. D., *Two Jamaicas: The Role of Ideas in a Tropical Colony* (Cambridge: Harvard University Press, 1955).

Dallas, R. D., *The History of the Maroons* (London: Oxford University Press, 1803).

DeCobineau, J. A., *Essai sur l'inegalité des races humaines* (Paris, 1953). (Quoted in Cheikh Anta Diop.)

DeLisser, Herbert G., *Twentieth Century Jamaica* (Kingston, 1913).

Dutton, Geoffrey, *The Hero as Murderer: The Life of Edward John Eyre, Australian, Explorer and Governor of Jamaica, 1815–1901* (London: Collins Publishers, 1967).

Edwards, Bryan, *The History, Civil and Commercial of the British Colonies in the West Indies* (London: J. Stockdale, Co., 2 vols. 1793; 3 vols., 1801).

Ethiopia Calls, vol. 16, no. 6.

Facts on Jamaica (Kingston, 1960 and 1965).

Gardner, William J., *A History of Jamaica from Its Discovery by Christopher Columbus to 1872* (London: Clarendon Press, 1873).

Garvey, Amy Jacques, *The Philosophy and Opinions of Marcus Garvey* (London: Frank Cass & Co., Ltd., 1967).

Garvey, Marcus, "African Fundamentalism," supplied by E. Monroe Scarlet in *Afro-West Indian League of Jones Town* (Jamaica, 1966).

Gerlach, Luther P., and Virginia H. Hine, *People, Power, Change: Movements of Social Transformation* (Indianapolis and New York: Bobbs-Merrill, 1970).

Gonzalez-Wippler, Migene, *Santeria: African Magic in Latin America* (New York: Anchor Books/Doubleday, 1975).

Herberg, Will, *The Writings of Martin Buber* (New York: The World Publishing Co., 1961).

Hume, Hamilton, *The Life of Edward John Eyre, Late Governor of Jamaica* (London: Clarendon Press, 1867).

Hyatt, Harry M., *The Church of Abyssinia* (London: Luzac & Co., 1928).

Isaacs, Ephraim, *The Ethiopian Church* (Boston: Henry Sawyer Co., 1968).

Jamaica Information Service, Fact Sheet no. 7 (Kingston, n.d.).

The Jamaican Daily Gleaner (Kingston, Jamaica).

Johnson, Carey, *The Fighting Maroons of Jamaica* (Jamaica: William Collins & Longate, 1969).

Jordan, Winthrop, *White Over Black* (Baltimore: Penguin Books, Inc., 1969).

Kerr, Madeline, *Personality and Conflict in Jamaica* (London: Collins Publishers, 1961).

Lincoln, C. Eric, *The Black Muslims in America* (Boston: Beacon Press, 1963; rev. ed., 1973).

Long, Edward, *History of Jamaica* (London: T. Lowndes, 1774).

Lynch, Hollis, *Edward Wilmot Blyden: Pan Negro Patriot* (London: Frank Cass & Co., 1967).

"Man or Monsters?" *The Public Opinion* (The National Weekly), vol. 30, no. 22, July, 1966.

"Marihuana: A Signal of Misunderstanding," *The Official Report of the National Commission on Marihuana and Drug Abuse* (New York: New American Library, 1972).

Mboukou, J. P. Makouta, *Black African Literature* (Washington, D.C.: Black Orpheus Press, 1973).

Morsley, Leonard, *Haile Selassie: The Conquering Lion* (London: Weidenfeld & Nicolson, 1964).

Nettleford, Rex M., *Mirror, Mirror: Identity, Race and Protest in Jamaica* (Kingston: William Collins & Sangster, 1970).

Newsweek, March 15, 1976.

Norris, Katrin, *Jamaica: The Search for an Identity* (London: Oxford University Press, 1962).

Patterson, Orlando, *The Children of Sisyphus* (Boston: Houghton Mifflin, Co., 1965).

Phillippo, J. M., *Jamaica: Its Past and Present State* (London: J. Snow, 1843).

Price, Richard, *Maroon Societies* (New York: Anchor Books/ Doubleday, 1973).

Ragatz, Lowell Joseph, *The Fall of the Planter Class in the British Caribbean, 1763–1833: A Study in Social and Economic History* (New York: Octagon Books, Inc., 1963).

The Rasta Voice (Jamaica, July, 1975).

Rotberg, Robert I., *Rebellion in Black Africa* (London: Oxford University Press, 1971).

Seligam, C. G., *Races of Africa* (London: Oxford University Press, 1968).

Semmel, Bernard, *Jamaican Blood and Victorian Conscience: The Governor Eyre Controversy* (Boston: Houghton Mifflin Company, 1963).

Simpson, George Eaton, "Religious Cults of the Caribbean: Trinidad, Jamaica, and Haiti," *The Institute of Caribbean Studies* (Rio Piedras: University of Puerto Rico, 1970.

Simpson, George E., "Political Cultism in West Kingston, Jamaica," *Institute of Social and Economic Research*, vol. 4, no. 2 (Kingston: University of the West Indies, June, 1955).

Sires, Ronald V., "The Experience of Jamaica with Modified Crown Colony Government," *Social and Economic Studies*, vol. 4, no. 2 (Kingston: University of the West Indies, June, 1955).

Smith, M. G., Roy Augier, and Rex M. Nettleford, "Report on the Rastafari Movement in Kingston, Jamaica," *Social and Economic Studies* (Kingston: University of the West Indies, 1960).

Stampp, Kenneth M., *The Peculiar Institution: Slavery in Ante-Bellum South* (New York, Vintage Books, 1956).

The Star (Kingston, Jamaica).

Stewart, J., *A View of the Past and Present State of the Island of Jamaica* (Edinburgh: Oliver & Boyd, 1823).

Tucker, Robert C., "The Theory of Charismatic Leadership," *Daedalus* (Summer, 1968).

Ullendorff, Edward, *The Ethiopians: An Introduction to Country and People*, 3rd ed. (London: Oxford University Press, 1973).

Vavoules, Alexander, and A. Wayne Colver, *Science and Society: Selected Essays* (San Francisco: Holden-Day, Inc., 1960).

Wallace, Anthony F. C., "Revitalization Movements," in *Reader in Comparative Religion: An Anthropological Approach*, 3rd ed., edited by William A. Lessa and Evon Z. Vogt (New York: Harper & Row, 1972).

———, "Revitalization Movement," *American Anthropologist*, Vol. 58, 1956.

Woodson, Carter G., *The History of the Negro Church*, 2nd ed. (Washington: D.C., Association Press, 1945).

Index